Breaking Better
22 armed robberies and one decision to change

Lennox Rodgers

REFOCUS
next generation transformation

Published by Refocus Project Ltd in 2019
Copyright © Refocus 2019

First Edition

The author asserts the moral right under the Copyright, Designs and Patents Act 1988 to be identified as the author of this work.

ISBN: 978-1-5272-3505-2

All rights reserved. No part of this publication may be reproduced, stored in a retrieval system or transmitted, in any form or by any means without the prior consent of the author, nor be otherwise circulated in any form of binding or cover other than that which it is published and without a similar condition being imposed on the subsequent purchaser.

REFOCUS
next generation transformation

I dedicate this book:

To the memory of all those young people who have lost their lives through violent crime

"Gone but not forgotten."

CONTENTS

Chapter One	Cherry Boy	6
Chapter Two	Loved in Different Ways	19
Chapter Three	Shoes in a Pillow Case	35
Chapter Four	Excommunication	47
Chapter Five	Glimpses of Another Path	63
Chapter Six	Turbulence	79
Chapter Seven	On Remand	93
Chapter Eight	Beginnings	105
Chapter Nine	Betrayed	119
Chapter Ten	Reputation	129
Chapter Eleven	Demons	144
Chapter Twelve	Pulled Deeper	161
Chapter Thirteen	Deals	175
Chapter Fourteen	Roots	187
Chapter Fifteen	Marley Chan	201
Chapter Sixteen	The Hand	214
Chapter Seventeen	Bali's story	227
Chapter Eighteen	Refocusing	241
Chapter Nineteen	Full Circle	256
Chapter Twenty	Looking Ahead	272

ACKNOWLEDGEMENTS

Firstly I'd like to take this opportunity to acknowledge all the people that have been the victims of the violence I've perpetrated, and to apologise for the hurt and pain suffered as a result of my actions. In no way is this book intended as a justification for my crimes. I can only hope you're no longer suffering any after effects and that you can find it in your hearts to forgive me. This also includes the police and the prison officers.

I know for some people that isn't going to cut it. I'll never be able to fully understand the hurt and pain I've caused. I'm genuinely sorry for my actions and their consequences, both to individuals and their families. I can only hope the work of Refocus, in some small way, is making amends and evidencing my commitment to turn my own life around.

I chose to write this book not to glorify crime or to polish my street cred, but to expose how damaged I allowed myself to become. I let my rage fester without seeking professional help, and took refuge in cannabis and other drugs that only served to make my actions more extreme and wicked. When I look at what's happening in our communities today, with young people being dragged into a world of crime in the mistaken belief it provides answers and fulfilment, I see a reflection of my teenage self. I feel compelled to speak up as a father and mentor — reaching out to young people through my own experiences and doing all that's humanly possible, through the earliest interventions, to divert them from making the same mistakes I made.

All events described in this book are based upon the story of my life from the early 1960s to the present day. However the names of some of the people and places have been changed to respect the privacy of individuals.

I'd like to thank all those without whose guidance and support this book wouldn't have been possible.

I'm forever grateful to Andrew Fox, Simon O'Leary and the Don Hanson Charitable Foundation. Andrew's support for Refocus, as an active and imaginative benefactor, has been beyond our wildest dreams. Often one feels small and insignificant in the ocean of charities and social purpose enterprises. Andrew's genuine inspiration and his response to my cry for help on LBC has turned my life around and enabled the writing of this book. Although we didn't have the privilege of meeting the late Don Hanson and his family, we can only marvel at the passion this wonderful man must've displayed to help those less fortunate.

I'd also like to thank Laurence Smith - Wow, what a journey we've been on together; your skills in helping to craft this tale have been invaluable, you've been fantastic to work with and we say a massive thank you for going the extra mile — to the extent that you actually brought your own son Harry and colleague Rita Sexton to the rescue when we were struggling for some artistic inspiration. I can't express how grateful we feel to all three of you. We hope this is the start of something wonderful.

I would like to say a big thank you to Mark my son, who has contributed to the beginning of most chapters with his fantastic artwork, of which I am sure you will appreciate just as much as I have.

I thank all generations of my family. To mum and dad: as you watch down from the heavens, I hope I'm making you proud. I've been honest in these pages about the difficulties of my early years growing up in Oxford, but I know deep down you loved me and wanted the best for me. I'm thankful that, in later years, we were able to resolve many of those issues and let things go. I look back on much of my life with you with fondness. To my dear sisters: I love you all and thank you for your contributions and support throughout my life. To my son and daughter: I love you both dearly. I will always regret not being the kind of father you needed, but I'm grateful to you both for permitting me, despite everything, to be in your lives. I'd also like to acknowledge the men who were exceptional role models to my daughter when circumstances (usually, being sentenced to serve time behind bars) meant I couldn't be the father you deserved.

I am truly thankful for having the Grants in my life — especially your willingness to take me under your wing and make me feel part of your family. I thank Chris, Mark, Sharon, Michelle and Georgina for sharing your amazing parents with me. Without you, my life could have taken a very different turn! And a special thanks to George Grant for being an incredible fatherly role model — space didn't allow me to fully do justice to your role in my life in these pages. And of course to 'Mummy G' - I love you dearly and will never forget the selfless love that you showered on me. I don't have the words to express the impact you made.

I'm grateful for schools such as St Edwards. Sometimes, it's only with the passage of time that one understands the magnitude of a school's impact on one's character. I thank all the teachers at St Edwards for your mentoring, wisdom and faith in the man I could (eventually) become.

A big shout out to Warwick, Jonathan and Kate – you've been my legal "A team", and I'll always treasure the memories, whilst being regretful of the circumstances that brought us together.

To Brian Greenaway, a special thanks, mate, for mentoring and coaching me and inspiring me through your book Hell's Angel to become a hope to others as you did to me.

John and Tamsin Pask – you took me into your home and helped me with a fresh start, supporting my rehabilitation and efforts to transform my life. You also introduced me to an amazing group of people who I now call family and of course my incredible lovely wife, Bali.

I am so thankful that my wife introduced me to families that have not just taken me in, but treated me as if I was one of their own. Once, I could only dream of being part of such a stable family unit. Malcolm and Margerate Irlam — thank you for trusting me with your front door key. Trevor and Linda Perry and your family, thank you for the grace and unconditional love you have shown me. It's an honour to know my wife Bali's family, especially her mum and the Dhillons, who I have grown very close to. The love and support from each of you has been humbling, and I'll always cherish you also as my family. A special thanks to Daniel for your inspiration and contributions towards the design of the book.

To the late Tim Griffiths, who was my minister, father in law and friend, and your wife Ceri. You welcomed me into your large and wonderful family. Ceri – you continue to help me to unpick the damage that lingers from aspects of my past, and have been relentless in ensuring I stick to my new path. I love you both.

To Roz Fox - you have been so steadfast in supporting me through many difficult moments, as have many other friends and colleagues..

And I can never forget all those who, in the early days of Refocus, saw my potential and didn't give up on me – Nick Ash, Carole Britnell, PC J Brooker, PC Hibbins, Rav Dhillon, Godfrey Featherstone, Helen Mchenry, Jean Parks, PWC, Alison Roper, John Shanley, Nell Shortis, Penny Stotesbury, and the Grey Zebra team.

To all the Refocus team – past and present. We've accomplished magnificent things together; I'm proud of every one of you. Jermaine Brown, Billy Bruce, Kelly Edmonds, Ashley Eldridge, John Griffiths, Julie Rye, Len Rye, Andy Watson and John W.

To the "Last Chance Programme" in Glen Parva, to Swalside Prison, Medway Secure Unit, Chelmsford Prison and Woodhill Prison for all the young lives turned around.

To our dear trustees — also past and present. Tim Griffiths, Genny Jones, Tara Keen, Andy Rogers, John Shanley, Karen Walker, Ricky Walker, Nancy Watson – and most of all Garnet Johnson, for your faithful support and commitment.

A special acknowledgment to those who have supported us financially over the years — including Bexley Youth Services, Bromley Probation, Kent County Council, Police Crime Commissioners, the Tudor Trust, the Colyer Fergusson Charitable Trust, Schools all over the South East of London and Kent, The Hedley Foundation, Henry Smith, the Kent Community Foundation and many more.

To all those in the media who've helped us raise awareness of the issues facing young people and the need to reclaim the streets from gangs — including Sky News, Colin Campbell, Ria Chatterjee, Ed Cook, Alex Bish and many more.

To my beautiful darling wife and soul mate, Bali. When the going gets tough you have always stuck with me. You have helped me to be the man I am today, truly another of God's wonderful interventions in my life. Thanks for who you are and all you do. I don't need to say too much about Bali, because readers will be meeting her as we progress through this story. In fact, she even hijacked a chapter for herself!

And finally, my thanks the "Big G", for the many times you've entered my life and protected me from the worst. Were it not for your divine intervention, I'd either now be behind bars, or six feet below ground.

On behalf of all those I've mentioned (and to all those I've overlooked, my apologies), if this book helps rekindle your faith in the power of hope and the ability of every soul, no matter how lost, to choose a brighter future, then it will have served its purpose.

"Rejoice with me, for I have found my sheep that was lost."

Lennox Rodgers
March 2019

1.
Cherry Boy

"Hello, Mrs Rodgers. Can I speak with Lennox please?"
"Who is dis?"
"It's Amy."
"Wha yo warnt im fa?"
"I'm his girlfriend."
"Wha yo seh?"
"His girlfriend."

At which point my mum, Zena Rodgers, slammed down the phone.

I hadn't gotten around to telling Mum about Amy, partly because it'd all been so harmless. It had been two days ago that, sitting together in a park, Amy had looked at the ground and whispered, "Am I your girlfriend now?" I'd mumbled a word that vaguely sounded like "Yes". She was very pretty. Also, she was white – that was a real bonus for an eight-year-old boy from the Caribbean. A smile lit up Amy's face. We kissed, exchanged numbers, held hands. An innocent, nervous start to a sweet child romance.

But to Mum, innocence was the last thing she associated with this news. The word "girlfriend" – and its many lustful associations – were swirling around in her head. She had inherited a strict and uncompromising view of the role of a young boy in the family hierarchy, one that was reinforced by the no-nonsense leaders at her Church. The efficient running of a large household — ten of us were living in a four-bedroom Council property in Wood Farm, Oxford – required rigid discipline, and everybody understanding their place.

As her youngest child, and her only son, my purpose revolved around being seen but not heard, obeying my parents' every command, disciplining myself by always doing my homework or reading books to show an interest in getting an education. On top of that, doing my share of what seemed like mundane, pointless chores mainly at weekends, when I yearned to race around outside with my friends, pretending to be James Bond or Tarzan, I'd be given a long list of instructions that took priority. Cleaning and re-cleaning the skirting boards to eliminate the faintest evidence of dust or grime was perhaps the least annoying of my duties, simply because it was so mindless.

As she smashed the phone onto the cradle, I was cowering at the far end of the hallway door. My instinct was to flee and hide, but my leg muscles weren't responding. I heard my mother emit a guttural sound brimming with disgust. Now she was striding towards me. For a moment, my panicky mind imagined I was in an episode of the Twilight Zone, and she was undergoing a terrifying mutation. With every step, her arm muscles swelling and her body transforming into something taller, stronger, more deadly.

"Bwoy, yo tink yah man?" she yelled. "Wah bwoy tink im a man?" ("One boy who thinks he's a man.")

I said something sarcastic in reply. I don't recall what.

"Yah too rude an outa arda. Bout yah tark to me like me ah yo a fren?" ("you think you can talk to me as if me and you are friends.")

Without warning, she slapped me on the side of my head. A clean, sharp smack. No echo.

Still rooted to the floor, I stared back defiantly. Mum hit me again, this time more powerfully. In her wrath, she never stopped after two blows. I'd never been in trouble before over a "girlfriend", but this certainly wasn't the first time my conduct had fallen short of her lofty expectations. Muddy and ripped clothes, returning late from school, playing truant from Church, no manners and respect, being rude and out of order, being a liar and a thief and more – each transgression was, to her, cast-iron justification for punishment. Severe punishment. Physical punishment.

Always physical.

Now she was unleashing a frenzied torrent of blows. The force of each slap and punch intensifying, as if that would reinforce the message that I was "outa arda".

I noticed two of my sisters sitting on the staircase, just out of Mum's eyeshot. They were slouched forward as if they had just come to the climax of a good film, all that was missing was their popcorn. They got pleasure from seeing my beatings and they smirked in agreement of my punishment. They used to say to me, "bwoy yo mus love licks," ("boy you must love getting beaten").

They thought that I was stupid to keep getting in trouble, knowing the consequences. Then a jolt of pain across my knees, sharper than any of the blows from Mum's hands, snapped me back to reality.

Mum had unbuckled her belt, and was using it to ramp-up the severity of the beatings.

Stubbornly, I refused to cry out or to plead. Instead, I imagined my future self. Aged 16. Burly, muscular. Endowed with upper-body strength greater than that of any other family member. My situation was agonising; but it was time limited. One day, I would have the power to fight back. I often found this a comfort when suffering under punishment beatings.

"Yo is ah narty bwoy, Lennox. Such a narty bwoy."

("You're a naughty boy.")

Mum was using the belt to whip not just my legs, but my entire body. The leather caught me across the cheek, and I raised my arms to protect myself against the next strike. I must've clenched my fists because she flinched, as if I'd been about to launch a retaliatory punch. That was when she summoned reinforcements. "Mack, Mack," she shouted. My dad, Mack Rodgers, who'd been fixing something in the back yard, was immediately on the scene.

Outwardly, Dad appeared the typical, respectable, first generation migrant. He was tall, and not too religious, almost always attired in a freshly-pressed, single-breasted suit but in an old cardigan and trousers for doing chores and DIY. His diligence in the workplace enabled him to hold down long-term employment as a porter at a nearby mental hospital. Yet he, like mum, regarded violent beatings as a routine solution for dealing with an unruly young boy. Their motto to me was, "Bwoy, if ya nah ere yo go feel," (Boy if you don't hear or listen, you will feel) I hadn't planned on the feel part but it was what I seemed to get on a daily basis.

"Im disrespeck, mi," explained my mum. "Im tink im a big man, wah gal karl ere and tark bout galfren, da bwoy tink im a man an im raze im han ta mi, wah fire lick afta mi."

("He disrespected me, He thinks he's a big man, one girl called here and was talking about girlfriend, the boy thinks he's a man and he's raised his hand to me to hit me.")

Dad was a man of few words, "Da bwoy raze im han ta mi," ("The boy raised his hand to me.") Mum shouted again. Dad is kissing his teeth, screwing up his face and his fist as the accusations mount.

I had no opportunity to deny these allegations before my father grabbed my head, using both his hands.

"Bwoy a baderation ya gimme? No hoo ya tark tu and no yah place," he grimaced.

("Boy, are you giving me badness? That means only one penalty. Be aware who you're talking to, and know your place.")

Then, as if it was the most normal thing in the world, he smashed my head against the wall. I shrieked at the searing pain and the sickening thud of the impact rang in my ears. My temple had clipped the corner of a framed photograph of St Vincent, which fell from its hook onto the floor. I stumbled but somehow retained my balance.

Then, an odd thing happened. The shock seemed to numb the pain I was feeling, and – at last – my legs summoned the energy to propel me from the scene. I staggered up the stairs where my sisters still sat enjoying the show, and – for some reason – lunged into my parents' bedroom to seek refuge. But, still dazed, I wasn't quite fast enough. Dad jammed his boot inside the doorframe, defying my pitiful attempts to shut myself in.

My recollection of what happened next is blurred, a series of disjointed fragments. In my mind's eye, I see my dad's fists striking down on my head. I remember collapsing to the floor. I feel the cold metal of his belt buckle slashing against my back, my thighs, my arms, my face – I still carry a scar above my left eye. I hear my own blood-curdling screams. I'm aware of my mum, finally realising this has gone too far, trying to restrain her husband – begging and shouting at the top of her voice:

"Murda, Murda, Murda Woy! Mack, Mack, tap yo go kill im, yo go kill da bwoy, tap."

I sense the presence of my relative, Thomas Brown, imploring my father to control his temper. Then, I'm aware that, although my mouth is open, I can no longer scream out. I'm losing consciousness. I can longer distinguish between the faces in the room. All is black.

When I awake, I'm sitting in my bedroom with my relative, who's applying a steri-strip to the cut above my eye. My arms are a mess of welts and bruises, and every time I try raising my hand, a sharp dagger of pain through my body forces me to be still. I don't leave my bedroom for the rest of the day. While my seven sisters share two bedrooms, as the solitary boy I have a room to myself. But it's barely a bedroom; in reality a converted box room, and there's barely enough gap between the bed and the wall to stretch out my legs.

And today the room was more claustrophobic than ever. Through the window, I could glimpse the world beyond my confinement – pedestrians and cars and trees. Wood Farm Road stretching away from the oppressive aura of my parents' home. But towards what? A world of freedom and adventure and joy? Or simply towards further, unremitting misery.

The year was 1971, when society regarded child beatings with a detachment that bordered on indifference. Our neighbours were aware of the suffering I endured – the houses were tightly packed, and my piercing screams were an almost daily occurrence. On one occasion, a nearby resident found me walking the streets late at night naked and dazed, but rather than offer comfort or make enquiries, I was simply returned to my home (where a special course of beatings awaited).

Some viewed my parents' attitude to household discipline as a deep-rooted feature of Caribbean culture – which had an element of truth, although the violence was excessive even by St Vincent standards. On two occasions, my screams so blood-curdling that concerned neighbours felt obliged to contact the police. Each time, the outcome was the same. An incurious officer made perfunctory enquiries, spoke mainly to my parents rather than to me, and concluded that – since this was "a domestic" – it was beyond the scope of law enforcement to interfere.

It wasn't only during the adrenaline rush of a beating that Mum called me "Narty Bwoy" ("naughty boy"). She used it as my nickname whenever she mentioned me to people within the community. At Church, I think more members of the congregation knew me as "Narty Bwoy" than as Lennox. Even one of the Church elders greeted me on Sunday mornings by exclaiming, "Hello, Narty Bwoy." Over time, unremitting use of this nickname had an effect not unlike the sound of water against tile from a dripping tap. I came to accept it as my fate. If everybody thought I was a naughty boy, surely that must be the essence of my personality. Gradually, but inevitably and often obliviously, I started to conform to my caricature.

Of all my sisters, during this period I only enjoyed a close relationship with Angela – who was closest to me in age. For as long as I could remember, she possessed an artist's knack for captivating imagery and design. She'd spend hours sitting in the house, or on the street, sketching anything that caught her fancy. Her pen portraits were stunning in their simplicity and beauty. Alone in the family, Angela felt a degree of sibling responsibility to help me find my way. She guided me in smartening up my appearance, explaining "the things that girls like". As I grew older, she helped me select "fashionable shirts", "a good haircut" and "nice toiletries", and she avoided becoming an accomplice whenever my more manipulative sisters were stirring my parents against me. Yet even Angela reluctantly sensed I was on an inevitable path of self-destruction, which nobody, herself included, could correct.

"You must love licks," she once said, "because you keep doing wrong."

The other sisters were more inclined to mimic my parents' behaviour than leap to my defence. Veronica, one of the oldest and most dominant, once laid into me and tied me to a tree in our back yard because I'd helped myself to some food without asking, before beating me with a slipper, stick and a coat hanger.

"Bwoy ya too lickerish."

("Boy, you're too greedy.")

Veronica was convinced I deserved "licks", and believed punishment would help to beat the bad out of me. If I objected, she parroted the same lines used by my father and mother.

"Yo is a crook". ("You are a criminal") Or, more poetically, "Yo is a liard an ah teef and yo tung go ketch fire ah yo gwarn bun in hell." ("You are a liar and a thief and your tongue will catch fire and you will burn in hell.")

Clear-cut. Unambiguous. Almost ritualistic.

Even after the most vicious beatings, such as the one provoked by Amy's call, my parents never spoke a word of apology or regret. For a casual observer, we could have been any regular family in the land. Until the next time I was seen to have breached "the rules", at which point the entire brutal cycle would start again.

It was a torrid childhood. And, inevitably, the beatings and insults were counterproductive. I turned inward, but never felt that the fault lay with me. Never once did it occur to me to apologise, or to conform with my parents' absurd and hypocritical demands. On the contrary, as the months passed, my frustrations built.

I hardly spoke again with Amy, since our gentle friendship had been the catalyst for so much trauma. But the sting of Dad's belt buckle had seared my psyche more than it had blighted my flesh. Confined to my room, sobbing into my cupped hands, an array of new, strange emotions welled up inside.

No longer was I being eaten with frustration. No, after being beaten with such savagery for something so trivial, the frustration was morphing into resentment.

And the first early stirrings of rage.

*

Rage was taking hold, and yet it's scarcely fathomable that only five years had passed since I'd been called "Cherry Boy" ("sweet boy") by friends and relatives throughout the Caribbean island of St Vincent, on account of my cuteness and a cheerful disposition.

Although born in England (in fact, the only family member with this birthplace), most of my first three years were spent in St Vincent. My dad had left the island in the late 1950s, believing – as did many others of his generation – that England offered unrivalled opportunity for prosperity, fulfilment and happiness. As soon as he'd saved enough to afford a second ticket, mum had joined him in Oxford, leaving my seven sisters in the custody of various cousins and aunts.

I imagine that, for both of them, settling in to their new life was uncomfortable, and sometimes perilous. They'd left behind a world where they enjoyed status and stability, for one that was baffling, broken and unwelcoming. Those "unrivalled opportunities" were notable by their absence, rather than their abundance. Even finding their first accommodation would've been an ordeal. Many guest houses in that era posted notices on the front doors declaiming "No Blacks. No Chinese. No Indians. No Irish. No dogs." As the years passed, it was apparent that Dad was struggling to cope with the changes of an alien culture, and yearned to return to a more familiar homeland. To this day, it astonishes me they both made such an effort to persevere.

I was born in 1963, the year of Beatlemania, "I Have A Dream", and the assassination of President John F Kennedy. Driven by her pride (and surprise) at finally birthing a son, I was barely six months old when Mum decided we should return for a short spell to St Vincent, so she could showcase me to the extended family like a prized trophy. We set sail as soon as arrangements were finalised, and remained on the island for the next three years.

A sovereign country in the southeast of the Caribbean Sea, St Vincent is one of the most densely populated, but also one of the most idyllic, islands in the region. It is dominated by thickly-wooded volcanic mountains, and ash from a 1902 eruption is said to have enhanced the soil's fertility, permitting cultivation of many exotic fruits and vegetables. Bananas have long been the island's leading exports, with sweet potatoes, coconuts and plantains also widely grown, and it remains one of the world's few arrowroot producers.

At various times, St Vincent has been a colony of both the British and the French empires, meaning that both languages are widely spoken by the population, as well as a local dialect called Patwa (essentially, broken English). During my infant years on the island, it was still officially a British colony, albeit on the verge of achieving "associate statehood" status, and then full independence in 1979. As with many Caribbean islands, St Vincent's demographics reflect the policies and practices of its former Colonial masters, in particular around the slave trade.

Two-thirds of the 110,000-strong population are of African descent, transported across the Atlantic to work on the plantations. Dad belonged to this community, although his choice of wife had been in defiance of both tradition and expectation. At just 19, Zenna had been half his age when they were betrothed; more controversially, she belonged to St Vincent's Indian community. Racism was rife on the island at the time, and I respect the courage of both my parents in shaping their own future rather than bowing to convention. To minimise rejection and antagonism, I understand it was even necessary to disguise Mum's heritage on official documents, especially the marriage certificate.

The Rodgers' family farmhouse was a sprawling residence a few miles from Kingstown port. I remember its improbably high ceilings and flamboyant pink exterior. The grounds were rich with herbs and fruit – mangoes, Rose plum, and of course bananas; and we let our goats and chickens roam freely (constrained only by their fractious, wary relationship with our six excitable and protective dogs).

With its tropical climate, open spaces, occasional thunderstorms and two hundred species of bird, it's no wonder the island's anthem starts "St Vincent, land so beautiful", and as a young child I delighted in this abundance. Although, even at that tender age, I winced at the rudimentary nature of the sanitation facilities – our farm had a single outside toilet, which consisted of a toilet seat atop a large hole, devoid of any type of sewage collection apparatus.

The local school was close to our house, and in the afternoon I'd sit on our front porch, waiting for groups of pupils to pass by on their route home. As soon as they came into view, I sprinted to the gate, beaming with pleasure as the school children gathered round, enchanted at my sprightly personality, making an almighty fuss over me.

"Cherry Bwoy look nice today."

"Gimmie a cuddle Cherry Bwoy."

"Wen yo geh big yo cah gwarn school ah da teacher dem gwarn love yo."

"Wah yo karl yo darg, Cherry Bwoy?"

("what do you call your dogs, Cherry Boy?")

"Yo warnt ah sweetie, Cherry Bwoy?"

"Cherry Bwoy, tell yo sista dem we seh howdy."

("Cherry Boy, tell your sisters we say hello.")

If my smile had been any wider, the top of my head would've fallen off.

Even when they teased me, it was always good-humoured, and without malice. With such a large family, Mum found it hard to maintain a full stock of clothing for every child and every eventuality, and it wasn't unusual for me to be playing in the yard in a hand-me-down dress. "You shouldn't be wearing girls' clothes, Cherry Boy," the school children chuckled at the gate. When I passed on this message to my mother, she wrapped her arms around me in a glorious and loving hug – exhibiting a level of affection that seemed to desert her in subsequent years.

"Yo mi one son," she laughed. "OK, I won't put you in your sisters' dresses, but mi nah ha more clothes fi yo carz dem a wash."

I adored the company of our animals, especially our dogs. They gave me, and all other members of our family, protection – yelping with excitement whenever we reappeared after a trip, slobbering with excitement hoping we brought them some food. No matter how long we played, they never grew bored, as they enjoyed this unusual relationship between owner and dogs. Deciding what to call a new dog – the more outlandish, the better – was always a major occasion. After fifty years, I don't recall the names of the dogs during my first stint on the island, but on later visits I met a 'Tiger', 'Gypsy Girl', and 'Black Man', and many others whose names I can't recall.

If it seemed too good to be true, it probably was. I was too young to appreciate it at the time, but there had been a serious altercation shortly after our ship docked. Mum had arrived, unannounced, at the homes of the relatives who had supposedly been caring for her daughters, only to learn that some of them had been treated little better than servants. Dirty, subdued, malnourished – they were barely recognisable as the lively and exuberant children she'd left behind.

*

St Vincent life and culture were visible throughout my parents' Oxford house – from the clutter of ornaments and pictures of family in St Vincent and the younger years, to the plaques in the lounge on which were carved scriptural verse, to the protective plastic laid over many of the carpets and settees. The kitchen had two pantries where the shelves were crammed with divine spices and sauces required for Caribbean cuisine, alongside oversized and colourfully-enamelled cookware.

Once a week, my mother liked to spend a morning baking traditional Caribbean breads – light banana fritters, or coconut buns with a sugary crust, or fried dumplings made from flour, baking powder and butter. I suspect the ability to bake a distinctive and irresistible bread is hard-wired into the Caribbean DNA, and despite nearly a decade in Oxford, Mum's ability with a baking tray and oven were undiminished. Invariably, she created more food than could be consumed within our household, despite its size, and I'd be sent on errands to distribute her produce to acquaintances. Especially to her friend Thomas Brown, my relative, who lived about ten minutes' walk away.

"Tek da bred ah yo god farda, dem like da sweetbread," she said one weekend.

("Take the breads to your relative's house. They like sweetbread.")

Mum chose one plain and one sweet bread, both freshly baked, and wrapped them in kitchen roll, and then called ahead to let the Kings know I was on my way.

I welcomed the opportunity to spend an extended period away from the house on legitimate business, and it was a mild afternoon I had stretched out the journey time by taking a detour to avoid local gangs who relished the chance to call me names and beat me up. So whilst avoiding alley ways and some parks, I imagined the gangs were Spectre agents from the James Bond films and The Man from U.N.C.L.E. which brought some fun to what often seemed like a horror movie. In this white fantasy world I was living in, couples weren't shouting at each other, nobody was hurling racist taunts in my direction, even the squirrels seemed calmer than usual By the time I reached the Brown residence, my spirits were lifted, and I swear there was almost a spring in my step.

I rang the bell, and Thomas's wife answered the door. When she realised it was me – and saw what I was carrying – she broke out in a lovely warm smile. Her daughter Pauline was standing alongside.

"Lennox, please, why don't you come in. Thomas, look. Cherry bring bred an ting fi we."

Thomas Brown was a slim, balding man, who portrayed an apparent gentleness of spirit. He worked in a car factory in Oxford and we all knew he adored his allotment, where he'd spend hours tending to runner beans and tomatoes, but beyond that he rarely revealed much.

When I arrived with the bread selection, he'd been reclining in his armchair in the front room (it was the sort of household where everyone knew that the deepest, most imposing armchair was his). But no sooner had his wife announced my arrival, then he catapulted himself to the hall, and was waving his nose back and forth above the breads, nodding agreeably at their rich aroma.

"Pauline," said Mr Brown, "go ask ya mudda ta mek sum tea." Bizarrely, he used his daughters to send his messages to his wife, despite all three of them standing less than a couple of feet from each other. Although framed as a request, the tone conveyed there was no room for debate. Brown's wife and Pauline scurried away, as obedient as a domestic servant in a country manor. There was no doubt about the power balance within this particular marriage. "Karl wen yo redy," he added.

"I hope you like them, Mr Brown," I said. "Mum worked hard to make them nice."

"Don't worry about that," he replied. "Now, come and sit here, and tell me about how you're getting on at school." I noticed he was speaking in English, rather than the Patwa he'd used to communicate with his wife.

He gestured towards the sofa. I sat on the middle of its three seat cushions, and gazed around the room. At the polished cabinet in the far corner. And the small table on which were scattered a handful of magazines. And a family photograph hanging on the wall – Thomas, his wife and his two daughters, Pauline and Lucy, sitting together on a park bench.

"Is Lucy home today?" I enquired.

"I think she's upstairs doing some homework," Brown said, still standing by the door, as if on sentry duty. "She's got a lot to do; it's probably best if we don't disturb them."

He looked at me with a stare that lingered for a few seconds longer than was comfortable. Then he made to sit down. But instead of returning to the favoured armchair, I suddenly found him seated right next to me. I squirmed with surprise and apprehension, but I wasn't quite sure why I felt such emotions. After all, my sisters and my parents often sat next to me on the sofa.

"That's better," he said. "Now we can talk properly."

"What do we need to talk about, Mr Brown?"

"School, like I said. Or perhaps how you're getting on at home. Or music. Whatever you like."

I noticed his leg was almost touching mine, so I shifted an inch to the right.

"I'm happy to talk about anything you want," I said weakly.

"Lang time mi no yo mudda ya no," he said, slipping into Patwa.

("You know that your mother and I have been friends for many years?")

He spread his hands as if to signify the passage of time, and one of his palms brushed against my shoulder.

I noticed he'd adjusted his weight, and once more his leg was against mine. Again, I eased to the right. And, again, almost imperceptibly, he nudged along in my direction. Two people, shuffling awkwardly along a single sofa. Literally and figuratively, I'd been cornered.

"Nah worry yoself bout nuting," Brown said, soothingly. "Yo no seh we arl love yo lang time, mi love yo tu yo no. We tek care ah yo."

("Don't worry yourself about anything, You no we have all have loved you for a long time. I love you too you know, we will take care of you.")

Now I could feel his hand sliding along on my thigh towards my groin, the feeling wasn't pleasant, I tried to wriggle away, but didn't want to antagonise him. So, trying to be casual, I pushed away his hand. I didn't say anything in case it would seem impolite.

"Wah apen, yo na war mi touch yo?" said Brown, as if insulted.

Stray thoughts were tumbling around in my head, but I still couldn't figure out what was going on. Why was he acting this way? Had I upset him? Was this normal behaviour from a family friend? Was he feeling lonely and in need of some company? I couldn't get anything straight, and all the time he was still talking about love and family. If I tried to say something, my mouth dried up and I struggled to formulate words of protest.

"Relax yoself," he said, "mi nah do yo nuting bwoy mi jus ah show yo, mi love yo."

("Relax I am not doing anything I am just trying to show you my love.")

Now his hand was in my groin area, stroking me through my trousers. He had tucked his thumb inside the rim of my trousers so that it made direct contact with my flesh. The harshness of his grope was jarring, and finally enabled me to give vent to the words that had been swirling around, unformed, in my head.

"Please, stop, I don't like it."

"Why? Don't you like it?"

"I don't know. I'm really sorry."

With one final caress, Brown withdrew his hand. But he didn't retreat along the sofa. Instead, motionless, he stared silently into my eyes. I blinked and looked away… Yet I could still sense his unrelenting stare burning into me. I glanced back in his direction. His face was twisted into a weird expression, one that I'd never observed before. The corners of his mouth curled upward into something resembling a smirk. His pupils were dilated. His brow was slightly redder that usual, with traces of perspiration. Only later did I come to recognise what this look signified. Stubborn, determined, unfulfilled lust.

The stillness was ruptured by a tap of a tray against the living room door. It was Mrs Brown.

"Come eat, man," she said.

2.
Loved in Different Ways

Oxford, the "City of Dreaming Spires," is admired worldwide as a centre of scholarship and the unwavering pursuit of knowledge. Its academic history is as illustrious as its architectural splendour. The city is home to the oldest university in the English speaking world; and the first museum – the Ashmolean – to be opened to the public. No wonder the finest young minds on all continents crave admission to its halls of residence.

Yet this idyllic vision couldn't be further removed from the experience of the city for someone growing up in a recently arrived migrant family in the late 1960s. To me, Oxford came to be associated with malicious animosity towards anyone seen as an outsider. In those days, racism wasn't concealed beneath a more accommodating veneer. It was brazen, especially in the school playground.

The number of non-white children at my junior school could be counted on the fingers of both hands, and we tended to stick together. We represented a microcosm of the planet's diversity, with one or two kids from Africa, from India, from China. Chris Grant was the only other pupil who shared my Caribbean heritage, and we quickly became close friends. Anyone with an Irish accident was also treated with venom by the older white boys, and had no choice but to gravitate towards our close-knit group.

The time of greatest danger for us was in the morning, thirty minutes before the school bell rang out. Until nine o'clock, no pupils were permitted inside the school buildings; neither could we loiter on the main road outside the gates or venture onto the football field. We had no choice but to gather, unsupervised, in the small tarmacked playground, enclosed by the main premises to one side, and the infant school to the other. A hundred and fifty kids crammed together with no adults to restrain any violent impulses. It was clearly a hotbed for bullying.

It was only my second day at Wood Farm Junior when I saw racism explode into violence. Stuart was the ringleader and the catalyst. One of the oldest and tallest boys in the school – perhaps he'd already hit puberty? – he strode to the centre of the playground, spat on the ground, his face twisted in contempt, and hollered his battle cry:

"Right, everyone. It's whites against blacks!"

The next thing I remember is the noise. Twenty boys rallying to Stuart's commands, and charging towards us, yelling and howling, leaving us in no doubt about their hostile intent. There was nowhere to flee, so our group – five of us dawdling in the playground corner – braced ourselves for the inevitable. It wasn't a long wait.

Within moments, I was lying flat on the tarmac. A brusque push to the chest had sent me reeling backwards until I lost my balance. I felt a stinging kick in the small of my back. We were hopelessly outnumbered, but instinctively I bounced back to my feet. They took aim at my legs – kicking at my shins, my calves, my knees – until I was once again stumbling around liked a dazed amateur boxer.

"Well, niggermind about that," laughed one of the boys.

"Wogamatter? Niggermind, you'll be all white in the morning." It was being sung like a times-table.

"Get back to the jungle, nigger."

"You swing from the trees, nigger."

"You're a jungle bunny a Sambo."

"Get a wash. You're white under that dirt."

I was on the ground again, and this time I curled up into a foetal position to protect my head. After a few more kicks, I felt one of the older boys grabbing me under the arms and hauling me to my feet. But I wasn't being rescued. Lifting me upright gave them the adrenaline rush of knocking me down all over again.

"Don't cry, wog – you'll be all white in the morning."

Until that point in my life, my entire experience had comprised three blissful years in St Vincent, followed by the nurturing simplicity of my infant school. So I was still naïve about how much spite and bile can dwell inside the human heart. Even whilst being beaten, it never occurred to me that my tormenters weren't telling the truth. If they assured me I'd be "all white in the morning," why would I doubt their honesty? So I was confused, the next day, when I scrubbed my skin to put it to the test, and my colour didn't change. All that happened was my skin felt sore, as if I had given myself a Chinese burn, and all the bruises and scratches and cuts remained as painful as before. Did my body regenerate at a slower pace than everyone else's?

And why did they accuse me of being from the jungle? I didn't remember where I lived any thickets of jungle vegetation on the island like on Tarzan – the landscape had been expansive fields leading to golden beaches. And I'd certainly never been allowed to climb trees. Let alone swing from them. How could they be so mistaken? Should I correct them?

The "whites against blacks" fights took place, always before and after school rather than during break times when teachers were assigned to supervise. But I can't believe the staff were ignorant of the harassment taking place on their premises. After a beating, I'd sit in class squirming and fidgeting and wincing as the pain lingered, my clothes dishevelled and sometimes ripped from the defeats. Sometimes I'd spot teachers watching the brawls through the classroom windows, as if they were the curious observers of an experiment, under an obligation not to intervene or as if they had placed a bet on a horse at the bookies. It was most hurtful when I saw one of the infant school staff members gazing at the fights from a safe distance – the same teacher who'd treated me with care and affection when I'd been under her charge.

In the early weeks, there was never any doubt about which side would emerge victorious from the fights. We were fewer in numbers, easily intimidated, inexperienced and we didn't have any combat skills. As time went on, the confrontations weren't always so one-sided. We developed some basic ability in self-defence and battle strategy. We'd design formations that protected our backs and made it difficult to separate us. Most importantly, we learnt to throw as well as receive a punch, often experimenting with moves we saw executed by James Bond, Tarzan or The Man From U.N.C.L.E.

The first time I heard a white boy yelp under a well-timed blow, I felt a great sense of euphoria and an overwhelming satisfaction, whoever said revenge was sweet, was right. In the second month, a couple of white Irish boys joined our side when they saw confrontation raging. I never figured out why; even with our enhanced tactics, we'd usually come off worse. They were either foolhardy, masochistic, or just desperate to get involved. Of course, we welcomed all volunteers regardless of their motivation.

Until junior school, I hadn't felt any real sense of an identity or belonging. I was a person, just like everyone else. Each of us had a physical body with hands and feet and eyes and ears. And we each had a soul; I'd been taught that at church. But I had no inkling that I was a particular sort of person; that there was a tribe to which I belonged, and other tribes from which I was cut off. I didn't define myself by adjectives. I wasn't a good person or a bad person; I wasn't a violent person or a peaceful person. Not a leader nor a follower. I was just me.

The taunts and insults from Stuart and his cronies became the trigger for my self-image and identity to take shape, a picture also influenced by the covert racism of the teachers, who seemed to relish gratuitous insults, and sometimes the slipper, whenever they felt I was struggling to understand a topic or paying insufficient attention. (I was also the last boy in class to receive a "10 yards" swimming certificate since fault was always found with a minor aspect of my technique; I was told that doggy paddling was the summit of my abilities.)

In the beginning, my self-image was little more than a series of snatched and scarcely understood words, none of which made any sense. I was a black boy. I was different. I was disliked. I was a victim. But, also, I was someone for whom fist were easier than words. Who could stand up for himself. Who could retaliate. And who, increasingly, found that being on the offence delivers results.

*

If I tried to discuss the bullying at Wood Farm Junior with my dad or mum, they showed little sympathy. They preferred to obsess about my unkempt appearance rather than the events which had caused it.

"Fix hup yoself bwoy, yo wah bring shame ah mi," Mum would say.

("Tidy yourself up, do you want to bring shame on me?")

If my trousers were torn, or my shoes were scuffed, they shouted at me and beat me as though it was my fault. It didn't take long for me to clam up. Better to take the blame, suffer the consequences, and get it over and done.

However, Chris Grant's mother was horrified and distraught on my behalf. Ceredwynne was no stranger to racism; although herself white and born in Oxford, her husband George was from Jamaica. Marrying across ethnic boundaries was, in the 1960s, as brave as it was rare. Ceredwynne found herself shunned by long-standing friends, and even family members. Her heart broke when her son told her about this "poor kid" who had "harmed no one" but for whom life was a daily ricochet between places of horror – punishment beatings at home, and racist violence at school. (Being of mixed race and head-turning good looks, and exuding an aura of coolness as he swaggered about, Chris rarely found himself the target of the racists' contempt.)

I'll never forget the day I first met her. The Grants lived immediately opposite the field, on a road called Titup Hall Drive (you can imagine the sniggering that provoked between young boys; I teased Chris relentlessly). With my parents both working until the early evening – it was the most natural thing in the world to accept Chris' invitation to meet his folks. Ceredwynne (who I came to know as "Mummy G") gave me the most fulsome bearhug ("Chris has told me all about you, you wonderful boy"), and when she released me, she unwrapped her arms carefully and slowly, as if she was petrified of what would happen if I slipped from her protection.

I tapped on the door at 7am and Chris shouted down to his mother, "Can Lennox come in?" Mrs Grant welcomed me into the house and looked at me and within minutes said, "Look at the state of you, you can't go to school like that." She had me up those stairs in the bathroom, cleaning and washing, and gave me Chris's clean pants and socks and I was back downstairs in no time. I was unrecognisable to myself when I looked in the mirror. This was my first ever experience of family life.

"You must need breakfast, are you hungry? I'm sure you are," she said.

I didn't know how to respond. I wasn't used to such exuberant displays of affection from white people. Should I say, "You're very kind," or "Can I help you?" With the words sticking in my throat, the manners and respect that had been beaten into me won through, and I said simply, "Thank you."

Chris and I often went to see his mum on a Saturday at the cinema where she worked. She gave us money to buy snacks, and we always selected the noisiest crisps or popcorn. We snuck in to watch movies we weren't meant to see, such as Jaws or The Godfather, and were never challenged because the staff knew Chris was the boss's son. We sat in the back row, mucking loudly, and pee-shooting sweets at the people's heads in front of us.

I spent an increasing amount of time with the Grants; it became my sanctuary for many years. The regular world had become a place of brutality and fear. The click of the latch and the sight of Mummy G's side door swinging ajar for me, like I was a member of the family, heralded entry into my safe haven. A place where words were used to encourage and praise, rather than to chastise; where love was offered unconditionally. Where, instead of telling me off for looking scruffy, Mummy G would kneel in front of me to help out – pulling up my socks, and wiping away mud stains with a damp cloth.

"I'm not letting you go around wearing old pants," she said. "Here's a pair of Chris's that I've just washed. Put those on instead."

One day, I was sitting on their garden step watching as George Grant showed Chris the basic functions of a car engine. "You could be a mechanic one day," he said to Chris, "It's a highly respectable profession." And I felt the warm wetness of tears running down my cheeks. It had never occurred to me that the parental role involves much more than never-ending condemnation; that fathers should be mentors, preparing their young to take their place in the world. It was a startling revelation.

Ceredwynne and George were careful how they involved me in family matters, since they knew I was damaged emotionally, but that didn't stop my excitable dreaming. One night, my imagination spilt over as it formed scenes of a possible new future. Going to St Giles Fair with the Grants. At the seaside with the Grants. Perhaps one day even taking the Grants to St Vincent, so they could see where I'd spent my early years.

I never learnt whether Mummy G made any serious enquiries about the adoption route. She never mentioned it to me again, and I respected her too much to ask. I adored her; in fact, she was the one person to whom I could never lie. What sort of person would I be, I asked myself, if I betrayed her unconditional kindness by disguising the truth, however hurtful that might be? She simply needed to say, "Tell me the truth Lennox," and the facts would tumble from my lips. Later, my inability to deceive or fabricate under Mummy G's gaze became a source of some friction between Chris and me. As we experimented in the world of petty crime, he would construct complex alibis to prove his innocence; but these efforts collapsed when I confessed to every offence under his mother's mild interrogation.

*

The trick was to wait until the cashiers were busy serving customers. When they were preoccupied with price tags and till receipts, they couldn't scan the shop floor for trouble. It was the start of the summer holidays, and I was evaluating the scene. One shop assistant facing off with an argumentative customer, the other ringing up the contents of an overfilled shopping basket. This created the ideal opportunity for a bit of thieving.

I was in the Headington branch of Boots the Chemist. It was not one of their showcase retail outlets. There were large stains on the carpet tiles, the paintwork was peeling, and the lights would flicker as if somebody had forgotten to top up the meter. It was the only brand name store on the block – I remember it being alongside a launderette, and a wine merchants and a newsagents. Crucially for my purposes, whoever had been making decisions about the store layout had little appreciation for how shoplifters operate. Portable high-value merchandise was placed on aisles just inside the entrance. The temptation was irresistible.

It was a year or so after a "whites against blacks" battle, and word had gotten around school that I had a knack for nicking stuff. Up to that time, it had all been petty thieving. Chocolate bars, magazines, small toys, even a jelly baby from a stash used by one of our teachers to reward diligent classwork. The most intriguing aspect of my burgeoning reputation was that, with the exception of one jelly baby (when my denials had been undermined by the powdery sugar on my chin), I'd so far evaded detection. As news circulated that I'd been caught taking sweets, I acquired a new nickname: "Stealer".

My eyes roved across the array of goods before me. Hairdryers. Electric razors. Women's toiletries. Mentally, I checked off how much I'd be able to conceal. My jacket had been carefully modified for the task; I'd removed the seams on the inner lining, and my hands could whip out through holes at the bottom of the pockets. With just one or two uncomplicated manoeuvres, it didn't take long to transport a medium-sized box from shelf to my person. And the jacket's ample padding ensured that the box remained inconspicuous, especially if I pushed it around the inside of the lining until it rested against the small of my back.

"Get ready, Lennox," an inner voice was whispering. "If you miss this moment, you might not get another chance today. And, as a little black boy, you can't be hanging around the aisles for too long, or people will get suspicious."

I glanced again towards the checkout. The argument was still in full throttle – something about "It was already broken? when I got home" – and an old lady with a walking stick was looking on impatiently. Neither of the cashiers seemed remotely interested in whatever might be happening elsewhere in the shop. I could feel the blood pumping around my body. What if there was an undercover staff member looking out for thieves? What if I dropped something on the floor in clumsy haste? What if everybody could hear the boom boom boom of my heart racing? A bead of sweat trickled down my forehead. I counted to three and then... Grabbed the box. Slipped it into the lining. Pulled my jacket tight.

A mere two seconds had passed, and the hairdryer was in my possession. A weird silence descended. I could no longer detect my heartbeat, but every other sound in the shop was magnified. A cough, the clink of change being handed over, the tap of the walking stick. My instinct was to run, but I knew that would serve to attract attention. I must remain inconspicuous. I shuffled towards the exit. No, that was no good. Too slow. Not natural. The more I tried to walk normally, the harder it became. I sucked at the inside of my cheeks, and put one foot in front of the other. Another step, and I was in the doorway. Another, onto the pavement. Outside. Free.

The hairdryer was being stolen to order; it wasn't the type of product a ten-year old boy from St Vincent would pilfer for his own use. As my reputation for being light-fingered had spread, one or two of the school racists had mentioned me to their parents. Before long, I was being given "wants lists". The hairdryer had been requested by the mother of one of the Wood Farm's nastiest pieces of work.

I was never paid for my enterprise; the racists would've seen that as preposterous. However, my success did win their grudging respect, albeit for a short while. Usually, we agreed they would wait just around the corner, so the item could be handed over moments after it had disappeared from the shelves. I liked it that way; if I carried stuff back to Wood Farm, I ran the risk of bumping into other local gangs – who would set upon me and rob me. It must've been an odd sight to anyone who'd witnessed the playground bullying and now seeing the racist tormentors with the black victim walking along the main road as if they were best buddies. It was certainly emotionally muddled for me. Rage at their viciousness still festered within; on the other hand, it was a relief to be in their presence for half an hour without a single callout of "nigger" or "wog". Instead I was being told "You're okay, it's the others like them Pakis and some of them other wogs."

Although I had a flair for self-preservation, not every one of my law-breaking escapades ended so happily. By the age of eleven, I'd been to court five times, usually for unruly behaviour or for petty theft. I'd also started thieving at home, and whilst Dad and Mum refrained from reporting me to the authorities, I'd still suffer the usual painful consequences.

On one occasion, I broke open the meter for the television, and took nearly five pounds in loose change; I'd used a screwdriver to snap open the device, and my attempts to disguise the damage were blatantly obvious. On another, I helped myself to "Partner Money", which my mum kept hidden in a cupboard in her bedroom. This was pooled funds, with contributions from most members of her Church, that was used as a kind of collective savings account. Comically, I advertised my guilt by spending my ill-acquired gains on a luminous yellow sweater and trousers.

When you're under age, court appearances can be surreal. Everybody around you seems ancient – far older than the teachers at school, possibly even older than the headmaster – and speaks about you as if you're not present. Token attempts are made for the proceedings to be intelligible, but for the most part everybody uses concepts you can't follow and terminology you don't understand. In the early 1970s, guilt was assumed. Nobody was arguing in my defence, and I don't recall ever being granted an opportunity to enter a plea. I wasn't even aware of the roles of all the adults in the room – terms such as "magistrate" or "clerk of the court" or "recorder" or "duty solicitor" or "probation officer" were banded around, but only later did I learn everyone's part in the proceedings.

The overriding memory is how glum and solemn the whole thing seemed. Nobody smiled, and everyone acted as though the severity of my misdemeanours was off the scale.

My dad was usually sitting next to me (Mum refused to attend out of sheer disgust), but was never invited to offer any remarks of mitigation in my defence. Of course, had he been asked, the likelihood is he'd have exacerbated my problems. On one occasion, while I was being quizzed by the police about an infraction, I'd tried to explain that someone else had been the instigator. Dad had shouted, "Bwoy yo tu lie, mi nah tell yo fi tap lie?" ("You're lying, we've taught you never to lie.") and to my shame slapped me in full view of the officers. They'd crossed their arms and nodded with approval at the sight of sound parental discipline being exercised.

By the time of the fifth court appearance, the system had clearly had enough. Before the official proceedings commenced, the duty solicitor sat with me for thirty minutes, explaining this would be unlike the earlier sessions. I was already under the mild supervision of Social Services due to the previous charges, but – the duty solicitor explained – it would be argued this had proven insufficient to curb the extent of my misbehaviour.

I was accustomed to adults trying to intimidate or frighten me with harsh words, but for the first time the tone of his remarks made me feel chills. Previously, the court sittings were concluded lightning-fast. This time, it seemed never ending. Social Services had turned up mob handed – I counted at least four representatives from the department, and they made a point of reciting, blow by unsavoury blow, all the charges that were racked up on my rap sheet. Having dissected the apparent failure of the efforts at mild supervision, they reviewed the pros and cons of a range of options before delivering their recommendation. There was a short break whilst the magistrates huddled for their deliberations. When the session resumed, the stream of words blurred into a background buzz while I glared from person to person, trying to suss out what was happening. Then, the eldest magistrate rested his spectacles on the desk, stared straight at me, and raised his voice a couple of decibels.

"Lennox Rodgers," he said. "It's been decided to place you into care."

A care order doesn't operate in the same way as a prison sentence. The guards don't handcuff you, and escort you from the dock direct to the prison cell. An hour after the court had adjourned, I found myself at home, watching television, as if nothing of any magnitude had transpired. By the following day, everything seemed back to normal. I rose, argued with my sisters about something trivial, turned up at the Grants where we had breakfast as usual and I collected my clean underwear, mucked around during lessons, stole a Mars bar from Tilly's on the way home and hung around in the park – where, I'd learnt, it was easiest to escape local gangs and "jungle" taunts due to the many escape routes. By early evening, the events of the previous day were fading from my mind.

It had just turned dark when the doorbell rang and Dad said:

"Bwoy come ya, sum people deh ya fi yo."

("Boy, some people are here for you.")

Two social workers and a policeman entered the house. While my mum was making everyone a cup of tea, the more senior of the social workers explained what would be happening. I wasn't asked any questions, or given any opportunity to respond. Her voice was polite but firm; this wasn't a matter for debate.

"We've found a very nice place for you to stay tonight, Lennox," she said. "The people who work there will look after you, and I'm sure you'll make a lot of new friends. You need to make a real effort to behave properly while you're away. I can't tell you how long it'll last, but it will be better for you if you make friends with the other children and obey your orders. Now I'll give you five minutes to go to your room and collect anything you'd like to take with you. Your mother has kindly already packed your clothes into a suitcase, but perhaps you'd also like a favourite book or a few comics, or one of your toys. We'll be waiting here, and we can leave as soon as you've filled your bag."

Upstairs, the enormity of this change finally hit home. I didn't bother with my books or comics; and daren't retrieve my stolen stash of notes. Instead I sat on the edge of my bed, overwhelmed by fear, and began sobbing. My cries must've been audible throughout the house, but no one came to comfort me. Except for my sister Angela. She tapped lightly on the door, and asked, "Do you mind if I come in, Lennox?" Sitting next to me on the bed, she wrapped her arm around my shoulder. With her other hand, she held mine, and intertwined our fingers.

"You shouldn't blame anyone for this Lennox," she said. "I love you. We all love you. You just need to find ways to stop stealing and getting into trouble. You're going away from this home, but not from our hearts. I'm sure we'll see you back here again very soon."

I stopped crying for a moment, and she wiped the tears from my face with her thumb.

"Say your prayers every night and never forget God."

It was a haunting, beautiful moment. I felt a tranquillity that, for the next thirty years, would elude me. Neither Angela nor I felt the need to fill the silence with words. We sat and hugged as if nothing in the world could ever interrupt us.

But, of course, the inevitable interruption wasn't far away.

"Lennox, bwoy ya nah ere mi a carl yo!" my dad was shouting at me to come downstairs.

Two minutes later, I was being escorted along the short path from the front door. It's eerie how many details from that day remain vividly scarred in my mind. The car that would be transporting me to my new home was a dull red Austin Morris, with light brown rubbery seat covers. However the most intense memory is of my mum's words, as I rested my bags in the car boot. She was standing in the doorway, Dad peering over her shoulder, calling:

"Tek im, tek im."

It felt as if a knife had pierced my soul.

*

Being renounced by my mother was a traumatic moment in my childhood. But it wasn't the worst. A year later, aged twelve, I contrived with my friend Alan to run away from Thornburry House, an observational assessment unit for pre-teens with behavioural issues. One evening, having been threatened by one of the more sadistic staff members, Mr Macho, that we'd be "locked away in a cell and left to rot", we tested the emergency exit doors until we found one that had been left unlocked. There was a short and ill-lit pathway. We checked that none of the security officers were nearby, and, hunched over, sped towards safety. We hadn't formulated any sort of implementation plan; we simply wanted to be on the outside.

"What now?" asked Alan, once we were beyond Thornburry's boundary.

I shrugged, clueless about how Assessment Centre escapees generally approach the next few hours.

We agreed to head to Oxford, despite it being over twenty miles away, for no better reason than I was familiar with the territory. After an hour or so, we figured that Thornburry Centre had probably alerted the police to our flight, and so we covered as much ground as possible out of view from the public highway. When we had no choice but to use the country lanes, we ducked behind bushes whenever a car came into view. Progress was painfully slow. Halfway through the night, exhausted, we crashed out in a field. Before we fell asleep, we reflected on what we should do once we reached the city.

"We can't do anything without money," said Alan. "Do you know anyone who might help us out?"

"There's a family called the Grants," I replied. "They've been very kind to me over the years."

"That sounds perfect."

"I don't think so. I can never lie to Mrs Grant, I call her Mummy G. If she asks what we've been doing, everything will spill out. I won't be able to stop myself."

"Well, Oxford is your base more than mine," said Alan. "Who else do you know?"

I ticked off the options. Clearly, there was no point making an appearance at home. "Tek im, tek im," encapsulated Mum's attitude to perfection. A long shot could be asking the racist bullies' parents. They might feel a soft spot for me on account of their hairdryer collections. But they'd never been willing to pay a penny beforehand, so were unlikely to start now – especially since I no longer had any immediate value for them. Which left Thomas Brown. He had been one of the few people who had never beaten me, never shouted at me, never belittled me. It was worth a shot.

By the time we reached Oxford, Alan was fed up and disenchanted with our adventure. I think he'd assumed I'd conjure a magical solution, but instead he'd had to endure a miserable day of sleeping rough, avoiding detection, and feeling hungry. It almost made him yearn for life back in Thornburry. He announced, "We've come this far together, but from now on, I want to do my own thing." He couldn't be dissuaded.

I was no longer just cold, hungry, tired and broke. I was also friendless.

Brown was alone at home when I arrived. After the ordeal of my flight from Thornburry, I must've looked quite a sight. I was finding it hard to express myself coherently.

"Please, Mr Brown, can you help me please? I was with my friend Alan, but he's gone now. I'm alone and don't know what to do. I need help. They told me they'd lock me up in prison so we escaped through a fire door. I don't know what else to say. The police are probably looking for me."

Brown rested a calming hand on my forearm. "I didn't understand all of that, but I got that you need help," he said. "Why don't you come in, and we can discuss it privately?"

"Thank you, Mr Brown."

"Don't worry bout noting. Come leh weh tark."

("Come let us talk.")

Brown indicated for me to rest on his sofa, and I shuddered involuntarily at the recollection of the times he'd touched me sitting there. But perhaps this time would be different, and at least he wasn't shouting at me or threatening to beat me. In fact, he offered to make me a chicken sandwich, and a mug of tea. After nearly two days without food or drink, I perked up immediately.

While Brown was in the kitchen, I looked around the living room. As with many Caribbean homes, it was characterized by clutter. Pictures, knick-knacks, ornaments, old magazines. Thick net curtains covered the windows, meaning the road outside was a jumble of blurred images. I guess that also stopped passers-by from peering in.

Brown returned with my meal, and I chomped at the sandwich heartily. It was nothing special – Caribbean-style chicken in hard dough bread but without the customary more rice and peas – but, after sleeping rough, it tasted like gourmet cuisine. Brown was sitting in his favourite armchair, with his legs wide apart, which was a bit strange. He straightened his cardigan, removed his spectacles, and stared at me intently as I ate. Unnerved, I felt the need to fill the silence, and said:

"I need some money, Mr Brown. Not much, just £10. Can you give me that?"

"If I gi yo dat, what will you give me?"

"I don't know, I don't have anything."

"Mi love yo yo no." Although I was still a few months away from being a teenager, I knew enough about the adult world to recognise a hint of lust in his tone. But I also recalled the precious love between George Grant and Chris. The memory of George talking passionately about mechanics flickered before my mind's eye.

"Love me like a son," I replied. It was a mixture of a question and a plea.

Suddenly, I was achingly aware that Brown's wife and daughters were elsewhere. Feeling the urge to leave, I rose, but I didn't want to make a scene. So, instead, I said simply, "I'll leave the plate by the sink," and headed for the kitchen. I could hear him calling after me, but my breathing was so short and deep that I couldn't make out his words.

When I returned, he was standing, and had edged closer to the door to the hallway, as if blocking off an escape route. I was about to make my excuses to leave when he said, "I love yo like dat an mi love yo anuda way as well." ("I love you like that, and I love you another way as well.")

Did he want to rub me again, like he had before? I couldn't imagine what else.

He hugged me, but it wasn't an affectionate hug. With his arms wrapped around me, he started turning me around, and I was surprised at the strength. Now he was standing behind me, so that I was facing the fireplace. An oblong mirror hung above the mantelpiece on the chimney breast. In the reflection, I saw his head tilting into mine until our cheeks touched. His mouth was so close to my ear that I could feel the warmth of his breath on my face, and I could smell the staleness of his last meal. His nestled his chin against the side of my neck, and moved it gently from side to side. His stubble scratched against my skin. There must've been a thousand hairs, and I was aware of the roughness of each one as it scraped my flesh.

Sensing my discomfort, he whispered:

"Why yo nah lem mi ha mi way wid yo?"

("Why won't you let me have my way?")

I felt his hands wandering over my legs and groin.

"If yo wah de money yo mus lem mi love yo my way."

("If you want the money, let me love you my way.")

Without warning, he unzipped my trousers and let them drop to my feet. I felt his hands wandering all around my pelvic area. My eyes darted around the room. I noticed the bronze shade of the mirror's frame, and the shapes of the decorative leaves which adorned it. And the faded wallpaper. And the red patterned carpet. Please let this be over. Hopefully, he'll touch me for a minute or two, and then it will be over.

His hands were no longer fondling me, but were now gripping the rim of my underpants. I felt the rub of fabric against my flesh as he slid them downwards, and I instinctively gathered them in my clenched fists to thwart his efforts. For a moment, we were pulling against each other, as if playing tug-of-war in the school playground.

"Tek dung yo brief," he said. "Or else you no wah appen."

("Take off your underpants or else.")

My mind filled with thoughts of prison. And my hunger. And being alone after Alan's desertion.

"Eh nah tek lang. Wait deh."

("It won't take long. Wait there.")

I didn't know what to do. I couldn't summon the energy for a confrontation, so – worn down and exhausted – I loosened my grip. In the mirror, I saw a smile spread across his face; the satisfied smirk of someone who has emerged victorious from a battle of wills, who has proven that the powerful will always triumph over the powerless. He let go of me. I was shaking but lacked the composure to move. I was vaguely aware of rustling as he searched in a cupboard drawer, and moments later, in the mirror, I saw him scooping his fingers into a tub of Vaseline.

Using the full weight of his body, he leant into me and forced me forward. I stretched out my arms to grab the mantelpiece, but my coordination was shot to pieces, and my flailing hands knocked against two ceramic figurines, sending them crashing to the floor. Finally, my fingers found the stone. As my body tensed up, I saw the blood veins on my knuckles widening as if fit to burst through the skin.

"Mi nah tel yo seh mi nah tek lang?" he repeated.

("told you it won't take long.")
The pain as he entered me was searing.

3.
Shoes In A Pillow Case

However much I scrubbed, I couldn't get rid of the sensation of having been defiled. The taps were turned to maximum, and the force of the inrushing water sent a spray throughout the bathroom, but the touch and smell and taste of Brown wouldn't wash away. So I emptied the bath and tried again.

I lathered the soap until I'd created an expanse of foam that roamed like a mountain range across the surface of the water, as if my encounter with Brown could be eradicated from history through the sheer volume of cleansing products I was applying. I tried lying in the bath until my whole body was submerged; and then standing up so I could vigorously rub my torso and my legs with a flannel. I made the bath too hot, and then too cold. I twisted and turned, hoping I could shake him loose. I tried thinking of something – anything – else. Wood Farm; Thornburry; Mummy G.

But, like an itch that gets more intense as you scratch it, nothing was working. My skin was crawling at the memory of Brown's breath, fingers, penis. And, against my will, my mind was re-living the nauseating detail of every moment in his house. I could even feel the clammy wetness of his ejaculate trickling down my leg, two hours after the event; so I grabbed a scrubbing brush and wiped back and forth across my thigh until I was bleeding. But it was no use; the wetness refused to budge.

Nobody had noticed as I'd crept back into my parents' house, but I couldn't stay invisible against the backdrop of the water's pounding sound. Dad had been informed by the police that I'd taken flight from Thornburry, so it didn't take him long to figure out who was in the bathroom. Oddly, his principal concern didn't seem to be my presence or my wellbeing or my behaviour. Despite not having seen me for nearly a year, his primary focus was my adverse effect on his ability to wash the dishes.

"Bwoy! ah yo use arf de warta?" he yelled, banging on the bathroom door and sucking his teeth.

("Boy, are you using off the hot water.")

I spent the next few hours lying alone in my bedroom, unable to get comfortable. Eventually, the smell of Brown's breath and the sound of his sadistic chuckling dimmed; but the feeling of his penis in my backside refused to fade. Every half an hour, I ran to the bathroom, convinced that I needed to defecate, only to discover my bowels were empty. Brown's corruption of me had disorientated my brain's ability to comprehend messages from that area of my body; I could no longer distinguish between normal bodily signals and the intensity of my reflex memories. It would be weeks until I was again able to sequence appropriate toilet visits.

My escape from Thornburry had ended in humiliation, and I knew it wouldn't be long before the police arrived to haul me back. But there was one person I yearned to meet whilst I was free. By now, Chris Grant would've been home from school for a couple of hours, so I stood below his bedroom window, whistling to attract his attention. Once he'd gotten over his astonishment at seeing me in Oxford, we headed for the Rec Park, where we sat on the roundabout, snapping twigs from a nearby tree.

"Chris," I said, "Something really weird happened to me earlier today."

Chris looked inquisitively. "Weirder than usual?"

"You know about sex, like, between men and women?"

"You know I do."

"I think my relative had sex with me. And I hated every moment of it."

Chris stared at me, his eyes widening saucer-like. I had no idea what I should do next. What's the normal chain of events when you're confiding in your best friend about being raped? Would he hug me? Should I hug him? Should I wait for him to say something? Would he suggest we talk with Mummy G?

Instead, his face broke into a grin, he thrust back his head, and he laughed. He was oblivious to my horror and distress, because we had spent many years laughing at the expense of other people's mishaps and now I knew what it felt like to be on the receiving end. During this time it was difficult for a child to accuse an adult and be believed; the thought of this increased my fears.

It was many years until I was able to confide in anyone else about my experience of being raped.

*

Before my escape from Thornburry, my encounters with the social care world had involved a blizzard of assessment centres, observation centres and care homes whilst the system strove to settle on the best solution for me. Being recaptured brought matters to a head. I was reassigned to St Edward's School as an alternative to the youth detention centre, an independent boarding school that specialised in handling children who'd exhibited the worst behavioural issues. Situated near Romsey, Hampshire, St Edward's is the former manor home of Lord and Lady Melchet, and it still conveyed the aura of a stately home. It was set in vast grounds with beautifully manicured gardens, an aviary and a stable block for retired race horses.

No-one was sent to St Edward's unless more tentative measures had proven fruitless, partly because the intensity of the supervision required a severe cap on the number of admissions. With up to a hundred pupils at any given time, the teaching was more intimate than at Eton, with class-sizes of perhaps five or six. Yet it would be nigh impossible to run such a school using ordinary teaching methods. Every child had either committed extensive criminal damage, or displayed unceasing hostility to authority figures including their family. The common factor was our immunity to all conventional attempts to control our behaviour. St Edward's' uncompromising approach to enforcing discipline – most of the teaching staff were ex-servicemen – made it an attractive last resort.

The Headmaster was Mr Bailey. We were woken just before seven by a burly staff member with the delightful name of Mr Harris, who would shake us from our beds with his trademark encouragement "frogs' legs for breakfast today." (After a while, I learnt to reply in similar vein, "Can't I have spiders' legs today instead, please sir?") Nobody was allowed to leave the dormitories with the beds unmade and the person on cleaning duties had to leave surfaces spotless. The dreaded punishment, should the skirting board next to your bed reveal any sign of dust, was "You're on scrubbing duties at break time." For serial offenders, this meant cleaning the gym floor with a toothbrush. On the other hand, passing the inspection was met with a ringing endorsement from Mr Harris: "All checked out! Now for your ablutions."

My first night in the dormitory didn't go well; not due to my inattentiveness to dust, but because – influenced by Angela – I still knelt by the side of my bed in prayer before tucking myself under the sheets. Making matters worse, I found it impossible to pray silently, and, for the battle-hardened boys to the right and left, this was the trigger for an induction with a difference.

"What you saying?" hissed one of the boys.

"Just a prayer," I said. "I won't be long."

I assumed that was the end of the matter, and resumed my petitions to the Almighty.

"Dear God, please look after Mummy G, and my sister Angela, and my other sisters..."

Whack! Shoes began to fly from all directions. Still in my praying position I continued with my short prayer, at which point I was surrounded by a group of boys who all had shoes in their pillow cases and took turns to continue to assault me as I came to the end of the Lord's Prayer. As soon as I finished, I got into bed and to my surprise they all stopped, I was left feeling bruised and beaten.

Every day, the military training of the teaching staff was tangible. At times it felt as if we were POWs in a war movie. At the first hint of disobedience in class, the blackboard rubber, or a set of keys, would be hurled in the direction of your head. If we fidgeted or were restless, we'd be curtly slapped down – the woodwork teacher Mr Waverley once yelled at me for being "up and down like a f-ing redundant yoyo." Headmaster Bailey insisted that, to celebrate his birthday, every year all the boys under his charge must participate in the outlandish ritual of a boxing tournament, run to a rather flexible set of rules that rewarded ultimate brutality. A makeshift ring was erected in the gym, and staff gathered around to watch the entertainment.

One of the teachers, Kitt Long, doubled as a boxing trainer. He was a short, stocky man (I liked to call him "two foot and a fag paper tall"), and his role was to incite us to remain on our feet long after a bout had been lost. Either he had a sadistic streak, or he genuinely believed being smashed around the brain was character building. If any of us showed signs of flagging, or wimping out, the headmaster would mock loudly, "What the ruddy hell is that?"

Inevitably, cliques formed amongst boys at St Edward's. I grew thick with a Luton lad, Timmy, who was universally known (even by the teaching staff) as Timmy Connor. He had an agility that contradicted his size; a prank he cherished was to slap you from behind on your forehead, and by the time you'd recovered your wits and turned around, he'd bolted beyond reach. He had a stubborn grit, and was determined never to display weakness. A couple of times, I saw him endure savage beatings from older boys on account of his girth, but he'd never plead for mercy or cry out in agony. Instead, at the end of a beating, he'd haul himself to his feet, and brush himself down as if he was recovering from an unfortunate slip. Once, this encouraged a renewed beating, which he took in his stride.

Timmy and I often indulged in skulduggery together. He was a year ahead of me, and had gleaned lots of covert information about the school's facilities. One movie night, when we were meant to be watching The Guns Of Navarone, he jabbed me in the ribs and muttered, "This is boring; let's do something else." Twenty minutes later we were in a field catching horses to ride bareback. He regarded rules as challenges to be overcome, rather than prescriptions to be obeyed.

Timmy's streetwise tips were especially valuable on disco night. It was the decade of Saturday Night Fever and Grease, and every term, as a treat, the school would arrange for three or four coachloads of girls to arrive at St Edward's for an evening where we could relax, socialise, and try to impress the opposite sex with our shimmies and spins on the dance floor. As we were queuing in the dining room for our last meal before the girls' appearance, Timmy warned me:

"Don't drink the tea. They put bromide in it to dampen your hormones."

I never learnt whether or not this was a legitimate suspicion, but the testosterone definitely pumped whenever I took Timmy's advice and spurned the tea. On one occasion, I'd been dancing with a girl a couple of years my senior, when our hands started wandering and our lips moved closer.

"Where can we go?" she whispered.

The dance floor wasn't a great place for intimacy, not least because teachers were prowling around with torches on the lookout for wandering hands and indecent behaviour. There were a dozen locations I could've suggested, but ludicrously the only one that popped into my head was the confessional box in the chapel. Des Daniels, the deputy head, spotted our escape, but to his misfortune so too did our legion of guests. As I was making out with my dance partner, two dozen girls formed a barricade outside the chapel doors, leaving Daniels to bawl "Rodgers, Rodgers, come out now," to no avail. I was living in the moment, carefree about the consequences, and even the psychological scars of being raped by Brown – which for years meant anything sexual was a source of dread not delight – temporarily evaporated. Admission to St

Edward's meant a claustrophobic existence; any craving for privacy should be left at the front gates.

Yet on this occasion, as the two of us kissed and fumbled, we were beyond the reach of anyone able to chastise us. Well, except for Jesus himself, nailed to his cross, watching over us from high above the altar.

It should hardly be surprising – given the emotional baggage of 100 teenage boys confined in close quarters – that bullying was endemic at St Edward's.

I'd only been there a day when I saw a boy bullying another boy in the corridor and I shouted at the bully to leave the boy alone. I wasn't sure whether he was going to ignore me, or turn on me, but in the event he did neither. It was the first time I'd been able to intimidate somebody through my physical bearing alone. Looking back I was lucky, these guys had issues like me and worse and I could have been assaulted.

Days later, I was talking to the senior boy Terry Matthews about meeting his sister in a previous children's home and out of nowhere he jumped on me and bit my nose as if it was a hot dog; it was a week before the teeth marks waned. But gradually I was learning to look after myself.

Tobacco was the cause of much bullying within the school. We all had a weekly allowance, but inevitably this led to a black market, and an unwritten rule that, once borrowed, smokes should be paid back double on the day you get your next spends. Inevitably, the older or stronger boys tried to control the deals, either by changing the terms of the trade retrospectively, or arguing about the amount involved (rollups came in four sizes, from "Borstalls" – containing a minute amount of tobacco – to "cigars").

If the other party to the trade tried to dispute the interpretation, the feud would escalate to a quarrel and then a beating. Having spent my junior school years on the receiving end of such treatment, the rage that festered in my heart wouldn't allow me to overlook such exploitation by those with strength and cunning on their side. Unconcerned for my own safety, I'd impose myself in the middle of the argument, and demand:

"Everyone must pay what they owe. Nothing more. Nothing less. If you cheat, you answer to me."

Increasingly as my authority and responsibilities grew, my interventions were focused on stamping out bullying and keeping the peace between the odd feuding group.

Every day, during break time, a local wannabe DJ manned the music booth in the main hall, and treated us to a selection of tunes he curated. Except none of us regarded it as a treat, on account of his miserable tastes.

After the third successive Neil Diamond track, we whipped up a coup. The DJ was ejected from the booth, and, until order could be restored and a better beautiful noise could be heard. St Edward's' corridors came alive to the immortal songs of reggae icons like Dennis Brown, Althea & Donna and Gregory Isaacs. The entire school population was united as one, regardless of colour or age or faction, as we swayed to the unmistakable beats of "Money in my pocket", "Uptown Top Ranking" and "Night Nurse".

Remarkably, by my final year, I'd been single-handedly responsible for the extraordinary feat of stamping out bullying at St Edward's. I hadn't accomplished this through the implementation of a carefully crafted strategy, still less at the request of the academic staff, but simply by standing up for the underdog whenever I saw trouble brewing, underpinned with an almost-blasé disregard for my personal safety perhaps because of my daily morning boxing training. It was the first time I felt a tinge of genuine pride in something I'd achieved using my own initiative. I was still haunted by the names "narty bwoy" (naughty boy), and "stealer" – the years of malicious insults and stereotyping couldn't easily be wiped away. But I'd seen a different aspect of my character, one I'd long suppressed, and that I'd never heard acknowledged even by those closest to me: It was my willingness to take responsibility when I saw injustice committed.

It's one of the ironies of my life that it took a brusque, no-nonsense, ex-air force headmaster, a traditionalist to his fingertips, and my polar opposite in so many ways, to recognise qualities within me that had been invisible to a near-endless throng of junior school teachers, social workers, family and friends.

In the event, so impressed was Mr Bailey at my ability to sort out bullying that, in 1979, he promoted me to be St Edward's Head Prefect. In theory, this position demanded a rigorous selection and vetting process, but one day, after he and I had been wagering cigarettes on the outcome of an England and West Indies test match, Bailey started referring to me as 'My Head Prefect' in everyday communication, and who was I to argue? I like to think that I discharged my duties in this role fairly and without animosity. Of course, I was now required to dispense the punishments I'd previously dreaded – such as the fabled "toothbrush to sweep the gym" routine – but I never condoned or conducted any physical beatings of younger boys. On my final day, Deputy Head Daniels announced publicly that, in his opinion, I'd been "the most upstanding Head Prefect in seventeen years."

Perhaps if Daniels had known about my activities away from the school premises and the countless fights it took to restore some sort of law and order in school, his praise wouldn't have been quite so high.

*

On the first Saturday of every month, St Edward's operated a scheme codenamed "Privilege", which essentially involved arranging a minibus or two to transport a student house group ten miles to Southampton, where we'd be deposited near the quayside and left to our own devices for several hours. Today, Southampton metropolitan centre, bustles with tourism and yacht owners, with the many business opportunities that spin off from its deep-water port (the original public quay dates from the thirteenth century). In the past decade, there has been a multi-million pound investment in the overhaul and redevelopment of the waterfront, involving spectacular business and residential premises, upmarket retail outlets, and ambitious leisure projects.

In the late 1970s, these were distant dreams. The dock area was seedy and – far worse – dull. There simply wasn't a lot to occupy young minds, so, instigated by me, it was necessary to make our own entertainment.

When I'd last been able to roam scot-free in a major city, I'd been the daily victim of racist violence in Oxford's Headington district. Now, half a decade later, I was stronger, more confident, and no longer alone. The rage was undimmed, but now I had the chance to turn the tables. For various reasons members of our group took a dislike to punk rockers and it was decided we would go punk rock bashing – we thought it was funny as we had previously been on the receiving end.

Punk rock had exploded overnight, seemingly from nowhere, with bands such as the Sex Pistols, the Clash and the Buzzcocks in the vanguard. The punk subculture involved raucous, often tuneless, music, an ill-defined anti-authoritarian ideology that sometimes encouraged self-harm, and attention-grabbing clothing, hairstyles, jewellery and attitudes. When two of more punks were gathered together, they were impossible to miss – spiky green hair, studded or spiked leather jackets, ripped T-shirt and trousers, all topped by large studs or chains dangling somewhere around their bodies in none-too-subtle invocation of a sadomasochist fetish. For a group of lads with control issues on day release from their approved school, the provocation was irresistible. This was my chance to wreak revenge. The fact that my Oxford tormentors were different individuals was, in my warped judgement, an incidental inconvenience. My rage could not discriminate between enemies; if punk rockers happened to be before me, it was punk rockers who would endure my anger.

I even led my peers in a rendition of "Down where the lights are flashing / We're going punk rock bashing" to the same melody as the chant about "nigger and Paki bashing" I'd suffered during my youth.

"What the f-, man?" squealed the nearest member of the group, as I winded him.

He was a painfully thin teenager wearing a 'Never Mind' T-shirt, and his skin was sallow, almost albino, probably from heroin abuse. He fell to his knees. I expected him to struggle, or at least to flee, but instead he was pleading pathetically.

"Don't do that, man, you got no reason," he begged.

I glared with scorn at the ridiculous cheap studs protruding from the side of either nostril. The sight was absurd; anyone who went around in public looking like that deserved to get beaten up I thought. I balled up my fist, and hit him on the bridge of the nose. He reeled in pain, grabbing his nose with both hands so that blood seeped out between his fingers. Woefully, none of his fellow punks sprang to his defence. I'd been anticipating a skirmish that would make the pulse pound, and was disappointed when the rest of the punk gang turned tail and fled, leaving the Never Mind junkie to our mercies.

One of the other St Edward's boys, Little Dread, stepped forward to administer the decisive blow. He landed a punch on the side of Never Mind's head, collapsing him to the dock like a sack of potatoes. Out cold.

Having satisfied our craving to see somebody suffer, we usually separated into smaller groups for the afternoon. Some boys headed off to chip-in and buy cheap beer in an off-licence, whilst others got up to mischief with the local girls.

In my third year at St Edward's, I was growing closer to Little Dread, partly due to our shared Caribbean heritage – although as a Jamaican boy he was contemptuous about my roots in St Vincent, dismissing me as a "smarl islan bwoy", (small island boy) or "Smarly" for short.

It was Saturday, and the waterfront area of Southampton was crowded with local kids on weekends and families relishing a seaside break. Even at our most impetuous, we knew better than to challenge punk rockers when the city was heaving. I was mulling options when Little Dread suggested a solution.

"I think it's time I introduced you to some people I know, Smarly. I think you'll get on well."

"Is it close?"

"Nicholstown. About fifteen minutes' walk."

Although I wasn't yet aware, it was notorious throughout the south as a long-established red light district, with a high crime rate, and had resisted multiple attempts to a clean it up. This reputation persists to the present day, even surviving a visit by the Queen and a Channel 4 documentary showcasing the poverty and neglect in particular areas.

The people who Little Dread had mentioned hung out (although they didn't live) in a two-storey terrace in the heart of the red light district. There was clearly a lot of activity in the house – chatter and music were audible from across the road – but Little Dread explained the front door was rarely used, and we'd need to approach via the alleyway that abutted the far end of the backyard. I suspected the alley was a dump with a load of broken bottles, fish and chip paper, condoms and syringes, but Little Dread insisted on using it for a last minute pep talk.

"When you meet my guys, you need to act cool, Smarly," he said. "I'm gonna give you a little weed."

He rolled a joint for himself, and sucked on it so the smoke filled his lungs as he twisted his natty dread hair (similar to dreadlocks) with a finger. Then he exhaled, slowly releasing the smoke from his nostrils and the corners of his mouth so that it formed a near-perfect circle in the air between us. As the shape expanded and dissolved into the atmosphere, he handed the joint to me.

"Now you try," he said.

I hadn't tried a spliff before, so the sweet taste caught me off guard, and I coughed heartily. Little Dread grabbed back the joint. "Yo smarl island bwoy," he scoffed, "Yer sarf bwoy So saaarf!" ("You small island boy, you're soft so soft!")

There was a gate leading into the back yard, and as Little Dread pushed it open, a guy in his mid-twenties wearing a loud shirt with a wide collar and a knitted red, yellow and green flat cap, approached us from the kitchen. He fist-bumped Little Dread, but looked at me quizzically.

"Ooh dis bwoy?" he demanded.

("Who's this boy?")

"Ah mi fren Lennox," said Little Dread. "He's cool."

("This is my friend Lennox.")

"Wah im warnt?"

("What does he want?")

"I thought he could be useful to us. He might join our business."

The guy cast his eyes over me in non-committal fashion, and motioned towards Little Dread with his thumb and forefinger to indicate he'd like a draw on the spliff. As he inhaled, a girl opened the backdoor and staggered down the steps, and the slow rhythm of a reggae drumbeat wafted across the yard. The horn section was playing an infectious counter-melody and I felt my legs swaying in time with the beat. Little Dread offered me another puff, and this time I exercised better control over my breathing, just about stifling a single cough. Little Dread grinned. "Yer still saarf," he said.

The girl had been joined by three others, and they stood close to us, swigging from a bottle of rum. One of them looked in my direction, but her eyes struggled to focus, and her expression was vacant. She was wearing hotpants, sandals, and a grimy T-shirt that had been ripped beneath the chest so that her midriff was exposed. I smiled but she turned away without acknowledging me, tipping back her head as she raised the bottle to her lips.

"You like her?" said Little Dread. "You want her?"

"Why do they look like that?" I asked.

"They've had a busy night," said Little Dread. "That's why this is good business, here. You can make good money if you're part of it."

"I see."

"You want her? I can make it happen. Straightaway."

I shook my head. "Not today. But I will have some rum and coke, please."

"Ha," said Little Dread. He slapped one of the girls on the backside. "Go and get my friend a rum and coke, that's good."

The girl whimpered obediently.

"You don't mind if I get myself some action, do you, Lennox?" he said. Without waiting for permission, he grabbed the hotpants girl by the forearm, a little too forcefully. She grimaced as he dug his nails into her skin, but didn't resist, allowing herself to be led into the house.

I couldn't help thinking of Angela, and Mummy G. My years of beatings had anaesthetised me to violence against young men, but the mistreatment of women still made me flinch, as if it awakened some ingrained protective instinct. Later, I would confront Little Dread about this, but he'd justify his roughness by explaining "They need to be kept under manhas" ("kept under control"), and "Be given wah bax" ("a punch"). I figured that, when I left St Edward's, there must be ways to make money that wouldn't make me compromise my morals.

So I declined Little Dread's offer to become an apprentice pimp, earning me the inevitable disdainful put-down, "Smarl Islan bwoy, yo tuh saarf." ("Small island boy, you're too soft.")

Apart from Southampton and the surrounding areas, the only city I was able to visit during my years at St Edward's was Oxford itself. Since our time in Romsey would inevitably come to an end, the school encouraged us to maintain a connection with our roots to assist with our rehabilitation into society. Uniquely amongst all at St Edward's, it was two years before the first visit to the school by any of my family members and eighteen months after before I got a second visit; nevertheless, I was allowed home leave. Since nobody in Oxford felt the inclination to collect me, the school gave out travel warrants so people could get trains and gave me a ride to the station from where I was to make my own way.

For me, with my rage burning, "home leave" involved minimising any actual time at home, and instead I spent the time either visiting the Grants or walking the streets. One Sunday, I rounded a corner near Wood Farm School, and realised I was face to face with Mark Fields – one of the racists who had taunted and beaten me years beforehand. Yet where he, and his accomplices, had once towered over me, he now looked fragile and diminished. My biceps had bulked out under Kitt Long's boxing training, but Fields just seemed weedy and pathetic, those of someone who would struggle with the simplest manual chore, let alone intervene in a heated dispute about tobacco rations, or fulfil an instruction to clean a gym floor with a toothbrush.

His eyes met mine and for a moment he struggled to recognise me. It couldn't have been more than a moment, because that was the time it took me to punch him in the solar plexus. He wrapped his arms around his stomach in pain, and lurched forward. At which point, I hit him again, this time to his face. He blurted something incomprehensible, so I seized his head in an arm lock, and snorted:

"Do you know who I am?"

4.
Excommunication

"I don't think I've ever seen you before."

"'Wogamatter, Niggermind, you'll be all white in the morning.' Do you remember saying that stuff to me? Every day. Before school. After school. Every f-ing day."

"It wasn't me. Honest. I don't know what you're talking about."

I cupped my hands around his temples, and lifted his head like an old football until his eyes were two or three inches from mine. Tears were forming in his eyelids, and his pupils were dilating, darting about, unable to return my stare. A brief moment of pity for him came over me and was gone as quickly as it came.

I had no idea what to do next. He had crumpled so easily, there seemed little point in hitting him again. And I could scarcely ask him to take me to the rest of his gang – I was pumped up with fury, but I knew I wasn't in some James Bond movie with a licence to kill. So I snarled, and said:

"I'll be watching you.

My final days at St Edward's were bittersweet. I'd secured the respect of the teaching staff and made some close friendships, but I was ready to move on. The burden of my responsibilities as Head Prefect increasingly weighed me down. I'd agreed to mentor many of the younger children who arrived at the school disturbed or insecure, without realising this could mean taking the full load of their problems onto my shoulders. A 13-year-old Spanish boy called Rio spoke hardly a word of English (he knew "Yes", but little else; it was the answer he innocently provided to every question, even when other boys demanded to know "Are you an idiot?" and "Are you a bastard?"). It fell to me to widen his vocabulary, and he followed me around the premises like a pet dog.

Another troubled youngster, Paddy, cut all the phone wires into the school; since the staff couldn't pinpoint the culprit, a smoking ban was imposed on all pupils, and I had to intercede to negotiate a truce. Worn down by these duties, one day I resolved to walk out of the school grounds and never return. I hadn't figured out my plan once I reached the gates, but I knew I'd had enough. My cover was blown when the Head of Education spotted Rio clumsily sauntering after me.

As my final day approached, I was the victim of much good-natured naughty school boy antics from the other boys. There were unannounced dorm raids, to short-sheeting my bed, a bucket of water over the door, boot polish on the toilet seats and of course that old classic – itching powder in your clothes. The gentle and affectionate teasing was in marked contrast to the pranks played in the film St. Trinians; in hindsight, being referred had been almost a blessing. During this period, the staff encouraged me to consider the next chapter of my life, and – influenced by their dignity and maturity – I concluded it should involve the army.

The school's many ex-servicemen were thrilled at my attitude. Les Daniels and others spent hours helping me to understand the diversity of roles available and the differences between regiments; they agreed it was the perfect calling, and I had the character and aptitude to be a success. I couldn't wait to get started.

After prolonged, emotional farewells, Mr Waverley offered to drive me to the station. He'd probably been rehearsing some heartfelt last words of encouragement ("Show 'em what you're made of, kid" and – one of my favourites – "Don't be farting about like a redundant fairy"), but Little Dread had somehow blagged the right to accompany us, and had no qualms about usurping the conversation. From the back seat, he recited the many advantages of an alternative career "with my mates in Southampton", craftily phrased in Patwa so our hapless driver had no inkling about the actual nature of the subject matter:

"So yo no seh we deesdent people don't it? and de barss go tek care ah yo."

("You know that we are decent people isn't it and the boss will take care of you.")

"Thanks Little Dread," I said, "but I'm set for the army. My mind's made up."

"Ah nuff monies yar mek yo no ah plenty gal go love yo, soon dem ah carl yo mr run tings an dan dada, smarly yo gwarn set fi life"

("You'll make plenty of money and lots of girls will love you, soon you'll be called Mr Run Things and Big Daddy.")

I couldn't be tempted, and three hours later, loaded down with bags, I disembarked on the platform at Oxford station. A short spell back in the city, and then the army beckoned.

Mum and Dad had agreed I could stop over with them until enlisting. In the five years I'd been away, family circumstances had changed, and although there were fewer people living in the property – four of my siblings had moved out – my bedroom was now used as storage.

This meant the sofa was the only place I could lay my hat, where I was joined nightly by our cat Timmy. But I wasn't fazed; within a couple of weeks, I'd have a proper bed in a barracks somewhere. I was itching to get started.

The only remaining hurdle was the army aptitude test, but that didn't seem a big deal. The staff at St Edward's had been confident and in the favourite phrase of headmaster Bailey, "I'd "ruddy breeze it", "with ruddy flying colours", and their assurances meant the world. I'd selected to join REME – the Royal Electrical and Mechanical Engineers – since I knew I had a good intuition for how machine components work together, especially in car engines. I rocked up at the test centre with a bit of a swagger, and breezed through the questions with five minutes to spare. The test paper was, I felt, rather elementary; I'd been able to jot down the answers that popped, instinctively, into my head, confident they were spot on.

Papers were marked, and results given, while you waited, and I spent the time calculating the maximum number of days I'd need to crash on the Wood Farm sofa before freedom beckoned. The blood drained from my face when I was summoned into the room, to be greeted with the news that:

"I'm terribly sorry, Mr Rodgers. The pass mark was 80, and you scored 75. Not bad but you have to wait six months to re-sit the test, so try again then.

And that was it. My dreams crushed in a moment. No advice on other army career options except the infantry. I'd fallen short of the threshold, so the British Armed Forces had no further need for my services.

The possibility of failure had never occurred to me, and I hadn't worked on a contingency plan. With the REME door slammed in my face, the way ahead was empty. Only my parents' sofa was certain; otherwise, the future was a void. I feared that days would turn to weeks, and then months, and then years. I felt rejected and forsaken. And that made me rash.

For the first time, I no longer needed to skulk around Wood Farm in fear of unprovoked beatings. But that didn't prevent family members from assassinating my character and denouncing my manifest shortcomings on a regular basis. After failing the REME test, I'd signed on to the dole, and on receiving my first giro check, headed to the pub with Chris Grant to drink through every last penny of my £16 pounds. Chris and I were both under 18, but I looked older so I was the "nominated purchaser", sneaking them to Chris who waited in the garden. This enabled me to guzzle a bit more than my fair share out of eyeshot.

Over three hours of drinking and oblivious to time, we enjoyed pint after pint of lager. By nine o'clock, even my double vision had double vision. Somehow, I staggered outside, leaning against a conveniently-positioned car. When the owner spotted me from inside the pub and all hell broke loose.

Chris ended up trying to pull this guy off me and was punched and lost a tooth in the process and I was raging incoherently about the ornamental sword which Daddy G, hung from the living room wall, which I seemed to think might assist the situation.

The next thing I remember was trying to get into the Grants' house to get the sword and being prohibited by Mark and his brother Chris and sisters Michelle and Sharon laughing at my drunken state and the funny things I said and did. Someone had called my sisters because Julie and Angela turned up to try to get me home but I reeked of the Crown and Thistle pub, a fact Julie took great pleasure in emphasising as she hated anyone in a drunken state forgetting that she herself had once been drunk.

"Get away from me, you're drunk."

At home, my father was giving a running commentary on my every move.

"Wach de bwoy, wach im no, im kya heven tan up straight," he scoffed.

("Look at the boy. Just look at him, He can't even stand up straight.")

It was true. I was unable to stand up properly for any length of time.

From the landing, Veronica joined the fray, hurling every colourful insult she could muster in my direction.

Through the fog of inebriation, painful memories bubbled to the surface – of years of beatings in this very place, at the hands of those who were now castigating me. I rose to my feet, waving around the deadliest weapon I could lay hands on – which happened to be the steel afro comb in my back pocket.

"None of you can give me beatings anymore," I wailed. "I told you that when I get big, none of you will beat me again! Now I'm the strongest."

At which point, I lunged my metal afro comb at Veronica, lost my balance and collapsed in a heap on the hallway carpet. The last thing I remember was a lot of noise around me and familiar voices shouting, "Tek im, tek im," being hollered more or less in unison to the police, who locked me in a police cell till 4am in the morning to sleep it off. My hope of a lift home was quickly dashed as I was told that the police don't run a taxi service and I was ordered to get myself home before they changed their minds and put me back in the cell.

When news of this incident reached her, my sister Angela was distraught at my distress, and she took it upon herself to nudge me towards a better path. She lent me a pile of religious tracts, miniature booklets each containing an uplifting story, often depicted in cartoon format. I remember one was about an American minister who confronted a gang leader of a notorious gang – his cross against their switchblades – and when they threatened his life, he responded simply, "You might cut me up, but every piece of me will still say 'I Love You.'"

Yet far from persuading me to trust in Godly judgement, the stories stoked my feeling of victimisation. All the characters in the tracts had somebody to support them. Someone to whom they could turn.

"Clearly, God has no idea of the people around me," I sneered when Angela asked about my reaction.

I even tried putting God to the test one evening, sitting on the floor of my parents' bedroom, challenging the Almighty to "prove you're real if you can." I waited five minutes, which I figured was ample opportunity for a being of God's supposed abilities to present me with irrefutable evidence. Disgusted at being ignored, I bundled up the tracts to leave on Angela's dresser, packed two suitcases and a rucksack, and strode out of the house without a single goodbye.

An hour or so later, I was on the M40 slip road, sticking out a thumb to hitch a ride. I hadn't prepared a hitchhiker's board since, I was living in the moment, I had no clue about my destination. All I knew was it must be away from Oxford. I figured, when the first lorry pulled over, I'd ask the driver where he could drop me off, and go with that.

*

The Bull Ring centre, in the heart of Birmingham, was unlike anywhere I'd ever seen. Built in the early 1960s, in comprises around 150 open-air market stalls with the country's first indoor shopping centre. Its architecture and maze subways create the impression of a concrete jungle, an image not helped by the drab grey nine-storey office block which towers over it.

I was immediately struck by the vastness of the place, as well as the unimaginable number of people, crammed together like farm animals. Many were as dark-skinned as me, while others were recognisably Indian, or from southeast Asia. I saw turbans and silk, beautiful colourful garments and headdress from a variety of nations, it was a breath-taking sight for me. The city centre was a dazzling kaleidoscope of bold colour and music. Unfortunately, the senses were also assailed by the sight and smell of dirt.

For all their shortcomings, my parents had ingrained in me a lifelong pride in the virtue of cleanliness. During my early childhood, one of the dislikes made about white people, was that "they never rinse their dishes properly and if they have dogs, they let their dogs eat from the same plates they use." As a rebellious child, I didn't heed my parents' advice not to have meals at my friends' houses. Mummy G, is white and had a dog and she was the cleanest person I knew at the time. As I wandered around the Bull Ring for the next few hours, these prejudices resurfaced. I saw adults urinating in corners, and beggars gorging on half-eaten sandwiches that they'd fished out of bins. It turned my stomach. Although I had scarcely a penny with me, and no means to earn money, I resolved that I'd never allow myself to plummet to such depths.

The city centre is built upon a sandstone ridge which spawns a steep gradient in the direction of St Martin's Church in Digbeth. There, I found a night shelter, and was thrilled that, by the time I arrived, there was still one unoccupied mattress which I could claim. My spirits, having been lifted, were quickly dampened as I realised the disregard shown towards basic principles of hygiene within the shelter.

Everything we used – cutlery, crockery, blankets — had been donated; they were nothing compared with the perpetual din of old men coughing. Not short throat-clearing dry coughs, but chronic splutters laden with phlegm and mucus. Nobody made the slightest effort to suppress their cough; it was as if they took pride in sharing the longest, wheeziest, most virus-ridden splutter of the evening for everyone to admire. I buried my head in the blankets, hoping it would shield me from the billions of microbes being propelled airborne with every rasp.

Strongly motivated to find alternative accommodation, I secured a bed in a youth hostel in Aston. My six co-habitees were thankfully free of viral infections, but compensated with a host of mental health issues. On my second morning, I was sitting at the breakfast table with a young man called Jack, when he announced:

"It's time to wash my hair."

At which point, he dumped his fingers into a tub of margarine, licked the scoop for good measure, and rubbed it fiercely into his scalp. Then he nodded at me, as if inviting me to follow suit.

To receive my dole money, it was necessary to "sign on" every day at the Unemployment Benefits office on Corporation Street. It would be hard to imagine a more thankless job than being one of the three counter clerks, for whom every day consisted of the repetitive cycle of locating, completing and filing forms – whilst never allowing a hint of a smile to flicker across the lips.

Moreover, taking a break was nigh impossible; as soon as the front doors were eased ajar, the queues built up, people of all ages, jostling and complaining, desperate for another giro to help alleviate the consequences of their own personal misfortune – rent arrears, or a bottle of Jack Daniels, or an each-way bet at the bookies around the corner.

Not everybody had to wait for counter service. Once, I'd been standing in line for an hour, inching ever closer to the counter, when there was a screech of tyres in front of the building. A silver BMW pulled up, reggae blaring, and two Rastafarians, dripping in bling, bounced into the dole office as if they owned the place. The taller man, aged around thirty and sporting a wool-and-felt bowler hat, walked to the front, pushing aside a white woman who was being served by one of the clerks, grunting "Outta mi way; move yoself." ("Out of my way, move yourself.") Then, he placed both hands on the counter, leant across, and said firmly to the clerk:

"Gimme mi bloodclart money, ya ere mi?" Roughly translated ("Give me my F-ing money you hear me.")

He sucked his teeth to indicate it was a command rather than a request, and the clerk fumbled around with his paperwork in meek compliance. Meanwhile, the woman who'd been displaced mumbled under her breath in protest, but was ignored.

"Urry up," said the Rasta, "mi hah tings fi do." ("Hurry up! I have things to do.")

Within five minutes, whatever paperwork was required had been processed, and I watched the Rasta slipping his cheque into his top pocket. As he left, he doffed his hat in my direction.

"Sary bout dat my yout," he said, teeth gleaming.

("Sorry about that my youth.")

The Corporation Street dole office was the site where I first witnessed reverse racism in action. If I, or another black man, was being served, the Rastas were content to wait until my business was concluded. But if someone white was at the front, it was a whole different scenario: they'd barge in, without any care, dispensing just enough intimidation to quell any backlash. Once, I saw a young white guy offer some resistance. The Rasta screwed up his face to look more frightening and aggressive, poked the offender viciously in the chest, and with gold teeth gritted, barked "Move yoself, yo bloodclart fool, or mi go do yo sumting." ("Move yourself, yo f-ing fool, or I will do something to you.")

Once I'd navigated the dole office and located sanitary accommodation, my time in Birmingham was primarily a story about a girl. Jennifer Robinson, slightly older than me, had recently fallen pregnant (although I didn't know that at the time). She stood out from the crowd – dressing smartly, and sporting braided hair and huge ear-rings. We met in the congregation at a local church and the church helped me to get a room – my own room – at a smart and well-ordered Christian hostel. I felt accepted and valued, and rewarded the Church elders by participating joyously in Sunday worship and volunteering to help with anything that needed doing. I was baptised into the faith by total immersion, and felt proud that, after all my setbacks, I was getting my act together.

Jennifer, who was the eldest daughter of a deacon at the Church, was fascinated by my clean-cut appearance, polite manners and – in particular – my accent, she called me the "Outa tong bwoy," ("Out of town boy"). When talking about me to her girlfriends as it was viewed in high regard or like some status symbol to have a boyfriend or girlfriend from another city and nobody could chat about you because your partner was unknown. One Sunday, she hopped aboard the minivan returning me to the hostel, and struck up a conversation. She was an astute observer of character, and I found her insights into the quirks of the Church elders hysterical. As our friendship developed, feelings were aroused in me that I'd never experienced before.

One afternoon, with no one else in her house, she took me to her room and started getting intimate. My mind was a swirling mess of emotions. As her hands caressed me, I flinched, reminded of the way Thomas Brown had touched me in his living room when he'd been grooming me. I knew the comparison was absurd; Jennifer wanted to express herself sexually out of tenderness, to symbolise her affection towards me – nothing could be further from Brown's warped and vile urges. And yet I was recoiling, physically as well as mentally.

"What's wrong?" asked Jennifer, sensing my anxiety.

For six years, since my clumsy exchange with Chris Grant, I'd spoken with no one about the abuse I'd suffered, and that wasn't about to change. So, I told her this was my "first time", and I was "nervous". I feared how she might respond to my inexperience, but she wrapped her hands about mine and said, "There's nothing to be scared about, Lennox. Trust me. Let me be your guide."

In the days that followed, Jennifer and I became inseparable, and this didn't escape the notice of the Church elders. Somewhat overawed by her status as the deacon's daughter, I hadn't fully appreciated the extent of Jennifer's reputation. Some of the elders regarded her as a lost girl, a "backslider". One Sunday, a pastor took me aside to offer a few cautionary words, which morphed into a no-holds-barred lecture about the sinfulness of young people in the modern world. He couldn't even bring himself to refer to Jennifer by her proper name. He labelled her dismissively as "that girl," or simply "trouble".

If I'd expected support from Jennifer's family, I was to be gravely disappointed. One Sunday afternoon, I was invited to join Jennifer and her parents for a Caribbean dinner – rice n' peas and chicken – and afterwards her father led me into a separate lounge area, the part of the house that was kept for best for a man-to-man conversation. It seemed everyone in the Caribbean had one of these rooms that was full of family memorabilia clutter laid out neatly, plastic covers on the chairs to keep them clean and in some areas of the room, even the carpet had a plastic covering. In their glass cabinets lay all the best China and glassware, everything was spotless.

"Brudda Lennox," he intoned, "I need to know... "Wah tis yar hintentions wid mi darta?"

("What are your intentions with my daughter?")

I was lost for words as I was not prepared for this kind of talk and hazy about whether I actually had clear intentions, and confused about what type of response would be regarded as most appropriate. So I mumbled:

"I don't really know."

"Brudda Lennox, that isn't good enough. We've welcomed you into our Church. You've been welcomed today into our home. I think you owe me a better answer than that."

As far as I was concerned, I owed him nothing, and I resented the line of questioning. Would I start asking him about the physical nature of his relationship with his wife? So I had no qualms about deceiving him.

"Mr Robinson," I said, "We're just friends. There's nothing more to it than that. I promise."

Rumours spread very quickly as Jennifer's pregnancy became more obvious, word on the street and in the church was that I had gotten Jennifer pregnant. These rumours caused Jennifer's mum to invite me round to their house again but this time for a coffee and a chat. I was a bit more prepared for an interrogation than before. "Tell me the truth, is this your child?" she demanded. Annoyed at her tone, but replying politely, "No I'm not the father," I said. "But you've had sex with my daughter," she accused. I stayed silent which seem to infuriate her and her language and demeanour changed. "Bwoy! Yo hiz nuting but wah dutty sin-bag so com out mi ouse an nah com bak ere." ("Boy you are nothing but a dirty sin-bag so come out of my house and don't come back here.") With that I made a quick exit.

The following Sunday, I was sitting with two other boys from the hostel in the third pew. The congregation had just completed a rousing chorus of "How Great the Power of Jesus' name", when the pastor ascended to the pulpit. He lowered his hands to indicate silence, and then, with an actor's timing, waited for the noise levels to subside. The Church was calm, except for the usual indistinct whisperings on the back row, where a collection of guys based themselves for their weekly pursuit of hot young Christian girls and some mothers trying to quieten their restless kids.

Eventually, the pastor said:

"Before starting my sermon, I have a sad announcement. Because of his refusal to heed multiple warnings about his unchristian relationship with the backslider Jennifer Robinson, it's my unfortunate duty to discharge Brother Lennox from this Church."

I felt the judgmental stare of a hundred pair of eyes burning into me.

"Ushers, could I ask you kindly to escort Brudda Lennox from the Church before we proceed?"

I was humiliated and disorientated. How could a loving friendship, that harmed nobody, be viewed with such contempt? Ours wasn't an adulterous or abusive relationship; it was an unexceptional romance between teenagers, the type of courtship which, I was sure, everybody within the congregation would've experienced at some stage. And yet, uniquely, I was being punished – excommunicated – as if I'd committed a crime of villainy. Even my appearances before Social Services never involved such an erratic, kangaroo court outcome.

Expulsion from the Church set off a chain reaction that, in time, caused me to abandon Birmingham, broke and depressed. Having been "discharged", I was no longer entitled to a bed at the Christian hostel, so Jennifer and I moved into a small bedsit where we could figure out our future together. By Christmas, she was a mother, and her newborn baby boy, Shakarn, brought laughter and excitement to three long weeks during which severe, unrelenting snow had brought the city to a near standstill. Eventually, the snows melted, and I felt the surge of euphoria, of liberation, at being able to roam further than the corner shop.

The birth of the baby did nothing to quell the rumours of me being the child's father, in fact it made them worse. Baby Shakarn, to me was too young to really tell who he looked like but it didn't stop people from saying how he looked like me and not once did Jennifer at any stage, come clean about who the father was and so tongues continued to wag.

As a result, I was somewhat irresponsible with my next giro cheque.

"Where is it, Lenny?" asked Jennifer, "we need it for shopping and the baby."

"I don't really have it anymore."

"What do you mean? You told me this was the day. We need the money."

"But you get your giro, and the Child Benefit so we should be okay still shouldn't we?"

"You have absolutely no idea how much I need for nappies, shopping and bills and stuff to give Shakarn the best start in life!"

"Not really, no."

"Now hand it over."

"I can't. It's gone."

"Gone? You mean, like, vanished? F-, Lenny. Just say what happened and where it's gone."

It was embarrassing to admit I'd been gambling on the fruit machines and lost and then lie to pretend I was trying to win more money for us. Thirty pounds and seventy-five pence. Every penny blown while standing gormlessly in front of the slot machine at the local cafe, and staring at the screen in case the next turn revealed a free nudge or jackpot. Or the turn after that. Or after that, sadly I was lucky to come away with my bus fare. The cafe was in Aston which would have been a long cold walk to Handsworth.

Understandably, Jennifer was unimpressed, and from that point our relationship disintegrated rapidly. If I tried speaking with her, she became reluctant to engage. If I reached to touch her, she moved. I learned that she bore a grudge for a long time. If I suggested we go to a movie, she said she wasn't in the mood. Within the month, the breakdown was beyond repair. She moved out to go and stay at her parents' house and through mutual acquaintances I heard rumours that she might have rekindled the relationship with Shakarn's father. Jennifer had got the house from the council because of the baby and it wasn't long before I was given my marching orders.

On the one occasion I did attempt to approach her, I was "dealt with" courtesy of a get-the-message visit from her five brothers. As a first-time offender, they chose verbal not physical intimidation (hospitalisation can involve such awkward police enquiries). But I was left in no doubt that, in the event of further transgressions, punches would not be the only thing pulled out.

It was more than I could bear. Like a human boomerang, by Easter, I was back in Oxford, reunited with both sofa and Timmy, to the bemusement and resentment of some of my siblings. I was almost nineteen, and could see no escape from the worthless drudgery of my life after St Edward's. The army had rejected me; the Church had excommunicated me; my girlfriend had fled from me.

Feeling worthless, heartbroken and devoid of purpose, I spent a lot of time with my friend and brother Chris Grant in between the odd jobs he got which never seemed to last long because they often asked him to do something more than his job description to help out and he was never shy in telling them what they could do with their job. I was on benefits and this wasn't much but it gave me something to get by on which was mainly spent on cigarettes, rum and occasional partying.

*

I'd been home for two weeks, and had barely exchanged a word with Dad. I suspected he was the culprit behind the occasional disappearance of cigarettes from the packet I hid under a pile of clothes, but otherwise we kept our distance. It wasn't long before I was able to move off the sofa and have my room back. Dad would wait for everyone to leave for work in the morning and then come to my room looking for cigarettes. He would search my clothes and my chest of drawers and when he couldn't find any, he would wake me up and say, "Bwoy, yo nah hah no cigarette kah gimme?" ("Boy do you have any cigarettes you can give me?") At which point I would reveal where I put the cigarettes, in my pyjama pocket, under my pillow and even in my shoe, then give one to my dad and off he would go. Dad had done this many times and it became like a game of hide and seek; I knew exactly when he would come in and so pretend that I was still sleeping and he would always search the last place where he saw me get the cigarettes from first, before tirelessly looking elsewhere. I often joined him for a smoke and we sat together on the dinning room sofa as if in the Kit Kat advert where we take a break from all the unpleasantness and we could be a proper father and son before the hustle and bustle of our family life continued and everyone returned home.

These were my favourite times with my father, nothing was secret and we talked like two friends about anything and everything we wanted. The first time we smoked in silence and this felt weird for us. The family knew I smoked, much to the disgust of my mother who hated the very smell of cigarettes but my father smoked in secret and nobody else knew and he was grateful that I got blamed if there was even the hint of cigarettes smell in the house but I ignored the nagging.

"Mi dun wuk now"

("I've finished work now." Retired.)

This was hardly news. In any event, he'd barely left the house since my return, busying himself in the garden and doing household chores like a house husband.

He explained the staff had been very kind on his last day at The Warneford Hospital, where he'd portered.

"Dem gimme wah new bran tankard."

("They gave me a brand new tankard.")

"You deserve it," I said. "You worked hard." It was a lovely pewter tankard engraved with his name on it and a lovely message of thanks for all his years of hard work.

"Eh fi de beer," he said, drawing deep on the cigarette, "an mi nah like ow eh tayse "

("It's for drinking beer, but I don't like the taste.") Dad much preferred drinking rum and Caribbean beers.

Dad had kept it as decoration but one day when I came home, I couldn't be bothered to wash the dishes to get a cup so I could make some tea, so seeing Dad's tankard, I made my tea in it, not realising the consequences. We both chuckled at the memory of me taking my first sip and how I jumped up in the air, as if I'd sat on a lot of drawing pins from the prank of some kid at St. Edward's school spilling and spitting tea everywhere, much to the amusement of my family who had knowingly kept silent.

"Life tuff yo no bwoy," he confided.

("Life is tough you know boy.")

"What do you mean Dad?" I asked.

"Now mi nah wuk, mi no hah much money."

("Now I am not working, I don't have much money.")

"You have your pension. And Mum earns her salary."

"Yeah bwoy but everyting ah jus bills all da time."

("Yes, boy, but everything is just bills all the time.")

"What do you mean?"

Dad reeled off a list of utility bills and a higher purchase agreement for some furniture they bought to take back to the Caribbean and retire there. I thought, that don't sound so bad and then Dad revealed some financial deal he and Mum did with some family member which involved selling our house that we lived in. He said it was meant to make things easier and give them some money to go back to St. Vincent with but instead it made things worse and increased their out-goings and now paying rent to family to live in their own house and more than what they paid the council.

I'd always treated cash as a tool for day-to-day survival, and had no conception of long-term budgeting, so I didn't fully join the dots about Dad's circumstances. If I'd been experienced in managing household finances, alarm bells might've been set ringing at his reference to paying family rent.

"Can't you, I don't know, borrow from the bank?" I asked.

"Bwoy dem people na heasy yo no, dem nah gimme noting, everyting arrda now bwoy ah mi nah no wah fi do nomar."

("Boy, those people are not easy you know, they won't give me anything, everything is harder now boy and I don't know what to do anymore.")

My dad was stifling a sob. Eventually, the barriers gave way, and the tears streamed down his cheeks. I realised the anger and rage rising up within me and my eyes began to water.

"Mi wah lef dis place ah go orrm wid yo mudda but ah plenty money we haf fi fine fi go."

("I want to leave this place and go home with your mother but we have to find plenty of money to go.")

It broke my heart to see a man who had once been a towering figure in my life, reduced to this shadow, and I made a commitment to help out, in whatever way was possible. The opportunity arose sooner than expected. My sister Julie had at long last got her council flat and moved her new boyfriend Kyle in with her and toddler son Jody. During this time I stayed at both my parents' house and Jen's spare room as I wanted to continue my cigarette chats with Dad.

He reminded me of the Rastas I'd met in Birmingham who seemed to have loads of kids from different women, and he already had a few kids with other women but he seemed to make my sister happy. Kyle had been badgering me to join him in a robbery and I was to do the dirty work and he was to provide the information and observe. "It's the easiest cash you'll ever make," he explained. "There are these two women who work for one of the local shops in the Cowley centre. Every Monday, late afternoon, they carry the weekend takings to bank at the Post Office across the road. Wham, bam, grab the loot, and we are on our way."

Initially, I'd been reluctant to get involved, chiding Kyle about a few concerns I had about his plan ("What if onlookers get involved? What if I'm recognised? Or they simply won't let go of the bag?"). But my father's woes changed my attitude. I wasn't really sure how much money was involved or how much Dad needed and if I got the money, whether Dad would take it, I didn't plan that far ahead. I just thought that this would help him he leave his worries behind and reboot his life, on the island he adored. His later years would be transformed, I had the power to make it happen. Four attempts later and I still couldn't do it and Kyle was so disappointed with me that every time I said I'll do it, he wouldn't believe me.

Finally, a cigarette session with my dad stirred me up, he was sobbing and I felt broken for him. There wasn't another option; I needed to play my part. Kyle wasn't persuaded by my change of heart. "You're unreliable," he scoffed. "You're a joker and I ain't taking that risk."

"In that case, I'll do it myself."

"You? Ha! That'll be the day!"

Kyle had misjudged my determination. I set aside the following Monday to do the job, borrowing some spare overalls, woolly hat and boots from an unsuspecting friend and stealing my mum's small vegetable knife from the kitchen drawer which would fit neatly in my pocket. I was worried that they may not let go of the money bag and my thoughts were to pin-prick their hand with the point of the knife to make them let go enough for me to snatch the bag and run. No need to case the job, (survey) as I'd been here a few times before so I knew the drill.

The key was to catch them by surprise so I found an inconspicuous blind spot on their route at the top of some small stairs and waited.

Finally, I could hear footsteps and voices of people approaching. I edged my head round the corner to take a look and my heart pounded and my adrenalin began to rush as I saw two women, one holding a carrier bag which had the money in it. Briefly I worried as it wasn't the usual man and woman that were regular from previous weeks. Too late to quit now I thought as their next steps would bring them level with me. Out I pounced in front of them, "Gimme da F-ing money," I shouted and grabbed the bag at the same time. I caused such a fright that they both screamed and the one with the bag held on to it for dear life, momentarily we were locked in a tug of war, then out came my knife whilst the screaming and pleas for help were shouted, I knew I couldn't keep this up for long so I quickly stabbed her hand with the point of the knife and she released her grip and I was off with the bag as fast as I could with screams and shouts of "stop" echoing behind me.

5.
Glimpses Of Another Path

Adrenaline was surging through my body. The beating of my heart was drowning out the background noise as it pounded like the steam pump on a runaway train. I'd seen reports on TV about people who exhibit heightened abilities during times of great emotional stress – such as mothers able to lift a crashed car to save children trapped in their seats – and now I knew the feeling. With the intensity of the moment, I felt like I had become superhuman.

With the bag, bulging with the weekend's takings, gripped firmly in my left hand, I was sprinting from the Cowley Centre with such speed I almost glided over the ground. I was acting purely on instinct, the pre-planned escape route had vanished from my memory. In the immediate wake of the robbery, I'd weaved through shoppers and round the back of the shops where delivery lorries and vans unload. I came to a main road and darting recklessly in front of an oncoming car, to the safety of an alley at the side of the local cemetery, where I stopped briefly to check if I was being chased. Not seeing or hearing anyone, especially the police whose station was less than a mile away, I opened the bag and there was a cloth bag stuffed with notes. Still observing my surroundings, I quickly removed half the money and stuffed them in as many pockets as I could and I stuffed the bag with the rest inside my overalls.

The alley was a potential trap so I climbed into the cemetery and ran through to the Iffley road which was at the other end and the timing was perfect as a bus going into the town centre was coming and I managed to get on, sweating and puffing and panting as I made my way on top deck at the back.

Police cars were rushing past in the opposite direction, sirens blazing, passengers chatting and guessing wildly about what could have happened, one lady guessed they may have caught the culprits responsible for a spate of recent car thefts on the Black Bird Leys Estate she said to her friend. I tried to remain hidden and wishing the bus driver would hurry up but school traffic slowed things down, mums and dads were still collecting their kids from a nearby school and a mum with two small children and a baby had got on which took ages. First the three people in front of her whilst trying to collapse her buggy with one hand and holding her baby with the other, "get on the bus," she shouted to the other two, and it seemed like it was going to take forever to get there. I wondered if I should get off and try to get a taxi but I didn't want to take the chance of being seen.

Finally in town, I needed to keep out of sight so I made my way to George Street cinema and paid to go in to watch whatever was on which just happened to be Cat People, with Malcolm McDowell and Nastassja Kinski. Hiding between the seats to avoid detection from the cleaners and aided by the fact that Mondays were not their busiest time, I watched the film twice before emerging from the cinema. It was now dark and I felt safer to venture out and so I got a taxi from the nearby coach station to Jen's new flat.

Kyle might have mocked my apparent cowardice and unreliability, but in my hands was the proof he'd underestimated me. For a moment as I entered the flat I had a disappointed look on my face and one look at Kyle's face said it all and, before he could say anything, I removed all the cash and threw it up in the air and it just rained five, ten and twenty pound notes. I was elated as we all laughed and celebrated.

Jennifer and Kyle helped me to calculate my newly-acquired wealth. One thousand two hundred and twenty-eight pounds. It was an almost incomprehensible amount, at a time when my dole money amounted to just fifteen pounds each week. I counted the cash a third time, just to make sure, sorting the notes into one-hundred-pound piles which I spread across my mattress. Then I stood back to admire the scene, as if I was a landscape painter taking pride in his artistry. This would surely be enough for Dad to get home to St Vincent, and help out my sisters (who had accumulated various debts), with plenty remaining for stuff I'd like.

Times felt good.

In the event, the cause that never benefited from my riches was Dad's passage to the Caribbean – which, ironically, had been the catalyst for the theft. My mum had a sixth sense about the money's origins and was resolute in her objections:

"Na tek de money Mack," she insisted. "Wah wok im do fi geh money like dat?"

("Don't take the money Mack. What work has he done to get money like that?")

"It's proper money," I protested. "I was working on building sites labouring and saved my wages."

Dad was nodding furiously in the corner, almost salivating at the prospect of beaches and fields and sun. But, when Mum's mind was made up, she was as unyielding as St Vincent's craggy coastline; and on this occasion there was no compromise.

"Da bwoy is a liard an a teef Mack, na touch de money, da money bad an mi nah warnt ti."

("The boy is a liar and a thief. Don't touch the money. The money is bad and I don't want nothing to do with it.")

Over the following days, Dad and I tried to concoct a scheme for transferring the money behind Mum's back. One idea was that I'd buy his collection of watches – he had over a half dozen in his collection. No matter how devious we were, she managed to catch us in the act. And, when she did, she was unyielding and hardline in her objections. I couldn't see the problem, we were struggling financially and I was coming to the rescue by hustling, how could she say no in the face of poverty, and make us do without. I know plenty of other parents who would have accepted it, but not my mum.

"Mi nah tel yo fi nah tek di money Mack? Mi trial ah crarses. Dem go lak yo up wid im. Ah wid yo teef money bwoy, da money will mek da police come tek yo an yo farda nah tek a penny frar im."

("Didn't I tell you not to take the money Mac? My trials and crosses; they will lock you up with him and with your stolen money boy, the money will make the police come and take you and your father, don't take a penny from him.")

She tried to snatch the money from him, but for a moment it seemed glued to his fingers. Eventually, Mum's willpower won through. Dad relented, his face etched with disappointment, and he dragged himself over to the sink where he stood muttering Caribbean obscenities at the kitchen wall through gritted teeth. Mum folded her arms and screwed up her face, and my mind drifted to an array of alternative uses to which the money could now be deployed.

None of my sisters, even my dad would never normally accept stolen money, as Mum's reaction displayed that we were not brought up like that and I would never even dare bring stolen anything round to the Grants and if I did, it wouldn't be long before I would have confessed all to Mummy G who would have marched me right back to where I'd stolen it from to return it. Only two sisters actually benefited from the money, Angela had got into rent arrears at her bedsit in Black Bird Leys and wouldn't take a penny of it even though I hadn't told her where I got it, so I asked her landlord how much she owed and paid it all off without her knowledge. Maybe, like Mum, she knew it was stolen. Jennifer being Kyle's girlfriend knew it was stolen but not the details, perhaps she would have kicked me out if she knew how I robbed it and stabbed a woman's hand to get it. Kyle only received money to buy alcohol and drugs as he forfeited his claims to any more by not being involved and I was left with the lion's share of the money.

I had previously applied for a fruit-picking job abroad with the hope I could help Dad out by actually doing a legitimate job, it promised long hours, overtime and lots of money. After the robbery, I received a letter of acceptance and it seemed like the perfect escape from all the police enquiries.

I had to get to a place called Goes or Gos which is pronounced (Huse) in Dutch, it took forever to get there because I kept using the English pronunciation and nobody knew where I was talking about, eventually I found just showing people the name on paper did the trick, then on to Zoetermeer where the factory was located. With no worldwide web available for fact-checking, I only got to see a small part of its lovely countryside, as I listened to exaggerated stories of Amsterdam's red light district teeming with available, insatiable women from every corner of the globe, of bars where mountains of drugs were piled high on the counters and tables, as if they were rounds of Stilton in a cheese store. It was a world where the only constraint on hedonistic excess was the limits to one's imagination. It sounded absolutely wonderful and was the most visited place at weekends that our workforce went.

So the money that Mum had spurned didn't go to waste. Holland's capital city is no place for the penniless, although I saw plenty of rough sleepers, beggars and drug dealers around the network of canals and bridges in the De Wallen neighbourhood. My wallet still hefty, I was able to relish the spoils. The processing plant adjoined barracks which had been built to accommodate the workers – meaning I had access to work whenever I needed to replenish funds. And with temptations almost literally on every street corner, even my Cowley Centre takings wouldn't last indefinitely.

Adversity taught me that, whatever its other assets, Amsterdam will never be synonymous with quality control, and in the first weeks we suffered the consequences of buying contaminated product from street vendors. My favourite outfit – bright, nicely cut, the best

Top Shop had to offer – was wrecked when Johann, a guy from the barracks, used it for target practice when retching from some brown weed that smelt of pesticide. Eventually, we figured out that the cafe shops were dependable sources of supply, and spent as much time smoking at the barracks as we did out walking the streets.

Inhabiting the barracks was like being resident in an Olympics village – it was almost a microcosm of the planet. I'd never met so many people from Asia, or from South America, and especially from Africa. Every nationality south of the Sahara was represented in abundance, and I marvelled at the Africans' ceaseless natural stamina. Not only did they look like Egyptian Mummies because during the first half hour of working with the onions our eyes burned before easing off and so they used rolls of loo paper to wrap around their heads to reduce the burning which never really worked but was a funny sight. After a gruelling twelve hours handling and pickling onions, their energy was undiminished. They just had an ability to keep going, probably driven by the thought of earning hundreds of guilders.

One evening, Johann and I were squatting around a small table in the corner of the barracks, cutting a lump from a hashish block of Gold Seal supplied by a Moroccan dealer at a coffeeshop in Handboogstraat.

"How long you reckon we'll stay here?" I asked.

"Until we get bored," said Johann, "and I don't see that happening until the next century."

I struck a match and lit the small rock of hash. It caught fire easily, and smoke was soon enveloping the table like a low-lying cloud. I placed a small glass beaker, upside down, so it covered the hashish, and my cupped hand could feel the surface warming as it filled with smoke.

"The next century, at least," he added. "Perhaps even the one afterwards."

I slid the beaker towards the table's edge, and placed my face a couple of inches from the edge. I raised the cup's lip, no more than a few millimetres, but enough for the smoke to escape. As I inhaled, the intensity of the drug was exquisite, filling my lungs. But I resisted the urge to breathe out, allowing the fumes to circulate around my system so that I could savour the full concentrated effect.

"You should see your face," teased Johann, whilst we sat with big grins across our faces

It was true. Increasingly, I was finding the buzz of drugs and alcohol helped me blot out the memories of sexual abuse, my dad's financial situation, the robbery, and keep a lid on the rage within me that still threatened to explode.

The memories of the scantily-clad women in the windows of Amsterdam's red-light district and the lines of drug dealers on the street shouting out the names of what seemed like every drug imaginable to passers-by kept playing back in my mind like a film on repeat as I floated on a buzz of euphoria. The night life in Amsterdam reminded me of the life offered me by Little Dread when we were in Southampton as kids. "Mr run tings," he said I'd be called, somehow through the buzz of it all, I just couldn't imagine myself as a pimp.

"Your turn," shouted Johan as he'd lit another rock of hash, which brought me round to the present. After I had taken in another gulp of smoke, I had such a coughing fit which made everyone laugh at first but as it continued for what seemed like ages and I thought my eyeballs would pop out each time I coughed it was so violent, Johan and some others patted my back then handed me a beer to calm things down. When the coughing finally eased, I had deeper voice than Barry White, "Don't hold it in so long next time," Johan shouted. After that I felt the blood rush from my head in one swift move and I collapsed in a heap on someone's bed to the cheers of everyone shouting, "he's done a whitey, he's done a whitey." A whitey is when the blood drains from your face, leaving a person pale looking and unconscious or just very drowsy. In the Caribbean circles, they call it "Lean" or "Mash up", not a lot of difference really as the condition is the same.

That realisation – that drug-fuelled experience – was the spur for the next bizarre twist in my early life. The next day at work, I was asked by some friends to travel different countries with them doing more fruit-picking when this job had finished. They made it sound exciting and fun and it certainly paid well and there would be lots more drugs and partying. Initially I had agreed but something happened to me when I was buzzing out of my head on drugs. I was having flashbacks of the story of the cross and switchblade about David Wilkinson, the minister, and the New York gang leader, Nicky Cruz. I didn't know what had happened to me because I passed out and I couldn't understand what was happening to me now. I'd gone to the toilet and found myself praying in a cubicle and asking God's forgiveness. It was the strangest feeling, almost as if something was compelling me to do it and having more flashbacks which was like watching a film but instead of seeing the original characters, I was seeing myself talking to the gangs.

So little time had passed since I'd been threatening and intimidating two blameless shop workers at the Cowley Centre; and yet even the memory of that evil couldn't dampen my newfound religious ardour. Back in England I had gone to see my mother to tell her that I'd changed and got God in my life and that I wanted to go to bible college. We chatted for a while and, without confessing any previous crimes, I apologised for being a "narty bwoy". My mum was almost beside herself with joy when I revealed that I'd "become a Christian." Overnight, she started treating me as normal mothers treat normal sons. She'd enquire about my day, check my health, offer to prepare a meal, engage in a proper conversation. Convinced, my mum showed her affections with a hug and with tears rolling down her cheeks said, " I have prayed for this moment every day and now my prayers have been answered." It felt like I was on a parallel universe, things were so different.

The police hadn't given up their search for the Cowley Centre robber and there was a photo-fit picture circulating in the Oxford Mail. I was on the list of suspects and subsequently arrested for questioning. In the police station, there was a Gideon bible in every cell. The detective sergeant and detective constable were playing good cop, bad cop with me. Before they got me a duty solicitor I had agreed to be interviewed without one because I was meant to be helping them with their enquiries. "We know you done it, Rodgers, and we have witnesses who can place you at the scene of the crime," said the DS bad cop. My trip to Holland helped and my alibi checked out but because my date of travel was after the robbery, bad cop continued accusing me. Finally DS bad cop threatened to fetch my mother and question her too. Well I nearly confessed there and then because my mother hates anything to do with courts and police stations and I wasn't going to put my new mother through anything like that, then DC good cop recommended I be put back in the cell to think things over.

In the cell, I realised I'd have to come clean, it was the only way out and the right thing to do. Seeing the bible next to me, I decided to see if God could offer any encouraging words, "It's a long shot," I thought, and not knowing where to look in it, I decided to read wherever I opened it at.

I opened it at the second Book of Corinthians, chapter five and started reading from verse one. After several verses, I almost decided to close the book and try again before good cop and bad cop return to interview me again. I didn't know what I expected God to say, since everything I did, went against all His moral codes. I was about to close the book when I glimpsed some of verse seventeen further down the page, which disclosed, that "when a man is in Christ, he's a new creation; old things are passed away, behold all things have become new." I thought about this for a moment to see if I understood what I read; to me, the meaning was very clear. "I didn't do it," I said to myself and then I kept saying it out loud to myself as I jumped for joy around the cell.

My elation didn't last long as I heard the familiar footsteps and rattle of keys outside my cell. DC good cop opened the door and asked me if I'm ready. Remembering the thought of DC bad cop contacting my mum saddened me and just before I walked through the door, defeated and ready to give up, DC good cop said, "Don't worry, we don't have any evidence, we are questioning all suspects like this." For a brief moment, I felt relieved at this news but DC bad cop to me seemed convinced he had his man.

"Before I charge you, we've arranged for you to speak with our duty solicitor," and I was introduced to Wilson Carter. Wilson was a tall slim middle-aged Australian man with bushy sliver hair. I was apprehensive of him initially because I'd heard stories of duty solicitors who help the police more than their clients, I was soon to learn that Wilson was not one of those but very professional and helpful. He explained that the police wanted to put me on an ID parade but was unable to find enough stooges similar to myself to make it fair so they decided to let me walk down the busy Cornmarket Street in the town centre and strategically place the witnesses on one side so they have a clear view of me walking by. The idea was that if the witnesses recognised me, the police would tap me on the shoulder and I would be arrested. Although it was legal at the time, it seemed pretty unfair, especially if I happened to be the only black male walking there at that moment, a problem Wilson helped rectify by insisting that the few stooges they could initially get, be allowed to walk there at the same time as well.

I did my walk twice and no tap on the shoulder but Wilson came up to me to tell me, apparently, he said, the witnesses only really got to see me for a moment the second time, because one bus was going in one direction and another bus in the opposite direction and before the buses blocked their view completely, they saw me briefly. This news meant that the police wouldn't be charging me and I would not be investigated further on this matter, however it didn't stop DS bad cop from giving me a word of warning, "I know you did it Rodgers, and mark my words, I will 'ave you one day," he said in a very stern voice. Whoever had been responsible for the

Cowley Centre violation was an old "creation", and nothing to do with me, I naively thought to myself.

Three months later, Amsterdam's debauchery was a thing of the past, as I enrolled in the Overstone College of Theology, near Northampton. From the first day, I threw myself with zeal into my new calling, determined to apply myself more diligently, and lead a life more blameless, than any of my peer group.

Whether I was studying Christian theology, or comparative religion, or obscure points of doctrine, I'd arrive at Overstone lessons having read and absorbed all the preparatory texts; afterwards I'd create meticulous notes to ensure all key points were absorbed into my consciousness. If my destiny was to be a Minster, I would try to prove myself the most dedicated, knowledgeable, devoted minister ever to graduate from the College – even though much of the material read like Japanese algebra to someone who had never studied beyond CSEs.

Mum knew nothing of my spell in the police station and I didn't see the point in sharing, especially as I didn't do it according to God's word. How different things would have been if DS bad cop had spoken to my mum about the robbery, I would have sung like a canary.

"Mi pray ah pray fi ah bwoy an geh wah lickle devil like yo, yo wus ah narty bwoy."

("I prayed and prayed for a boy and got a little devil like you, you was a naughty boy.") Were now replaced with simply, "good boy."

But I could overlook these quirks in light of the broad grin and robust bearhug which greeted me whenever she opened the door. Finally, twenty years too late, I felt I'd gained a mother.

Being enrolled at Overstone was not merely a matter of attending lessons and studying; the students were encouraged to travel to Churches across the country, ministering, mentoring and singing.

For many parishioners, when the Overstone choir was in town, it was as if Hollywood celebrities had arrived. A dozen of us – six guys, six girls – all fresh-faced, respected, honourable. What Christian parent wouldn't be sizing up our merits as spouse material for any eligible offspring? It was during one such visit that I'd been introduced to Susan Parks, a singing instructor from Woolwich, and a member of the London Community Goopel Choir (LCGC for short). Susan was a smart dresser – she worked by day in an insurance company, and had appeared in tabloid adverts for hair products and makeup – and she made quite an impression with her wide eyes, saucer-shaped face, and lavish perm. She quickly decided that I was "the one" and began bombarding the College with messages of lavish affection. The other students couldn't resist teasing me, but were also filled with envy that I was being pursued by a "London model and singer."

After the pain of my separation from Jennifer Robinson, I hadn't planned to rush into another romantic relationship; but I was flattered by the attention, and increasingly spent my free time in her company.

The amount of "free time" would soon swell, for all the wrong reasons. One Tuesday in late May, I was summoned to the office of the Dean of Students. Although I was in his presence for a short time, the echo of his words had reverberated throughout my life.

"I'm afraid, Brother Lennox, the Church which has been funding you is unable to continue its contributions. I don't have any information about their reasons, but those are the facts. Unless you're able to find an alternative source of funding by the first day of next term, we'll have no choice but to terminate your studies with us. I'm sure this isn't the news you wanted to hear, but there's little I can do about it." He advised that I may be able to work and study and pay my way that way.

For a moment, I felt the rage returning, but contained the anger long enough to reach Overstone's lakeside, where I sat for an hour, yelling and screaming at the breeze. At God.

"I don't understand," I screamed. "Why would you allow me to come here and put me through this, only to have my studies terminated?" I gave God a chance to answer my question but there was no answer and no noise except the sounds of nature around me. Frustrated and angry, I wanted God to set aside his heavenly duties, and appear before me, so I could release my rage on Him – physically if necessary. I didn't understand what was happening and why, so in my ignorance I told God what I thought of his love.

"Your love is like a parent who sends their child outside in the cold to play and doesn't give them a coat to wear," I yelled into the air as if I was talking to someone way up in the heavens and not someone who is all around us. Again I yelled out what seemed like another proverb of my own, "Your love is like a parent who sends their child to school and when they get there, there are no teachers but a pile of books and a note saying, educate yourself."

It was an act of rebellion and frustration; it was also symbolic of the mess my life had suddenly become. I felt robbed and abandoned, helpless and still God didn't answer me or I was naively wrapped up in my own thoughts and emotions that I couldn't hear Him.

*

That summer was a tornado of increasingly desperate attempts to rustle up the finance needed to continue my studies. I pleaded to no avail with the Church that had cut off funding; the reasons were unrelated to anything I'd done, but they were unwavering. Mum's advice was to pray and trust God to sort it all out but my lack of understanding about how God really works led me to leave Oxford and take up residence at Acton's Heartbreak Hotel – which was nothing to do with Elvis, and was about as far as you could get from Graceland's Mansion.

The sinks were ingrained with grime, the beds were infested with bugs, cockroaches patrolled the corridors, and the single communal TV hung precariously from the wall with live wires dangling on either side. I suppose that, strictly speaking, its claim to provide bed-and-breakfast was accurate, but it did test the limits of truth in advertising: breakfast comprised a cup of lukewarm tea and a single thin slice of buttered toast. Nevertheless, London was then, as now, the place to secure paid work fast, and it was essential I had somewhere to stay overnight. For seven straight days, I worked ten hours daily on a labouring site in Chiswick – walking the five-mile roundtrip since I couldn't afford the bus fare, and avoiding meals (other than the slice of toast) for similar reasons. By the end of the week, I was exhausted and weak.

I could barely recognise myself in the mirror – my cheeks had lost their chubbiness, the skin receding around my bones, and my eyes were deadened, devoid of sparkle. I lacked the willpower and physical strength for another week at the construction site, and so stuffed my belongings into a bag and headed towards Paddington – broke financially and spiritually. To make matters worse, abandoning my job meant I was never even paid for the week I'd spent on-site. To this day, whenever I hear people speak of London being "built on the back of cheap labour", I can't help but grimace.

That afternoon, I sat at Paddington Station, watching the world go round and wondering how I was going to pay my school fees, more importantly, how I was going to get immediate food and shelter as I had no more money to afford the three-pound per day charge to stay at Heart-Break Hotel. During the summer months, central London shops heaved with crowds, especially tourists who often seemed in competition with one another to spend as much local currency as possible on overpriced tat. I noticed how easily shop assistants were distracted by argumentative customers or by their questioning ("Can I get batteries for this back home?" "I haven't got my receipt." "Can I exchange this?"), and I noticed in the open-plan newsagents, John Menzies, that when serving customers they often left the tills open for brief moments. I tried to avoid thinking about stealing it because I wanted to live a changed life, but desperation got the better of me. I now knew what I was going to do next and, shortly after, I was running down a main road with a hundred pounds in my pocket.

Uncertain about the next steps, I moved to Woolwich; at least, I'd be close to Susan and with her help, I was now sleeping on one of her church friend's sofas. It wasn't a palace, but it was a step up from the Heartbreak Hotel. She insisted I meet her family and I was soon having regular meals with them. Her father, Caleb, a skilled carpenter and cabinet maker, eventually took me on as his apprentice, perhaps to invest in a future son-in-law but I thought; I've tried bible college, construction work, and fruit picking – why not dabble in some woodwork to extend the list even further? It turned out that I had a modest flair for the trade, having had some practice at St Edward's School with Mr Waverley. I was soon assisting Caleb with more advanced projects such as first and second fixing. I had much to learn and Caleb was a good teacher.

I'd barely settled in – when I heard the news that Susan had been rushed to hospital. By the time I arrived at the Casualty unit, she was under sedation in preparation for the operating theatre, tubes plunged into her mouth as if she was the victim in a horror movie, surrounded by a busy-looking medical team and banks of monitors that displayed her vital readings. My head was still spinning when one of the nurses sat me down to tell me Susan had taken a suspected overdose. I could barely process the information. Not Susan, surely – the smart, sassy, career-minded choirgirl?

My sister Veronica had met Caleb Preston a couple of weeks beforehand, and had recommended I should "stay clear of him and Susan, he's got a screw loose," but I'd attributed that to a clash of different religious beliefs. As far as I was concerned, Susan was flawless. How could somebody so composed, so together, possibly find herself in this predicament?

Caleb was already at the hospital when I arrived, and, while we awaited an update on her condition, he took the opportunity to grill me about my relationship with his daughter.

"Do you want to be with her?" he asked. "To marry her?"

His tone was uncannily reminiscent of that used by Julie's dad, when he'd probed my intentions towards his daughter. But this time I was better prepared.

"I think we're both happy to take our time," I said, "and see how things develop. Neither of us wants to rush matters."

He placed a hand on my shoulder. But it wasn't a comforting or consoling hand.

"Perhaps I didn't make myself clear, Brudda Lennox," he said. "You need to marry my daughter. To take her off me."

I hadn't fully appreciated the Prestons' domestic situation, but quickly leant that Susan's relationship with her father was far from healthy. He resented her presence around the house, and she loathed his controlling influence. They had frequent heated rows, which often resulted in objects being hurled.

"She's a lovely girl," I said. "Let's see what happens."

"Brudda Lennox." Charles lowered his voice so it was barely audible, but there was no mistaking the firmness of his intent. "Unless you agree, this moment, in the eyes of God, to marry my daughter, then I'll call Overstone College and tell them you're fired as my apprentice for bad behaviour," (implying my intimate relationship with Susan could be mis-understood and ruin a minister's reputation) "and that I recommend that you not be allowed to continue your studies. I trust I've made myself clear to you." Caleb held a high position in the Church and had influence.

"Oh, I see. That's very clear, sir," I said.

It was a few more hours before the doctors revived Susan from her induced coma. Never having proposed marriage beforehand, I wasn't certain of the etiquette, but decided it would be polite to dress smartly, brush my teeth, and offer a fine bouquet of flowers. I had tried to anticipate her reaction – would she be surprised, overjoyed, apathetic, horrified, dismissive? As she came round, it was nothing like the movies, when patients switch in seconds from "out cold" to "fully alert". Susan was still dazed and a bit groggy as I popped the question, but her gentle nod was unmissable There'd be a Mrs Rodgers before long! I was even convinced her forehead rippled in an expression of mild surprise, but nothing like the shock I experienced when she remarked:

"This is probably a good time to mention something else. I'm pregnant."

"You mean, like, having a baby?"

"That's usually what it means, yes."

"And I'm the...?"

I trailed off in mid-sentence as she gave me a withering "what sort of girl do you think I am?" look.

From the moment our engagement was announced, Caleb Preston attitude towards me underwent a massive change. He'd never been the warmest person, but up to that point I'd regarded him as a perfectly reasonable prospective father-in-law. Suddenly, his behaviour became that of a petty, heckling bully. He docked me a day's wages when I spent two hours away from the workshop, organising a photographer for a wedding that he'd instigated. At the family home, Susan locked herself in the bathroom to escape his prying questions and presumptive interference into every aspect of her life. Nevertheless, I wanted to be a dutiful son-in-law, so when he offered to host an engagement party at his house to celebrate our union, I persuaded the Grants and my sisters to set aside their reservations and join the festivities. I wasn't above blatant emotional blackmail.

"It's a really special moment for me," I implored. "It'll mean so much to have you there."

The engagement party, in fact, only served to strengthen their scepticism. Whilst not expecting lunch at the Savoy, they did anticipate – having travelled from Oxford at my request – at least some basic hospitality. And the did, admittedly, lay on some food. It was neither appetising nor plentiful, but at least it existed. The problem arose with the unexplained absence of drink. And I'm not referring to the lack of beers or wines; there was literally nothing to drink. Intrepid as ever, Chris located a glass on a kitchen shelf, and was pouring himself some tap water, when he found himself at the sharp end of Mrs Perry tongue.

"There'll be none of that," she instructed, "Not in my house. Not until after you've finished eating."

"In that case," said Chris, "I don't think I'll stay in your house." He signalled to the rest of my guests, and the entire group departed en masse towards the pub across the street, leaving me facing an unsavoury dilemma: the family with whom I'd grown up, or the family into which I was marrying. To my regret, I chose the latter.

The reality quickly dawned on me that, with marriage and baby both imminent, it would be impractical to resume my biblical studies, even if I'd managed to cobble together sufficient finance. Two weeks before the wedding, I wrote to the College, expressing sorrow and regret that I'd be unable to return. It took three redrafts until I was happy with the tone, but in retrospect I was far too apologetic. I took onto my own shoulders the responsibility for failing to complete the programme, but in reality I was the injured, aggrieved party. I'd committed no shortage of deeds for which apologies were due, but dropping out of Overstone shouldn't appear on the list. Events had conspired against me; ones with lasting consequences.

After the engagement party fiasco, my family understandably boycotted the wedding itself. Mum and Dad had a legitimate excuse; they'd finally stumped up for two flights back to St Vincent, and, by the date of my marriage, were in the Caribbean making their retirement plans. Nobody else had the stomach for another day like the last, and sent a lot of flimsy excuses. "But it's only a single day for you," I moaned inwardly, "As for me, I'm facing a lifetime of it."

My sister Veronica made a point of phoning me to justify her non-appearance and had been quite negative about Caleb Preston , having bumped into him in Norbury and had a cup of tea.

She was still struggling to comprehend the wedding.

I'd been treated to so many silly remarks from my sisters over the years that I didn't pay any heed.

Nevertheless, I did appreciate that, if I let my relationship with Caleb spiral any further downwards, the day might come when my festering rage would explode, and I might harm him physically. So I used the arrival of our baby to engineer an exit from his carpentry business. On my final day at the workshop, I praised him effusively for his wise teachings and kindness, hoping he'd reciprocate my warm feelings. It wasn't until some weeks later that I discovered how wrong I was.

In the meantime, events moved quickly. Our baby entered the world in September 1984 – a chuckling, lively little imp we named Mark, in honour of the American rhythm and blues band who had recently topped the charts with their insanely catchy hit 'Love Train'. For the first time in my life, I knew what it was like to love another person unconditionally. One night, while Susan slept, I whispered to Mark that, whatever the future held, I'd always be there to support him; I'd never let him down. He raised his tiny hands and gurgled.

For me, that was cast-iron acknowledgement. The deal was sealed.

After the disappointment of Overstone, I finally landed a job which gave me high hopes for a worthwhile career, as a security guard on a building site. The role was tailor-made for my abilities. I was physically strong – five years of boxing training at St Edward's, under the intense teaching of Kitt Long, had seen to that. And I didn't scare easily. When you've stood up to racist bullies, it is hard to get intimidated by the occasional trespasser. As my probationary month went by, I found myself given more responsibilities, and the foreman spoke encouragingly of a "prosperous long-term future" with the firm. Had I found my destiny? From the despair of the Heartbreak Hotel to a beautiful wife, adorable son, and promising career – all in the space of a few months. I glimpsed the road ahead; it seemed almost… tranquil.

The glimpse was shattered on the final day of my probation, when the senior manager on site invited me into his portacabin. He wasn't exactly in tears – you never see that on a building site, but he was stammering as he broke the news of my situation.

"You've been a model worker. You haven't put a foot wrong. This is the day I was planning to make your position permanent, and offer a hefty pay rise. But I'm not going to be able to do that, I'm afraid. In fact, we're going to have to let you go."

I heard the words, but they made no sense. I rocked back in my seat, and stared at the ceiling. Was this a wind-up? A test of my resilience? My overactive imagination?

"We received a reference from your former employer. Which is usually routine. But in this case, he was damning. Across two whole pages. Unreliable, dishonest, prone to mistakes. And that's just the first paragraph."

So this wasn't a test.

"And what makes it even stranger is, as I'm fully aware, the reference was written by your father-in-law."

As I changed out of my security officer outfit for the final time, I was suddenly reminded of Veronica's phone call, shortly before our wedding day – the one I'd dismissed as stirring trouble. Veronica had assured me that, upon finishing his cup of tea (and leaving her to pick up the tab), Caleb Preston had leant across the table and said something so chilling that she'd physically shivered; so unexpected that she'd mentally rechecked the words, in case she'd misunderstood.

"It was unmistakable, Lennox," she'd said. "He told me: 'Two bulls can't live in the same pen. Don't get too fond of your brother, Veronica, for one simple reason. Because I'm going to destroy him.'"

6.
Turbulence

My relationship with Caleb Preston deteriorated rapidly after the "employment reference" break-up. He was interfering in every aspect of my marriage to Susan, even criticising the settings on the thermostat. ("I'm just trying to keep Mark warm," I pleaded in mitigation; "You understand nothing and do everything wrong.").

One day, I confronted him about the stream of verbal abuse he'd penned to the construction firm:

"I was doing really well, and needed the income to provide for my wife and son. Your letter cost me my job."

I expected him to be defensive or embarrassed about his critique, but he was neither:

"I stand by every word of it. If you lost your job as a result, that's too bad. But it's your fault – not mine."

I couldn't figure it out. This was the same man who had begged – in fact, blackmailed – me to wed his daughter, and now his actions were throwing both our marriage and our livelihood. Whatever the motivation, I feared his extraordinary determination to "destroy" me would follow me like a shadow into any new ventures; my only strategy was to escape beyond his reach, along with my wife and child. Oxford was the obvious choice. I was making arrangements to stay (again!) with Jennifer during my hour of need, when, out of nowhere, I learned that my in-laws had brought forward their plans to relocate to Florida.

"Are you certain?" I asked Susan, as she broke the news. "He never mentioned anything like that when I was in his workshop, not a single time."

"As far as I understand, he's been planning it for months, but kept it under wraps in case they declined his visa," she said. "Apparently it ticked the right boxes that his brother already lives there, and has a steady job."

"As far as I'm concerned, they're welcome to him. Their loss, our gain."

It was an unexpected turn of events, and I never found out precisely what had sparked it. Preston wasn't someone to act on impulse, or take a life-changing risk. Yet, here he was, uprooting everything for a new start in the sunshine state. In truth, I wasn't too bothered about the explanation; I couldn't wait for him to be on the far side of the ocean, a fading memory and no longer an influence on my life.

With Perry imminent departure, it was possible to concentrate on searching for a new job, without suffering renewed anxiety that he'd sabotage it. Susan and her father had experienced a slight reconciliation in the days before he left – partly triggered by me. When helping in his workshop, I'd once heard him say, "she never says sorry for anything," so I'd suggested to Susan that when the opportunity arises, a mild apology might help to reset the relationship. At first, the defusing of tension was a welcome development, although sometimes it seemed I was now the one being frozen out.

Susan had always wanted to live in Florida, it was her dream but because of her turbulent relationship with her dad, he wasn't going to help her to go with them and I was happy that we could make our own plans; but her dad had other ideas and decided that if Susan wanted to go, he'd pay for it and make the arrangements. A blazing row followed and I told Caleb to keep out of my marriage and he refused and I stormed out and headed back to Oxford to cool down.

I came back one week later to find everyone gone except Caleb; he came home from work and found me there. He didn't lie about Susan's whereabouts when asked but led me to believe Mark had gone with her too. We didn't argue anymore but the atmosphere was tense. He was leaving for Florida in two days and invited me to stay in the house as all bills were paid up, a nice gesture that almost seemed kind. It wasn't until I spoke to Veronica again that she told me to get out of the house now and that Caleb had planned for me to be in the house when the council turn up and evict me and all utilities get switched off.

Whilst staying with my sister Veronica in London Road Norbury, I became a shop assistant in a branch of Scholls, the feet specialist and immersed myself in the world of insoles, orthotics, hosiery, moisturising foot creams and treatments for fungal nail infections, corns and cracked heels, with a promise that I'd be trained in chiropody. These weren't subjects to which I'd given a great deal of thought when I'd been sanding wood or guarding a construction site. I was selected as the standout candidate for the role because the other staff had other ambitions for their careers and were mainly middle-aged women with families. In any event, for a few peculiar months. I was the man with a plan for people of all ages concerned about their verrucas, ingrown toenails, athlete's feet, or simply excess dry skin on their heels, It was a surreal time.

I had imagined Mark's face in Disneyland as he enjoyed meeting Pluto and Mickey Mouse, theme parks, animal shows, waterparks – and I couldn't have been more thrilled for him but angry at the way things had turned out, which made it a little unsettling to learn, a few weeks into their move to Florida, that Mark had never left the country. Martin Crown – a London acquaintance who'd gamely stood in as best man when Chris boycotted my wedding – called in a state of puzzlement.

"I don't want to cause any alarm," he said, "But I'm sure I saw Marl this morning."

"No way, he is in America with his mum, that's what I was told."

"You see, here's the thing. He wasn't with Susan."

"You must've imagined it."

"It was at the Blackheath Baptist Church, in Charlton and he was with a family I've never seen before. A woman with a few other children was bouncing him on her knee, as if he was her own son."

This must be a case of mistaken identity, I was sure. It'd be an easy error to make; babies look near-identical – but I couldn't get Martin's words out of my head. I pestered him with calls for more information, and eventually – feeling some responsibility for my distress – he offered to track the family's movements after the next weekend's service. "If I get you the address," he said, "You can take over the investigation. My job will be done."

Martin delivered his findings: the family in question resided in a semi-detached home a short walk from the Church. I arrived at the property after work one evening, but the curtains weren't fully drawn and it was possible to crouch by the windows and peer directly into the living room. There was Mark, beautiful Mark, so innocent, lying on a play mat clutching a furry teddy bear, while two young girls I'd never seen before played peek-a-boo as their presumed mum watched television.

It could've been a scene of perfect domestic bliss, except for...

My brain was spinning. My son, my first born, in the company of strangers. This was not a matter that could be allowed to stand. But what should I do? Smash down the front door? Rant? Threaten?

Plead? Argue? I managed to suppress my instincts; my primary concern was for Mark's wellbeing, and I'd had enough brushes with authority to know that making a scene wasn't conducive to a good outcome.

So I waited until the next day, when I was in a calmer frame of mind. I knew I'd need to confront the mum but I wanted to rehearse exactly the words to use, and ensure that, regardless of how the conversation developed, I'd neither threaten or use force. For once, composure was achieved and maintained.

Introducing myself and explaining with surprising calmness that I was Mark's dad, I wanted to know why they had Mark. At first she denied any knowledge, but admitted being relatives of the Prestons. I tried to be reasonable and ask her to continue to look after Mark during my work hours and I would pay her. When I mentioned "Don't make me contact the police," sweat burst across her brow and her disposition changed. I provided my contact details at the Scholls store; if I hadn't heard from her by noon the next day, I'd have no hesitation in notifying the police.

The deadline worked a treat. Twenty-four hours later, I was reunited with Mark and in the unusual position of being a single parent. Apparently, Caleb had agreed to pay Susan's fare to Florida only if she left Mark behind, said the relatives and not once were they contacted or sent any money for his keep since moving to Florida. I also received a message from Susan via one of her friends who saw me shopping at Woolwich market. She said that Susan was sorry about how things turned out and that her relationship with her dad broke down a few days after they got to Florida and she wondered if we could sort things out and try again. I was still angry and hurt about it all and wasn't willing to try anything again.

It had taken me a few weeks to acquire competence in basic carpentry, but I didn't have that luxury with the infinitely more complex task of caring for an infant. From day one, I needed to be proficient in nappy changing, preparing meals, bottle feeding, and – crucially – knowing how to react when the screams and cries just won't cease. My sisters shared a few handy pointers, but mostly I needed to figure the stuff out for myself.

With Mark now a permanent presence in my life, there was no time left for Scholls. I was a few minutes from quitting when they beat me to it. "On your application, you said you had no ties. Clearly your situation has changed so you have to choose, a career with us or parenthood." It was a no brainer, I wasn't going to abandon my son again. Ironically, they'd been first to realise my days were numbered, since they'd taken the call from the Perry relatives from Charlton.

The next few weeks were amongst the most blissful of my life. Mine was the first face Mark saw every morning, and he gurgled and chortled with glee. Ours was a precious bond; we played and laughed. I spent long evenings telling him meticulous and detailed stories, knowing he didn't understand a word – about "Cherry Boy", about Mummy G, about St Vincent, about his aunties, about St Edward's, even about his mum. I bought him the best of what I could afford from the Mothercare range, and passed the hours pushing him up and down the Cowley Road, or hopping on a bus into Oxford, so I could tell him about where we were born and no matter what I said, he'd respond with a chuckle.

We were a unit, and for this first time I noticed that other pedestrians would look at me with huge smiles as they passed by.

This was also a period when money was plentiful, despite the loss of my income from Scholls. Being a single dad unlocked my entitlement to various benefits that were otherwise not applicable, and social services helpfully guided me through the maze. The health visitors were adamant that accommodation must meet exacting standards of hygiene, and provide ample room for play, and arranged an extended placement at one of east Oxford's most upmarket B&Bs. And I had no qualms about supplementing my benefits with extra cash to which I wasn't strictly entitled to.

"Aren't you a little smartly dressed to be on benefits?" asked the counter clerk. He was wearing a moth-eaten sweater, and stared at my suave attire through his horn-rimmed glasses with unhidden envy.

"Listen mate, just because I'm on benefits, doesn't mean I have to look like it!"

"Fair enough, I suppose," he said, and he initialled my documents.

With no sign of Susan returning to England, I applied for – and was awarded – full legal custody, helped by glowing reports from social workers about my parenting skills. With divorce proceedings also underway, I was making a clean break with the past. We were a great team, Mark and me; whatever mistakes I'd made over the years, here was something I'd get right. He would grow up as a happy, cared-for, provided-for child. Of that he had my vow.

I'd adapted to my role as a single parent when, unbidden, Susan re-entered my life. Her honeymoon period had finally reached its end, and she managed to track me down.

"Now I'm back in England, I'd love to catch up," she said when she called.

I was furious about how she'd abandoned Mark; she was tearfully apologetic, explaining that her father was only prepared to fork out for a single airline ticket. We agreed a meeting point – for old times' sake; it was a café in Oxford city centre where we'd spent one of our earliest dates.

She cooed with admiration when she saw how Mark had grown.

"I'm so happy for you, Lennox, that you have custody," she said. "You're devoted to Mark, and he's so fond of you."

"Thank you; I've been trying hard."

"I know I made a mess of things. You're doing a far better job than I would've managed. It's all worked out so well."

"I hope I can keep it up. Some days are tougher than others. But, so far, it seems to be OK."

"Y'know, I don't have any mementos of Mark. Do you have a couple of photos, perhaps a copy of the birth certificate? It would be lovely to have some things to remember him by."

"For sure, I don't see any problem. In fact, I'd be very happy to dig out more things. If you like, you can have some of his baby clothes; he's grown out of them – it's better for you to have them. I'd only throw them out."

Susan was on a roll and she had one more favour to ask. She was "so sorry" about the recent misunderstanding, "I would really like to take Mark on a holiday to see Mom and Dad. I promise he'll come with me this time. You can even wave us through the barriers at Heathrow, if you have any doubt."

I was reassured by her offer; I couldn't face the prospect of finding Mark once again left with random strangers. If, with my own eyes, I witnessed him checking in for the flight, what could possibly go wrong? She'd hardly take a detour on her way to the terminal gate. I even offered to contribute towards the flights, although Susan declined.

Having seen them off – all smiles and hugs – waiting for their return was miserable agony. My body clock had adapted to the routines of being a twenty-four-hour carer, so there was an unbearable Mark-sized void in my day. I felt eerily alone, but comforted myself that he was away for a mere two weeks. I'd even converted the number of days into hours – 336 in total – and, each time the minute hand reached zero, I'd count down "one less hour to wait."

Finally, the date of their return arrived. I bought chocolates for Susan and a huge cuddly toy for Mark, and was stationed in the Arrivals Hall a full sixty minutes before the plane touched down. I imagined their movements. "Now they'll be leaving the plane… now they'll be queuing at Immigration… now they'll be waiting by the baggage carousels…" and, the best one, "Now they'll be walking through the 'nothing to declare' lane, approaching the sliding doors, and standing right in front of me in Arrivals."

My pulse accelerated when a group of bronzed holidaymakers, one sporting a T-shirt with "I love Florida" emblazoned across the chest, walked through the doors. The first passengers from their plane. I knew that mothers-with-babies can be amongst the last to disembark a packed flight, so I wasn't worried that Susan and Mark weren't present in the first wave. Ten minutes later, a few nebulous doubts were starting to form. Thirty minutes later, my mind was reeling with panic.

It would be another twenty-two years and nine months before I saw Mark again.

*

The next few months were a haze as baby milk bottles gave way to bottles of a very different description.

Unable to punish anyone else for what had happened, my liver bore the brunt. When I wasn't unburdening my sorrows over a Caribbean Rum with a bored barman, I could be found with a can of Special Brew or Crucial Brew somewhere, or collapsed in my apartment, my face flat against the floorboards. Social services were scathing in their assessment of my plight. When I'd renewed contact with Susan, I'd flown full-square in the face of their advice, her mental instability having been cited as a factor in my favour during the custody hearing.

More to the point, there was no disguising the stench of alcohol on my breath. Even if they had the resources to launch international proceedings against child abduction, my rapid descent would've killed off their inclination.

Chris tried his best to raise my spirits; but if anyone could, he could but it troublod him to walch his closest friend on a path of self-destruction. One weekend, he bought tickets to a dinner-dance in Blackbird Leys, whether it was calypso, or ska, or reggae, we'd launch ourselves around the dance floor like an idiots, just for laughs and helped on by generous measures of rum or Red Stripe beer. Chris realised I was in a really bad way when he spotted me opening the pull-tab of my next drink whilst still swigging the dregs from the previous one. When eventually he persuaded me of the need to leave, I couldn't navigate the short path to the main road without Chris's support. Nor without spewing half the contents of my stomach across the concrete slabs.

"Couldn't you at least have aimed for the lawn?" groaned Chris.

I was wrecked but the night wasn't finished. Staggering down the Cowley Road, we heard music coming from a house somewhere in James Street and some people walking there. The reggae beat was wafting hypnotically through the house as the base vibrated loudly and threatening to crack the windows.

These house parties were called Blues, and people all over Oxford had them weekly. People often went to night clubs then afterwards to a Blues Party. The house was rammed on both floors, bodies were packed tightly along the hallway and up the stairs, and manoeuvring from the front door to the lounge was fraught with peril, as it's hard to find any space that someone else's foot wasn't occupying and mainly guys lined the hallway and unsuspecting girls who were trying to get past, ended up doing the Caribbean version of dirty dancing with every guy they passed. Chris inadvertently stepped on the crocodile-skin shoes of a hulking, blinged-up man in his mid-30s.

"Yo! Yah mash mi carn bwoy; a wah do yo?" he exclaimed then sucking his teeth in vexation.

("You step on my corns boy; what's wrong with you?")

We noticed his hand plunging into his pocket, as if checking for his knife.

"I'm sorry man," said Chris, and moved on quickly before he changed his mind.

Chris's apology diffused the situation. We'd avoided a fight and instant eviction – a fact for which I was especially grateful when, reaching the lounge, my eyes alighted on a skinny girl in a tight-fitting top and hair gloriously highlighted with bright red streaks; she wasn't chatting to any other guys, so that was good enough for me and with hair of the dog helping me to sober up, and vomit breath, I sidled towards her.

"Would you like a dance?" I hollered in her ear. The DJ had just put some lovers' reggae, with its slow rhythmic beat, on the turntable.

Neither of us could hear a word I'd uttered – she was standing right next to a massive speaker, and the pounding of the base drowned any conversation. Nevertheless, my meaning must've been clear because she immediately wrapped her arms around my neck, and writhed in time with the beat. The music seemed even louder than before, our bodies vibrated every time the bass sounded, and we danced obliviously.

Moments later, our lips locked. The stench of vomit must've been unmissable whenever I exhaled, but she clearly didn't care. This was one night that wouldn't go to waste. With the excitement, I felt my skin glistening with sweat. That hadn't happened for a long, long time.

Somehow, despite the noise, we arranged to meet the following day.

Neither expected the other to show, but in the event we both made the effort. I learnt her name was Natalie Masters, of mixed race – half Indian, half Arabic. She had a feisty, rebellious nature, and a chaotic approach to everything from conversation (her speech was very fast, and she was forever in scrapes for speaking her mind too bluntly) to personal finances (not for the last time, she was being evicted by her landlord for non-payment of rent). I'd never met anybody who exuded such mesmerising charisma, and I was quickly captivated. We drank like sailors, we fought like ferrets. It was a high-intensity relationship and we became inseparable.

No longer holding down single-parent responsibilities, I had time on my hands for a bit of hustling, and teamed up with an Italian guy from Headington, nicknamed (with typical gang humour) since he was always behaving like a black dude despite being the only white. Yardi and I devised a sure-fire method to scam Radio Rentals, pocketing £500 between us each time. The scheme was as audacious as it was simple. We used other people's stolen identification and sometimes borrowed, usually just a library card and a rent book. The controls at Radio Rentals being less than foolproof, these were accepted as conclusive evidence of our credit-worthiness, enabling us to hire top-of-the-range camcorders with all the accessories.

By the time the head office ledgers flagged there was a "problem with the account", we'd repeated the deceit at half a dozen stores in the region. The only ceiling on our ambitions was the number of outlets around Oxford; if I'd had my way, they'd have been as plentiful as post boxes.

I had many fiery arguments with Natalie, but none as intense as this. We were not in the best place, emotionally or financially, to raise a child, so – as diplomatically as possible – I suggested an abortion. Natalie wouldn't agree to it – amongst other reasons, she experienced a break-up from her own parents. She carried the baby during a rollercoaster nine months, during which we were evicted, slept rough, lived in a shelter in central London, and eventually was housed.

We drifted apart, we made up; we shouted "I never want to see you again", we kissed and pledged "I'll never leave your side." It was dizzying, intoxicating, addictive; from one day to the next, I was unsure whether she was my lover, or a bitter ex. Fortunately for both of us, we were on good terms the day Karen was born. I was on the maternity ward throughout the labour, and was invited to cut the umbilical cord. I'd fathered two children into this world; hopefully my bonds with my daughter would be built on more secure foundations – such as living in the same continent! – than those with my son.

I'd been unemployed since leaving Scholl, and was only able to afford a decent lifestyle through what I received from benefits. I was concerned this was not a sustainable solution to our family finances. It was time, once again, to make plans for a proper career, and top of the list was returning to carpentry – at least I'd already displayed a level of proficiency. Natalie was supportive, in typically forthright language:

"Anything that gets you earning some money."

With Karen's arrival, Natalie had leapt to the top of the Council flat waiting list, and the authorities had already identified a few alternatives which matched her needs.

I enrolled on a carpentry programme at the Skills Centre in Perivale, West London. Successful completion of the programme would provide me with a City & Guilds certificate in Carpentry and Joinery, and this would open opportunities both for securing jobs on building sites, and for pursuing the self-employment route. I couldn't afford the daily commute to Perivale and had no independent means to reach the centre by nine o'clock Monday to Friday. For the first three months on the programme, I made the return trip the only economic way – by walking nearly five miles from the hostel to the M40, then thumbing a lift from any driver who happened to be heading to the capital and was in need of company to ease the boredom.

To guarantee punctuality, I set the alarm for three o'clock. The teaching staff were impressed with my time-keeping albeit perplexed at why my eyes would start drooping towards the middle of the afternoon.

What nobody realised – not Yardi, not Natalie, not my carpentry lecturers, not Chris Grant – was the rage hadn't left me. It hadn't boiled over recently, not since I'd exacted brutal revenge on the racist Mark Fields a few years beforehand. It had been contained but it hadn't been eradicated. And as circumstances were placing me in situations of mounting stress, I faced triggers that risked rekindling my rage, causing it to erupt in ways which would be devastating not just for me, but for those I held dear.

*

It kicked off on a Friday afternoon, when an attempted hustle had backfired.

Through quick wits, I'd narrowly escaped arrest, but seethed that Yardi had abandoned his 'lookout' post, leaving me perilously exposed. When you're thieving with a partner, you're as reliant upon one another as any effective double act – Batman and Robin, Starsky and Hutch, Morecombe and Wise. Your wellbeing – and potentially your liberty – is placed in the hands of that partner, and breaking this trust is an unforgivable act of delinquency. I did not react well to Yardi's behaviour. It wasn't in my nature to sit down for an in-depth appraisal of his performance, or to draft a development plan. It wasn't the first time the trust had been broken, he was caught swindling me out of money before too. My method of feedback was somewhat more explicit.

"You f-ing idiot!" I shouted, slamming him against the bonnet of his car.

"Hey, man, no need to get mad. It worked out, didn't it."

"I could've been locked away. I got a kid, and I could've been locked away. F- you!"

We'd met at the rendezvous point – under an archway on an estate in Pudding Lane, near the town centre, where, despite being in broad daylight, some of our encounter was hidden from witnesses. This meant there was no need to hold back my anger, or to pull my punches. I smashed Yardi's jaw and he stumbled backwards, then I rained blows and kicks on him and raised my fist to strike again.

Yardi was a wreck, quivering like jelly; a patch of urine spreading across the front of his trousers.

"You're crazy," he said, "I'm getting out of here."

He fumbled in his pocket, drawing out his car keys, which he jabbed in the direction of the car door. But he was too shaken to hold them steady. The key missed the lock, scratching the paintwork instead. He tried again, with the same result. His shaking fingers were unable to muster a third attempt, and the keys fell in a heap on the gravel.

My knuckles were throbbing from the blows I'd already inflicted, and, looking at his car, it dawned on me that physical pain wasn't the only way to exact revenge. Yardi adored the vehicle, a classic three-door sport hatchback, a 1974 Volkswagen Scirocco, named after the Mediterranean wind. He oozed affection for the vehicle, talking to it when it purred dutifully ("Good girl, fine girl"), and – armed with a bucket of steaming soapy water – set aside an hour every Saturday to restore it to its gleaming, pristine condition. It was like a child to him, perhaps more than a child.

So I opened the car door. Fired up the engine. Released the handbrake. And guided the Scirocco to the edge of the gravel, and into the River Thames.

I smirked at Yardi, readying myself for a stream of abuse. But words deserted him – he was shocked into silence by my actions. He stared down, whimpering, colour drained from his complexion, a broken man.

I felt exhilarated, and hurt at the same time, our friendship was broken. I went home to recover from my headache and aches and pains from the onslaught of violence. The other reason was everyone on the estate now knew about the car in the Thames and it wouldn't be long before the police showed up.

Natalie was in the kitchen, breaking the leaves off a lettuce while her sister, Tara, was wiping dishes.

"Where's Karen?" I asked. After losing Mark, checking my daughter was nearby had become a daily reflex.

"Don't worry, Lennox, she's fine," said Natalie, rinsing the lettuce under the cold water tap.

"I hope she hasn't been anywhere near Whitney today."

"What's it to you? If I want Whitney's help, I'll ask for it."

"I've told you before I don't want her looking after Karen."

Whitney and Natalie had been tight throughout their teen years, but the woman was gay, and that made my skin crawl. Growing up, my family had never discussed homosexuality; and throughout my schooling, sex education was confined to conventional male-female relationships. This was not unusual during the 70s and 80s; just three years after Karen's birth, the Thatcher government was to pass the notorious Clause 28 amendment to the Local Government Act which made it an offence for local authorities to "promote the teaching in any maintained school the acceptability of homosexuality as a pretended family relationship".

Nevertheless, even by the standards of the time, my aversion to gay and lesbian sex was extreme. I found it impossible to separate the generality of same-sex relationships from Thomas Brown's abuse of my 12-year-old self. Tainted by that horror, and consumed with prejudice, my brain couldn't conceive of Whitney as a doting, big-hearted babysitter. All I saw was another Brown, skulking and scheming in the shadows.

"You can't tell me who I can have as a friend. Whitney's a good person, and you need to get over your hang-ups."

Tara had set the crockery down on the draining board. She was clearly itching to make a point. "Like Natalie says, just get over it." She then levelled some racist insults, which sounded odd given her own ethnicity.

"You stay out of this. This is between me and Natalie."

Feeling extremely paranoid I sensed them both forge against me, I felt the situation slipping from my control.

"F- off, Lennox," said Natalie. "Let her speak if she wants to."

"Look, perhaps it's best if I stay with my sister and then see Karen everyday so you can play happy families with your sister and Whitney."

Natalie put her hands on her hips. "If you go," she muttered, "you'll never see Karen again."

"Why," I said, "this isn't good for us or Karen."

"That's the choice," she said. Tara sided with her sister and butted in with her own comments, saying that I didn't deserve Karen and how I didn't want her anyway.

A switch flicked in my head. It was almost two years since I'd handed over my son to his mum, little realising he wouldn't be returning. Now I was being threatened with a second loss. And this time, of my darling Karen. My baby girl, whose face lit up whenever she heard my voice. Anyone who menaced me like that was low-life scum.

Without warning I reacted by hitting Tara and she grabbed the kitchen table to break her fall.

"You're a monster," she cried fighting back, "You f...ing Monster," then she lunged for the front door. Driven by fear, she dodged my attempt to haul her back. As she ran from the property, she screamed over her shoulder, "I'm getting the police, you bastard." My thoughts turned to Karen. I needed to check she was safe; that Whitney hadn't mistreated her.

She'd been asleep in her cot in the main bedroom, but had surely woken with all the shouting from the kitchen. I eased the bedroom door ajar, and as it creaked on its hinges, Karen opened her lungs. I couldn't bear the thought of my baby daughter in distress, and moved to pick her up. Natalie was shouting at me to "Get out of the house."

As she turned to walk away, it was clear I couldn't take any more of this and so I flipped and completely lost control to my anger and rage.

There was a thud, and she lost consciousness immediately, dropping to the floor. Her sprawled body, prostrate on the rug.

My rage still hadn't faded. I gripped her hands, and hauled her to the lounge. Despite her slender frame, her body was surprisingly heavy, but my anger and rage spurred me on.

7.
On Remand

It was as if two forces were battling for supremacy within my brain – and the one imploring me not to hurt Natalie was winning out.

"You mustn't do it," whispered a disembodied voice; bizarrely, the calm tone reminded me of Reverend Urman, from bible college.

"I want to kill you. But God won't let me."

I threw the cushion into the corner of the room. Disgusted. Ashamed, I didn't recognise myself and I felt evil.

And then spasmed with terror at what might happen next.

I had no idea how much time had passed since Tara fled the scene, but – if she was true to her threat – it wouldn't be long before the police were banging down the front door. What would happen then? I needed help. I called the Grants and luckily Chris answered. Panting, panicked, I asked him to rush over.

"What's it about?" he probed. "You sound awful."

"I can't... I can't tell you now. Just hurry. It's an emergency."

I looked at Natalie; she looked almost peaceful. But what if she denounced me to the police? Accused me of hurting her? What if she had injuries that could incriminate me.

When Chris arrived, his jaw nearly dropped as he surveyed the situation barely to comprehend the scene.

I babbled, "It was her fault, Natslie's fault," but Chris was oblivious to my pleas, looking at me with disbelief.

"Lennox, tell me the truth. Did you do this?" In truth, I couldn't believe it.

I was still sheepishly attending to Natalie, when the police arrived. They were collecting anything that might be useful evidence. Meanwhile neighbours were gathering. It wasn't an everyday occurrence to have the street filled with the blue flashing lights of an ambulance and squad cars, let alone the swarms of emergency personnel, and they were peering through the doorway and windows.

Answering questions from the officers at the scene, I was barely coherent, and it never occurred to me that every nonsensical claim I made might be used, one day, to persuade a jury of my guilt.

Did I expect the officer to yawn, close his notepad, and file everything away under "No suspicious circumstances"? If so, I'd be sorely disappointed. It wasn't long before handcuffs were being locked around my wrists.

"Lennox Rodgers, I'm arresting you on suspicion of assault. You do not have to say anything unless you wish to do so, but anything you do say may be used and given in evidence in a court of law."

I was in a trance.

"Do you understand me, Mr Rodgers?"

Karen's cries bought me out of my daze; it was as if I was only tuned to her voice.

Tara had been too afraid to enter the flat whilst I'd been inside, but as I was led away I heard her shout "Bastard," as she raced to find her sister.

My brain was a mess as I saw medics race into the flat.

Then I was wondering who'd look after Karen while everyone was in hospital. Chris was last man standing – I felt assured he'd take care of things.

The slamming of the car doors after I'd been bundled into the back, and the arresting officer's voice as he barked "Suspect in custody" into his radio, snapped me back to reality.

*

The magistrates' hearing wouldn't be until Monday, so the next two days were spent locked in a dank police cell at the St Aldates police station, my only company being a couple of drunks arrested for disorderly behaviour. A duty solicitor explained the magistrates' procedure, and a succession of officers who hauled me into the interview room for further questioning whenever they obtained an additional nugget from Natalie, who was now increasingly able to provide them with an accurate version of events from her hospital bed.

The hearing was a formality. I spoke only to confirm my name and address. The duty solicitor made a cursory application for bail – "My client has family in the area and I'm sure they'd be prepared to vouch for him and ensure he complies with any conditions the court wishes to impose" – but the prosecution swatted this aside, arguing that Natalie and Tara both lived within the vicinity and would be understandably terrified lest I make contact, either to influence their testimony, or worse. The severity of the charges – the police were alleging Attempted Murder and Actual Bodily Harm – also weighed against me.

As I'd been warned, it wasn't even a finely balanced decision for the three-strong magistrates panel. They consulted with the clerk on a point of law, and then the most senior spoke to formalise their decision. "Bail is denied and the accused is remanded in custody pending Committal Hearing and Trial on dates to be set."

A police guard grabbed hold of me, pinching my upper arm with gratuitous vigour, and escorted me to the court's basement cells, where I'd be left to fester and stew for six long hours, until there were a sufficient number of us to justify readying the police van for the short journey to HM Prison Oxford.

*

If, gentle reader, you're one day unexpectedly incarcerated, you are strongly advised to avoid the bottom bunk.

Oxford Prison had been built amidst the ruins of a moated Norman medieval castle, after being largely destroyed during the English Civil War. Its original watch tower, St George's, survives to this day – built of coral rag stones, and Grade One listed, it was once a dominant feature of the Oxford skyline. A few years before my arrival, the prison was briefly notorious for a rooftop protest organised by the Preservation of the Rights of Prisoners. And an interesting footnote to its history is that, in 1996, long after my time finished, it was converted into a Malmaison Hotel, with many of the cells refurbished as guest rooms (shrewdly the areas used for hangings were set aside as offices rather than public space).

Arriving in jail for the first time can be nerve-wracking. I'd been transferred as part of a group of six, and a senior prison officer asked each of us to verify our identities and the nature of the charges against us. This was valuable intelligence keenly noted by the Reception Orderly, an inmate who'd been selected to assist the officers in handling newly-arrived prisoners. The Orderly paid particular attention to any Rule 43 prisoners, those alleged or convicted of sex offences, and would ensure the grim details spread like wildfire throughout the prison population.

Then, it's time for "Processing", which sets the tone for prison life. Any desire for privacy or dignity should be abandoned at the prison gates; every step involves obeying rules and instructions, with no scope for discussion or argument. Personal possessions are the first to go; most are kept securely with one's civilian clothes, to be returned on release but some – such as my half-finished packet of cigarettes – were thrown in the wastepaper bin (I noticed the Orderly gleefully fishing them out, as soon as backs were turned).

After an intrusive strip search (I'll leave the details to your imagination, but it involves squatting), I was provided with my prison garments. Ripped, worn and ill-fitting ("We're out of size 34 mate, how about 38; no size 8 shoes, mate, best we got is 7 or 10," said the Orderly), with a number on the back that bore no relationship to my prisoner number. I was also given my kit bag, containing a swanky blanket, two sheets that resembled tablecloths, cheap toiletries, a comb not designed for my afro hair, a toothbrush, a roll-on deodorant, soap, plastic cutlery and crockery, spare underwear, and a piss pot.

One of the most aspirational possessions in jail is a proper bucket, complete with handle and lid. I'd need to work my way up to such exalted luxuries – on day one, all they had available was a shallow, lidless container roughly the shape of a frying pan.

We were deposited for the first couple of hours in a holding cell, where we received no information to help acclimatise or prepare. The only way to pass the time was through sharing stories, and the seasoned hands relished this opportunity to alarm and dismay the novices in the group:

"What you in for, mate?"

"I got given two years for a dwelling." (meaning, a robbery)

"You was lucky. I'm here because my mate grassed me up."

"How 'bout you?" asked a bald guy in his fifties, staring at me.

"They say it's Attempted Murder and ABH," I answered.

"Bloody 'ell, mate; you're looking at twenty years, minimum. Maybe life."

Gloriously, my starter pack included my weekly supply of tobacco – half an ounce, the cost of which would be deducted from my allowance. It took me a while to appreciate that, on the inside, the value of "half an ounce" is massively inflated. Naively, I shared my supply with every crafty prisoner cadging from me – "Gissa some baccy", "Yeah okay, this should be enough for a rollup." Only after I'd exhausted a full week's tobacco within four hours did I realise how long I needed to wait before replenishing my stock.

The final stage of processing was to confirm my religion. This was required to complete my Cell Card, a record of basic information about each inmate which was hung outside one's cell.

"Pentecostal," I declared.

"What the f- is that?" asked the officer, screwing up his face.

"It's a type of..."

"Never mind what the f- it is. The only options are Roman Catholic, C of E, or no religion. Pick one of them."

My cell was on the third floor of the main block – number 3-21. I'd be sharing with a Jamaican armed robber called Elvis but in prison he went by the name Toby to stop jibes from other inmates (he rarely sang, and when he did, it was like a banshee's wail). He hadn't been warned that a cellmate would be coming, and he scowled as I was ushered in. I tried striking up a conversation, but it would be a few days before I elicited anything other than mumbles.

Of course, he'd already snagged the top bunk, and at two in the morning I realised why this was such a benefit. I was woken by the high-pitched squeaking of his bed as it rocked backwards and forwards, accompanied by wheezy snorts and groans which Toby made no attempts to disguise. Looking up, there was an object poking through a hole in his mattress. Seconds later, a rather unpleasant substance was hurtling in my direction.

In previous years, I'd stayed in a few places – such as the Birmingham night shelter – where levels of hygiene had fallen short of the standards obsessively observed during my upbringing. My parents had taught me that cleanliness is close to godliness, and I still recoil from the stench of unwashed clothing or bodies. One of the harshest adjustments during my first week in jail was being surrounded by noxious odours and unrelenting grime – and, once I'd come to terms with the pervasive filth, by how hard it was also to keep myself clean. Generally, we washed in basins, but were permitted into the communal showers once a week. I was given a small sachet of shampoo; I squeezed out a pathetic glob of slime which resembled dish water, which wasn't enough to wash my hair.

Then, I'd stare in despair at the obligatory block of white Windsor soap; black skin needs and deserves cocoa-butter to keep it moist. The worst was yet to come: one minute for soaping, one minute for rinsing, then the water supply was cut off. I never knew showers could be so rushed. On the first occasion, I mistimed everything, and spent the rest of the day covered in crusty dried soap, that absorbed moisture from my skin until I was itching all over – my face, under my arms, around my groin. It was agony.

Life was hard for regular prisoners, but our every discomfort was magnified for sex offenders.

For their own protection, they were segregated into a different wing, but it wasn't practical to keep them entirely separate. At the slightest glimpse – for example, when one of them was being escorted to the library, or the exercise yard, or the chapel, or the medical centre – a barrage of taunts would fly ("You f-ing nonce", "You perv"). The worst treatment was reserved for the meal times. The sex offenders were served last, but one day I was at the end of the line for regular inmates, which meant I saw the prisoners on serving duty abusing the rations before doling them out to the sex offenders. They'd spit in the soup, wipe snot into the mashed potatoes, run their hands up their backsides before handling the bread rolls. When the prison officers weren't turning a blind eye, they'd be chuckling with implicit approval.

Oxford represented my first experience of actual imprisonment, but I was no stranger to surviving inside an institution – and my years in the care system had taught me invaluable life skills. In particular, I knew the value of never exposing any vulnerabilities, no matter how anxious or jittery I felt. A pack of lions will instinctively set upon the weakest – if you're potential prey, survival depends upon there being another weaker, more terrified than you. I knew I was doing something right when I was spared – in fact, I was invited to observe – the grisly initiation ritual endured by some new prisoners. The startled victim would be held face down, just above a bucket of cold water, while a comb is scraped against his windpipe, and red paint squirted onto the water's surface. The effect is uncannily realistic. The inductee assumes their throat's been severed, and they're bleeding to death. Any inmate who sobs like a distressed infant is teased mercilessly for at least a week.

Once you've found your feet, the prison authorities won't allow you to pass time chilling in your cell. Everyone is expected to undertake one of the myriad of menial jobs that need to be performed, from sewing mailbags, to joining the so-called Shit Patrol Squad – which was charged with the task of picking up from the grounds next to the cellblock left overnight (wrapped in newspapers and hurled from the cell windows by prisoners who were loathe to have rank stench of a filled bucket in the corner).

The officers presumably decided these elevated responsibilities were beyond my capability; hence they charged me with the more mundane role of mopping the prison's landings, walkways and corridors. One day, I was mopping outside a first floor cell, when its occupant whispered to me:

"Oy, you, come over here."

I recognised Malcolm, one of Oxford's longest-serving prisoners, who'd been convicted of manslaughter in the late 1960s, and, having served much of his time in Gartree, was still a few years away from eligibility for parole. The younger inmates gave him a wide berth; he had a fearsome reputation, aided by a hulking body shape – his head seemed to merge into his shoulders without the need for inconveniences such as a neck. I didn't hesitate to obey.

"I seen you around," he said. "You that new kid who's in for Attempted Murder."

"Well, I ain't been found guilty yet," I said. "I'm hoping to get off."

Malcolm roared with laughter. "That's what they all say! Listen, you got a name?"

"Lennox. From cell 3-21."

"It's your lucky day, Lennox. Cos I got a job for you."

He rummaged around in his kitbag, and handed me a ball of paper.

"You know what this is?"

I looked at him surprised. Obviously I knew what it was. Rizlas – tobacco rolling paper. Probably king sized, given its bulk.

"I need you to take this to cell 2-02."

Aha – it finally dawned on me. He wasn't referring to the Rizlas, but to its content.

"Do this properly and I'll have another job for you tomorrow and I'll give you something for your troubles."

When I rounded the corner, safe from prying eyes, I unrolled the Rizla. Concealed inside were two tabs of LSD. I'd been on the streets long enough to recognise them, despite never experimenting myself. Blessed with Malcolm's encouragement, I didn't remain an LSD virgin much longer. The recipient in cell 2-02 couldn't contain his excitement. I put it in a newspaper and slid it under the door, whilst making out I was still mopping. And so began my career as Oxford Prison's most fresh-faced drug runner (aka Malcom's skivvy) – a task well-suited to a seemingly humble cleaner. I now had the ideal pretext to roam freely around the block, collecting and delivering packages as I went; the prison officers didn't pay too much attention to the black bloke shuffling along the landing with his mop and bucket, as long as I seemed trustworthy, and stayed unobtrusive, I was generally left alone. Access to free drugs was a fringe benefit that helped me escape some of the horrors of life inside.

Having satisfactorily fulfilled an initial batch of orders with a few close shaves, I found myself with a growing number of orders from clients eager for continuing service, and my ambitions grew.

Before long, it was impractical to fulfil everyone's requirements through moonlighting while on cleaning duties, and I needed to establish alternative means of distribution. One of the most direct was to hide the product in a sock which I'd tie to the end of the ripped sheet, and then either lower it or swing it from my cell window into the eager hands of the recipient. In practice, this wasn't a straightforward manoeuvre. The cell window was only reachable by standing on the thick pipes which ran along the back walls of every cell, stretching over, and using a small plastic prison mirror to work out where to swing the line. My first attempt ended in farce. I got a good swing going, but forgot to keep a tight grip of the sheet when it reached its highest point.

The sheet, laden with its marijuana-filled sock, soared like an eagle through the early evening skies, before landing with a plop at the far end of the exercise yard. The following morning, the Shit Patrol Squad courteously returned my bedding and footwear, albeit the more valuable contents seemed to go missing in transit, and I was told to "work back the loss" to avoid a beating.

Half way through my time in Oxford, I was introduced to the devious Trevor Smart, who became something of a personal mentor. On the outside, he was every parent's worst nightmare, since he was prone to bribing kids to misbehave at home for the sheer hell of it. ("I'll give ya a couple of quid if ya cut elbow holes in yer dad's best suit.") In jail, he'd rile the staff in the canteen shop by spending his weekly takings from sewing mailbags – which, at his most productive, could reach £3.50 – on Black Jack chews, aniseed flavoured sweets that were popular at the time. He had no great yearning for Black Jacks, but insisted the shop assistant count them out individually, all three hundred and fifty of them, to ensure he wasn't short-changed. It was the type of harmless but irritating prank he adored.

Trevor found ways to extract advantage from his ill-fortune. He wore a glass eye – I never learnt the story, but presumably it resulted from a fight – and, if a conversation bored him, he'd pop the orb from his head, and deposit it in the middle of the table, peering around so everybody had an unforgettable view of the empty hole that remained. As party tricks go, it certainly livened things up. On other occasions, he'd drop his glass eye into someone else's pint while they were at the toilet, and roar with laughter when they did a double-take at the unsettling object staring at them from their glass.

His mentoring, especially in the early days, focussed upon survival techniques and schemes for thriving whilst incarcerated.

"Get hold of a copy of the prison officers' Standing Orders from the library," he advised. "If they haven't got one in stock, place an order. It's worth its weight in gold."

"It sounds dull," I said.

"Anything but. You'll see."

Trevor was partially right. The rule book wasn't the most riveting read – I don't think it'll be nominated for the Nobel Prize for Literature any time soon – but awareness of where prison officers have (and don't have) discretion was priceless, and helped level the playing field in the never-ending battle of wits between screws and jailbirds.

Armed with this insight, I kept a notepad in my jeans' pocket, and a pencil tucked behind my ear. Whenever an officer picked on me, it quickly became a situation where the proverbial pen is mightier than the sword.

"Get back to your cell fast, you f-, or I'll have you on solitary."

"Wait one moment, please, I need to write that down in my notes."

Under Trevor's criminal mentorship, I identified officers' weak spots, and exploited them mercilessly. When it wasn't raining, we were often allowed into the yard for so-called exercise (in reality, half an hour spent walking in a circle). Returning, we'd be subject to body searches in case any contraband had been thrown over the prison walls for us to collect and distribute. One day, I was being checked by an officer who'd wound me up in my first few weeks, ridiculing my mania for cleanliness. Now it was time for revenge.

As his hands checked my inner thigh, I leaped backwards, shouting to his superior officer:

"Boss, this f- just touched my knob."

The incident wasn't deemed serious enough to warrant a thorough investigation, but I took a malicious delight in seeing the officer nemesis redeployed.

Until the week before my trial, I managed to stay clear of any violence. However, one of my drug-running clients – Darius – had previously defaulted on his obligations, and I couldn't let matters stand. I melted the stem of my toothbrush, and before the plastic solidified, jammed a sewing needle into it. I had my weapon! But I hadn't counted on Darius's cocky streak. He wouldn't surrender easily to a punishment beating. When I confronted him, he lashed out viciously, and within moments we were rolling around on the floor of his cell. At last, I got the upper hand, and rained a series of blows against either side of his head until his body went limp, but I respected his fightback so never resorted to my adapted toothbrush – reserving it to threaten onlookers who I needed to back off.

But what to do next? The bloody bruising, especially around Darius's left temple, was visible from the opposite walkway; I couldn't afford awkward questions this close to my court appearance. Usually, the prisoner code requires us to say "I slipped, sir" if questioned by officers about injuries, but on this occasion, the Standing Orders provided better inspiration. We sneaked some butter from the kitchen and, having smeared it on a flight of steps en route to the cell block, submitted an official complaint that Darius's injuries had arisen from a fall caused by prison negligence. Someone in authority must've been alarmed at the potential consequences, and insisted on a quick out-of-court settlement.

Darius and I divided the £800 award equally; it was more than enough for any blame or recriminations about past events to be quickly forgotten.

Which brings us back to my spell in solitary, which arose halfway through my incarceration at Oxford. Trevor Smart's mentorship had worked wonders, and I'd used his wise insights to establish respect and status amongst my fellow inmates. Case in point: I helped convene "associations"; two hours when well-behaved prisoners were allowed "games privileges" – table tennis, pool, table football. I regarded associations as the perfect cover for less wholesome activities, and plotted to host drug parties in our cells instead.

Whilst the greener inmates were pocketing eight-balls, the rest of us were inhaling industrial quantities of cannabis, in ways which – we hoped – wouldn't leave a lingering scent in the air (in brief, we'd cut the bottom off a large bottle of Coke, stand it in a bucket of cold water, and place cannabis on foil that we'd punch with holes and stretch across the bottle's mouth; as we raised the bottle from the water, the smoke would be sucked into the bottle until it was full of smoke from the dense concentration – and perfect for inhaling). But we'd reckoned without the weed's ability to release its sweet aroma, spreading through the tiniest spaces – and despite our efforts to disguise the smell through mists of talcum powder around the cell doors, it wasn't long before the prison officers were breaking up our pot parties and we refused an order to go back to our cells.

When the incident was written up, it somehow morphed from a harmless cannabis party into a full-on prison riot, providing the ideal payback for getting this officer's friend redeployed to another wing – I was swiftly sent to the punishment wing, where I was to spend the next four weeks with my party of friends.

The first thing you notice "in solitary" is the harsh nature of your accommodation. It isn't long before any jailbird confined in this way is yearning for his regular cell. The combination of loneliness and boredom often arouse thoughts of suicide, so the cells are bare but for the essentials, all designed to minimise any risk of self-harm.

The three principal objects are a plastic bucket (to be used for slopping out), a bed (bolted to the ground), and a mattress (two inches thin, and heavily stained with bodily fluids). I barely slept during my first night in solitary, partly because I was still high, and partly because the bed's sagging caused excruciating backache. On the second night, I experimented with placing the mattress on the floor, in case that provided comfort; unbelievably, it was worse – every ridge of the tiles could be felt through the foam, and the floor was not only dusty, but (scrubbing notwithstanding) still smelt of dirty protests.

If I hoped for companionship from prisoners in neighbouring cells, I was to be disappointed. The soundproofing didn't allow for any private conversations. This was quickly exhausting, and also drew the attention of the screws. Three times daily, I could exchange a few short words with whoever delivered my meal. Something to which I could look forward to. Which was more than could be said for the food itself. The menu was rarely more ambitious than toad-in-the-hole – hard, burnt batter, indigestible sausage, lumpy potato, and bland gravy which was sometimes half skin. It must require a highly skilled chef to prepare food quite so unappetising.

Every source of torment was exacerbated by the presence of cannabis in my system – it would take nearly a month to fully flush out. The drugs mingled with the lack of nourishment, and the isolation, and the grim environment. And the result was Thomas Brown flashbacks. Searing flashbacks of the act and abusive words.

"Leave me alone. Get out of my mind!"

I screamed, and smashed my head against the cell wall, so forcefully the room was showered with flecks of dislodged paint, leaving me dizzy and in pain. At last the commotion had attracted the attention of the screws. One grabbed my arms, and locked them behind my back; the other pointed the tip of his baton between my eyes.

"You gotta help me," I stammered.

"Fat chance of that," comes the reply.

Besieged by flashbacks, I made two clumsy suicide attempts. The first was to stockpile paracetamol, rationalising that, if I complained of headaches for a few days, it wouldn't be long before I'd collected enough drugs to overdose. It didn't occur to me that, conscious of this risk, inmates are provided with pills of lower strength than those available over the counter at Boots – and in the event I suffered nothing worse than a queasy stomach.

More experimental was my effort to puncture my heart. A safety pin had been left in an item of clothing by the prison laundry, and I unravelled it to create a miniature spear. Surely, this was long enough to pierce one of my heart's chambers, or at least reach my coronary artery. I wove my device into the mattress, testing its rigidity when pressure was applied from above. And then dive-bombed – the centre of my chest aimed full-square at the pin's tip. Needless to say, I didn't suffer instant death. In fact, the only evidence of contact was a tiny graze, more modest than a blood test pinprick. I was bewildered. How low can you sink, when even ending your own life is a task far beyond your capability?

The only medicine that worked was patience, waiting until the passage of time cleansed my system of the drugs and brought closer my release from solitary.

8. Beginnings

After nine months on remand, the trial date arrived. Bleary-eyed from lack of sleep, I was introduced to my barrister, who asked me to confirm how I'd be pleading and gave me a whistle-stop summary of how the trial would unfold. He estimated the proceedings would take around three days, followed by the jury's deliberations which, in cases such as this, usually took no more than a couple of hours.

Standing in the dock, hands sweating, mouth dry, struggling not to move, with my life on the line, must be one of life's scariest experiences. I was conscious of nearly one hundred pairs of eyes – court officials, members of the jury, journalists, friends of Natalie or Tara, members of the public with nothing better to do – all boring into my soul, seeking the slightest clue in my appearance that might shed light on my guilt or innocence, but I stared dispassionately into the middle distance.

One of the journalists was a wise gentleman in a tweed jacket, who – barely a year beforehand – had commissioned me to erect a nursery for his wife's playgroup, including a huge Wendy house equipped with cooker, washing machine and phone booth. He and his wife had lavished me with praise, cake and drinks; I'd felt warmly welcomed into their family's embrace. Now he'd be reporting, no doubt in excruciating detail, on my fall from grace. I choked back the tears, humiliated, barely retaining my composure.

With the jury sworn in, the most agonising period of the trial – the first day-and-a-half – was underway.

This was the opportunity for the prosecution to set out its case, and they attacked the task without mercy. It was bad enough listening to the testimony of Tara and Natalie as, prompted by the prosecution barrister, they recounted my actions leading up to and during the attack – literally blow by blow. I shuddered at their accounts. I'd spent almost a year regretting my actions to myself. Now, finally, I was forced to hear the events described, unfiltered, by people with a very different perspective. Next, I squirmed through the testimony of Chris Grant – although not a witness of my actions, he'd been first on the scene, and the judge ruled that his testimony about what I'd said, and how I'd acted, was admissible. Was it really me who'd inflicted these injuries?

My head was swirling with confusion and self-doubt.

With the initial testimony complete, the prosecution called various police and medical witnesses. Their remarks provided little new information, but the cumulative effect was proving devastating. I felt like a lost boy in a mountain range, hoping to spot an escape route. Whichever way I turned, safe passage was blocked off – either by a doctor, or by a detective, or by the victims themselves.

But I'd chosen to deny the charges, and had no alternative but to stick with this course.

It was time for the defence to argue its case, threadbare as it might be. I was in the stand for no more than twenty minutes. My barrister was gentle, walking me through my version of the evening's events.

Then it was the turn of the prosecution.

"Mr Rodgers. You claim Tara Masters assaulted you, unprovoked, and you retaliated in an act of self-defence; is that correct?"

"Erm... Yes, it is."

"How would you assess her strength and body weight compared with yours?"

"Erm... I don't know. Hard to say. I suppose I'm stronger."

"I think everyone in the court would agree with that. Moving on, whereabouts on your body did she attack you?"

"Erm... erm, I don't recall. Perhaps my face."

"I see. Did you sustain any injuries as a result of this unprovoked assault?"

"Erm... I'm not... erm... sure."

"You don't recall?"

"Erm... No."

At each answer, the barrister rolled her eyes, as if scarcely able to believe the nonsense spewing from my lips.

"Now, let us turn to Natalie Masters. You claim you found her on the sofa, after she'd harmed herself ."

"Erm... Yes, I did."

"Was this before or after your altercation with Tara."

"Erm... Afterwards."

"So let me ensure I've got the sequencing correct. You claim that Tara assaulted you. You fought back, so Tara fled to fetch the police. Leaving you and Natalie alone in the house."

"That's right."

"So, with you in the house, and with her sister having just fled from your beatings, that's the time she chose to self harm."

"Erm... I didn't beat Tara."

"Just answer the question, Mr Rodgers. Was that the time she chose to harm herself ?"

"Erm... Yes."

"Don't you think that timing seems a little odd.

"I... erm... suppose, so."

"Which she managed to do without leaving any fingerprints? Did she wipe them clean while she was bleeding?"

It was a great question; she was filleting my case like a salmon. If only a trap door would lurch open in the dock, and I could tumble away from her cutting cross-examination.

"I... erm... yeah, suppose."

"You've described yourself as her saviour. But I'm interested to understand, when exactly did you realise that she was trying to harm herself? ? You were the only two people in the property, and it isn't large. Did you notice while it was happening?"Erm... erm... I don't know. I really don't recall."

"Now the axe. According to your account, she must've hit herself with force on the back of her head. Do you know how hard that would be?"

"Erm... don't know about any axe. The bruise on her head er... erm... was from a fall."

"Oh, she fell before she self harmed did she? Did you see her touch the axe at all?"

"Erm... I didn't."

"So how do you explain her hair and her DNA on the blunt end of the axe?"

"Erm... I really don't know."

"There seems to be rather a lot you don't know, Mr Rodgers."

As she sat down, one of the members of the prosecution team patted her on the shoulder, congratulating her on a resounding demolition. I sneaked a glance at the reporter whose nursery I'd built; he was looking at me wearily, with a hint of pity.

The judge asked my barrister whether he'd be calling any other defence witnesses. In previous discussions, I'd asked my lawyer not to solicit any character witnesses; I was too ashamed of my circumstances to beg favours from Daddy or Mummy G, and I was far too embarrassed to consider an approach to Mr Bailey, or other members of the St Edward's teaching fraternity – who'd all assume I was now four years into a flourishing army career. But it seemed one person, having learnt of my predicament, did approach the court, unsolicited, to provide a character reference.

"Your Honour," said my barrister, "I'd like to enter into the record the testimony of my client's relative, Mr Thomas Brown. Mr Brown has written a wonderful and touching letter to the court. Allow me to quote from it, "I have known Lennox Rodgers his entire life. I cannot speak of the events in question, but from my own contact with him, I know him to be an upstanding person of high moral integrity.'" I realised that Brown, having been absent from the court throughout the procedures, was now sitting alone in the back, head bowed. I looked away before I could be overwhelmed with nausea.

*

My barrister's prediction that the jury would require two hours proved excessive. Around forty minutes after being instructed to consider their verdict, the jury was back in court, a sheet of foolscap paper held fast in the foreman's slightly quivering hand.

"Foreman of the Jury. On the first count, the Attempted Murder of Miss Natalie Masters, do you find the defendant guilty, or not guilty?"

"Not guilty, Your Honour."

My heart raced. This was a magnificent outcome; I turned towards my barrister. For a moment, I thought I'd won. But my barrister wasn't smiling, and I remembered there were two remaining charges on the docket, one of which had been introduced by the prosecution midway through the trial, as a fallback in case they couldn't make the 'Attempted Murder charge' stick.

"On the second count of the Grievous Bodily Harm with intent of Miss Natalie Masters, do you find the defendant guilty, or not guilty?"

"Guilty, Your Honour."

"And on the third and final count, the Actual Bodily Harm of Miss Tara Masters do you find the defendant guilty, or not guilty?"

"Guilty, Your Honour."

My barrister muttered words of consolation, but they were drowned out by the spontaneous cheers erupting from the far side of the courtroom. A group of Natalie's friends were hugging one another.

*

It took me a while to appreciate how lucky I'd been.

My barrister certainly realised it. With the two guilty verdicts passed, he'd been warning me of the prospect of a significant custodial sentence, possibly around five years. At the sentencing hearing, he requested the court to exercise leniency and paraded the usual checklist of mitigating factors – a tough childhood, this being my first serious offence, my young daughter shouldn't be deprived of her father-figure – but, even to my ears, these sounded pathetic rather than persuasive.

When the judge made his determination, he whizzed through a blizzard of numbers – "Two years for Grievous Bodily Harm", "Six months for Aggravated Bodily Harm",

"To be served consecutively", "Nine months on remand". Once the data had sunk in, my barrister had helped run the maths: I'd be in jail for just another eleven months, followed by eight or nine months out on licence.

"Congratulations, Lennox. That means less than a year until you're basically a free man." He emphasised the words "less than".

According to rumours, the prosecution was appalled at the inadequacy of my sentence, but they had no room for manoeuvre, and the matter was considered closed. It wasn't until the Criminal Justice Act 1988 received Royal Ascent that Law Officers had the power to apply for leave to review any sentences which, amongst other things, could be construed as "unduly lenient".

My sentence would be served at a different jail – the second I'd experience (I was totting up prisons like a football fan checking out every ground in the first division). But, in the days before the transfer would take effect, I had to attend to some unfinished business in Oxford.

One of my contacts on the outside had been sending me small supplies of weed and cannabis resin for recreational use. "I miss my size eight trainers" during a phone call was (admittedly unsophisticated) code for "Tell Des to bring me an eighth of an ounce". In hindsight, I can't believe the actual meaning escaped the deciphering skills of the eavesdropping officers, but assume that, amidst the violence and intimidation, low-level smuggling wasn't rated a top priority. At other times, our code embraced terminology such as "red beard" (weed with ginger strands), "soap bar" (average quality cannabis resin) and "gold seal" (top grade).

In any event, for three consecutive weeks, supplies had gone missing. I couldn't rely on a stooge to fix matters, so concocted a scheme to break out of prison and wreck revenge on Des myself.

"You'll never bust out of here," asserted Carl Simons, my post-Toby cellmate. "Not unless you can turn invisible or leapfrog the walls. I know you got an ego, Lennox, but you ain't got superpowers."

"Whoever said anything about busting out of here?" I said.

"I don't follow."

"Security's tight here, granted. But if I need hospital treatment, bingo! You ever seen a hospital with high walls?"

It was a lightbulb moment for Carl. "Lennox," he said, "You the man. [pause for reflection] But... you don't need hospital treatment. So how does that work?"

"That, my friend, is where you come in."

I recalled viewing a TV programme about surgeons who specialise in broken hands. According to my warped logic, this proved conclusively that a hand injury was one of the straightforward routes from HMP Oxford to the John Radcliffe. Carl had been born with a sadistic streak, and didn't require much persuasion before signing-on as my enthusiastic co-conspirator. His first proposal was to bash my knuckles with the leg of the bed. After three attempts, there had been plenty of screams and much bruising, but nothing that might justify a trip to the infirmary.

"Don't worry," he said, "I got me a blade. You too much of a wuss to cut yourself, so I'll need to get the job done." I tried using the razor blade on myself but my attempts made Carl laugh because I didn't even need a plaster for what I did, so he volunteered to cut me.

"Not too deep," I said, looking at the ceiling.

Carl wasn't impressed at my inability to watch the deed. "I said you was a wuss," he scoffed, as he buried the blade so deep in my hand that I swore I could feel it pressing against the skin on the far side.

Half of the plan worked like a dream. After a cursory examination, the hospital doctor concluded the injury was "way above my pay grade", and arranged emergency transportation to the John Radcliffe. From the taxi, I looked eagerly at the rows of terraced houses, and hundreds of people going freely about their daily business. It wouldn't be long before my scheme reached its heroic climax, its peak, and I'd be joining their number. At liberty, at last – let Des beware!

Unfortunately, the second half of my plan encountered unanticipated complications. Namely, that Home Office policy required hospitalised inmates to be handcuffed, either to a prison officer, or to the side panel of a hospital bed, at all times (other than when under the influence of general anaesthetic). My mind raced for solutions to this fiendish obstacle, and, with a flash of inspiration, I reckoned a visit to the toilet might provide the opportunity to escape. Once again, I was outwitted. The toilet had no window; in any event, a lengthy chain was attached to my handcuffs so the officers would be immediately aware of any sudden movement. In addition, the hospital had a greater-than-usual police presence due to the football match taking place on the same day.

In the operating theatre, as the anaesthetic started coursing through my veins, I was just as scared about the operation as if I was getting a tetanus injection. My overriding emotion was humiliation at my amateurish incompetence.

That evening, I must've been the subject of discussion in quite a few conversations throughout Oxford. My getaway crew waited for five hours in a layby near the hospital before resigning themselves that I was a "no-show". Carl did a doubletake when I returned to our cell, identical but for the colossal bandage wrapped around my hand and the sling around my arm.

I lay on my bunk cursing the fact Des wouldn't face the music for at least eleven more months. I rolled towards the wall, and pain shot through my body at the pressure on my hand as the drugs started to wear off. In fact, thirty years later, the tendon still hasn't fully repaired, and I rarely feel any sensation in my thumb or forefinger.

Since the authorities never deduced my insidious plans, the decision to transfer me wasn't in jeopardy, and the following weekend, I was included in a select group bundled into a coach for the 100-mile ride through Newbury and across the Salisbury plains, to HMP Shepton Mallet. The highlight of the trip was lunch, half way to our destination, at the Pucklechurch Remand Centre – a specialised women's institution. As we were escorted in handcuffs and chains to the kitchen, a dozen inmates crammed at an upstairs window, lifting their tops (we sang "Got yer tits out for the lads" in encouragement).

Shepton Mallet is the country's oldest operational prison, but also one of its smallest and least economic.

This has led to significant problems with overcrowding: in theory, the jail's capacity was 169, but by the mid 1980s, it had reached 260. For over a century, policymakers had struggled to find a solution to its lack of scale. Throughout the 1930s it had been empty, save for a caretaker, on the basis of a recommendation from the Prison Commissioners, but with the outbreak of the Second World War, and the urgent need for military accommodation, it was hastily reopened – firstly to house British service personnel, and latterly for use by the American military (when it was gruesomely used to execute eighteen army privates found guilty of sundry offences, generally murder or rape, by court martial). The execution block was a two-storey red brick building near the back of the prison, complete with gallows. There has subsequently been some controversy about the racial profile of those condemned; thirteen of the soldiers killed by capital punishment were either black or Hispanic, in an army that was at the time overwhelmingly white.

Having been returned to civilian use in the 1960s, Shepton Mallet found something of a niche for itself as a training prison for inmates serving sentences below four years, preparing them for release into society with a focus on education and trades (its many workshops included scrap metal recovery, tailoring and plastic moulding). For no better reason than the reference to my City and Guilds carpentry certificate in my pre-sentence probation report, this was deemed an appropriate destination for the balance of my sentence.

While in Shepton Mallet, I shared cells with a couple of memorable characters. Ben was a mixed race Londoner, addicted to exercise. He found a broken broomstick, and tied it with shoe laces to the air vent near our door to create a chin-up bar. He could complete 50 chin-ups straight off, as well as press-ups on a single wrist; possibly his most impressive feat was 20 press-ups in a minute, clapping in mid-air between each one. When he wasn't getting his muscles into shape, he'd spend days crafting, in painstaking detail, model butterflies from matchsticks. When they learnt of his talent, the screws offered to buy his creations at knock-down prices, no doubt selling them at a substantial mark-up on the outside.

My next cellmate was Prince Abubu, a wide-eyed Nigerian with a Jekyll-and-Hyde personality. He'd been imprisoned for a series of white collar frauds, and was famous for his unfussy appetite. I once saw him devour a barely cooked chicken. Most of the meat was raw and soaked in blood, as if it was from a carcass killed a few moments beforehand.

Unless any newly-appointed Shepton Mallet prison officer has a stomach to match Prince Abubu's, I'd strongly advise they steer clear of the coffee. In the welding workshop, where the screws naively commanded workshop orderlies to make their coffees on the hour, it was common practice to add a complementary teaspoon-sized helping of spittle. In fact, refusing to add a dollop of spit would get you tagged as an officers' grass – and subject to an inevitable beating!

*

Released on probation from Shepton Mallet, I found it difficult to resettle in Oxford – too many memories were still fresh, and prospective employers informed me almost everything I'd learnt in jail about welding was "Years out of date and incompatible with modern health and safety." I called Chris, and others, and whilst nobody slammed down the phone, their tone was matter-of-fact and standoffish. It would take time to rekindle trust, friendship, and love – if that's what I wanted. Frankly, I wasn't yet sure.

I was also plagued by guilt at how I'd treated Natalie. For weeks, it was hard to watch television because even mild violent action sequences towards women would trigger memories of my violent crimes, leaving me sickened. So I arranged to look after the flat of a distant relative (a nephew's aunt), who was out of the country for a few months. My probation officer was enthusiastic, mistakenly assuming I'd now be far from temptation. Little did she appreciate how trouble follows me from one city to another, like a star-struck groupie.

I'd been in Southampton for barely a day when, out of courtesy, I checked in with my relative's brother, who, as the Head Chef at Southampton General Hospital, was no doubt a pillar of the community and a person beyond reproach. In fact, Peyton ran a lucrative side line dealing cannabis – he invited me to his place, and with great dramatic flourish, lifted a couple of floorboards to reveal five or six kilos safely hidden away.

It didn't take me long to appreciate the beautiful harmony between his position at the hospital and his entrepreneurial activities – they were almost tailor made for one another. Not only were the doctors and nurses among his most loyal customers, but he had access to a steady supply of patients in need of effective pain relief. (His trademark quip was, "How would you like one of our new, homemade biscuits?"). He also had free rein to employ around a half dozen orderlies, who he used as runners for his endeavours. I had to admire the panache and style with which he ran a drug dealing operation, not in the shadows, but hidden in plain sight.

"Always have legitimate employment," he counselled me. "You're less likely to face questions about any unexplained wealth. If I'm ever quizzed about a couple of extra grand in the bank account, I've always got a valid answer. I ran the catering at a mate's party, or a wedding, that sort of thing. Saved my bacon a couple of times."

Peyton was forever on the lookout for opportunities to expand his reach, and was instantly fascinated by my network of connections in Oxford. "Take a couple of ounces to start you off and if you get rid of that quickly then come and get more and pretty soon, you'll be buying your own ounces off me yourself next time you're heading back," he suggested. "No need to pay upfront – you're family, so I trust you. If you skim a bit off each deal, you should be able to undercut the competition, make a nice margin for yourself, and see me right."

Peyton had a natural understanding of the supply chain economics, and he described the division of spoils with the clarity of a forensic accountant. He became an early mentor in the business side of the drug trade, and it was with great sadness, decades later, that I learnt he'd destroyed himself, mentally, physically and financially, when he'd succumbed to the lures of his own product, ending his days with a crack cocaine addiction.

Eventually, Peyton's encouragement gave me the confidence to lay my hat, once again, in Cowley (my probation officer's head was spinning at my frequent relocations). I took a week-to-week rental, and my punters soon made sure word spread quickly that "Lennox has come across top grade hash." I woke early to get prepared, but unfortunately was a touch hyper, and over breakfast indulged rather too heavily in the product. This is never advisable, for the same reason that teetotallers make the best pub landlords.

My first customer – Rob – came via referral. Since I'd be selling to a stranger, it was necessary to take a few precautions to ensure I wasn't being introduced to an undercover cop – or someone casing the joint so they could steal my stash at a later date. Rob was briskly told to wait outside whilst I had a word with my friend for putting me in such an awkward position:

"What yer doing bringing people I don't know here to my house? Yer know the rules, I'll do it for you this time but next time arrange to meet at the pub and I'll serve your new buddies there, okay? Now, how much does Rob want?"

Eventually, I consented to allow Rob through the door. My eyes were bloodshot and there was an ashtray full of smoked spliffs on the floor, next to where I sat cross-legged. So it was probably self-evident that I was high and paranoid!

A few minutes later, Rob and my friend were on their way, with an eighth that was nearly as big as a quarter. In fact, I graciously lent my friend a knife so he could take a cut as well. In my doped state, I still hadn't twigged that I was handing away freebies, as if I was running a special "help yourself" promotion of buy one get one free.

As realisation of the incredible value sank in, my friend was back within ten minutes – this time wanting a stash for himself. He'd even negotiated to borrow money from Rob to front the payment. News of the "deal of the century" spread like proverbial wildfire. I was doling out increasingly generous portions to all comers, especially white dudes (who, unlike Rastas, tend to prefer weed to hash), who'd been having difficulty with their regular suppliers. Some of them would wander around the block, before coming straight back – just enough time to satisfy themselves the deal was as good as it seemed.

It only dawned on me that I was virtually giving away my weed and hash when I was clean out of stock, yet with my money belt only half full. Of course, my absence of basic business acumen was no excuse to default on my obligations to Peyton. I headed to Southampton to make a fulsome apology. It would take me many weeks of hard graft to fully pay my dues.

*

With family members still keeping me at arm's length, I found it easier to forge bonds with low-level criminals, where mutual respect could be rooted in shared experiences and outlooks. I grew tight with a hustler called Matty Rourke, who I first met at a dance competition in the Cowley Centre (he took away first prize due to his mean shuffle). Matty was a loner by nature and preference; he wasn't close enough to be accepted as a gang member, so he hovered on the periphery, as a kind of associate – somebody who could be a source for stolen goods, or might have a group of buyers, rather than a member of the inner circle. When Trevor Smart learned I was spending time with Matty, he cautioned me to keep my distance. "I can smell a bad 'un a mile off," he said. "No good will come when Matty's around."

Trevor and Matty's rivalry came to a head one weekend when they'd been drinking heavily in the same pub. I'd left early to smoke some pot alone in my flat, so missed the genesis of the argument (I learned later it kicked off in the pub car park when Matty questioned the virtue of Trevor's mother; Trevor responded by calling Matty "pondlife", and soon the insults were descending into threats of violence). Aware of my 'no-nonsense' reputation, Trevor's girlfriend Grace Watson concluded I was the only person in the vicinity who could stop their confrontation spiralling out of control. She raced to my place, and hammered on my door, begging me to intervene.

"They'll kill each other," she shouted. "But they'll listen to you."

I'd been savouring a rare moment of quiet with my spliff, but like a moth drawn to a light, couldn't resist the lure and the adrenaline rush. I grabbed a kitchen knife (could be useful, you never know), and charged with Grace back to the scene. By the time I arrived, Matty had the upper hand. Blood was smeared across Trevor's chin from a split lip, and he was reeling from a fresh onslaught of blows. Knowing of the glass eye, Matty was cunningly dodging and weaving to Trevor's left, where his visibility was most impaired.

"Oi stop!" I demanded.

"You one of them now?" said Matty. Where Trevor was English to his fingernails, Matty and I shared a Caribbean heritage.

"That's not what it's about and you know it," I said, lunging at Matty, and judo-throwing him to the floor. As he fell, the knife slipped from my top pocket and scraped his arm.

"Blacks should stick together!" he said, humiliated and angry.

Grace was urging Trevor away from the scene, so she could tend to his wounds. "You're a good mate, Lennox," she said.

And that's how matters would have rested, if Trevor and Matty hadn't both been taken to the same Accident and Emergency unit, for a precautionary check for broken bones. While waiting to be triaged, the bickering inexplicably reignited. "F- you, State," wailed Matty, climbing onto a nursing station. "No, f- you," shouted Trevor. As you can tell, it wasn't exactly the Queen's English. Panic erupted; there were a number of people in the waiting area – the usual Saturday night pub and club brawlers – and, as punches flew, they were screaming and fleeing in random directions.

Two burly security officers were quickly on the scene, and brought order to the evacuation. Then blue flashing lights, and a cluster of squad cars rocked up.

"You with them?" one of the officers yelled at Grace and me.

Still feeling the effects of my last spliff, I said, "Yes, but…"

"Don't bother. We're arresting the lot of you."

I assumed we'd be held in a police cell for a single night, at worst, even joking about this with one of the officers who detained us ("We'll be outta here in the morning, you guys ain't so lucky"). So I was grossly unprepared for what happened at the next day's magistrates' hearing. Trevor and I were denied bail on account of Matty's testimony – he alleged I'd repeatedly stabbed him in a frenzied berserk rage. Astonishingly, before this act of treachery, Matty had orchestrated his own release without charge, and wasn't even in the courtroom alongside us.

"I've done a ton of crap for which I could be locked up," I groaned to Trevor. "Breaking up your fight isn't one."

We were snookered. Unaware of Matty's conniving, we hadn't prepared a defence, and, knowing of my reputation, the police were ill-disposed to offer support. Matty's testimony had the inevitable result – Trevor and I were remanded in custody. That afternoon I was back behind bars at HMP Oxford, re-familiarising myself with the rulebook, reviving old friendships. What a shame they didn't provide "loyalty points", Holiday Inn - style.

After two months on remand, the date fell due for my committal hearing, when the prosecution was required to present additional pre-trial evidence to justify a further period of lock-up. I was represented by a feisty Australian lawyer called Wilson Carter from the local firm of Laurence & Harvey's, a 20-partner practice, who wore his hair in a stylish quiff with tapered sides.

His straight talking manner endeared itself to me. Over the coming years, he'd represent me on numerous occasions, and was always precise in his demolition of flaws in the prosecution case (I'd sometimes refer him to associates in need of representation, with a glowing testimonial). At the committal hearing, he was typically merciless:

"There isn't a shred of evidence that my client assaulted Mr Rourke with a knife; the medical report doesn't even mention a plaster. My client is paying the price because a known criminal filed trumped-up charges out of pure spite."

Thirty minutes later, I was on the courthouse steps with Wilson breathing the cool open air, a free man.

"G'day, Len," said Wilson, exaggerating his Aussie accent for comic effect. "In the nicest possible way, I hope I don't see you next time."

We shook hands vigorously. There was no doubt in Wilson's clever detective mind there would be a next time.

9.
Betrayed

I was on Cloud Nine, strutting through the town centre like a king, but a double tragedy was soon to strike. Chris Grant had recently fathered twins, tragically one of them hadn't made it past his first few weeks. On the way to the baby's funeral, I'd bumped into one of my sisters who asked whether I'd heard the news about Dad.

"I know he's living with Mom in St Vincent."

"Not anymore. Lennox, he died last Monday."

My mouth hung open, as if I was a ventriloquist's dummy and one of the strings had snapped. How could this be? Surely he was going to be around forever? Could she have confused him with someone else? But her face told a different story. I muttered, "It's not true, it can't be true," but knew in my heart that it was.

Dad had suffered declining health for a number of years. It hadn't been helped when he'd accidentally hit his leg with a cutlass while tending to overgrown weeds. Too embarrassed to discuss the mishap with my mum, infection had set in, which in turn affected his blood circulation. Eventually, the leg had been amputated below the knee, and Dad spent his final years on crutches or an ill-fitting prosthetic limb. My suspicion is that, no longer able to lead an active life, he'd simply lost the will to live.

What triggered my rage was that, because I'd been on remand, I was hearing the news many days after the event. I hadn't been able to call Mum to pass on my condolences. I hadn't been able to fly out for the funeral. I hadn't even been able to send a card, or prayers, on the day he'd been buried under the mango tree of his local church.

And there was only one person to blame. The f- who'd stitched me up. Matty Rourke.

He'd overstepped the mark. Dad's passing made this a family matter, a matter of honour. Matty needed to be dealt with, as soon as I'd finished a period of respectful mourning, assisted by twice my usual consumption of marijuana.

I saw Matty from across the road, I asked him to come with me, "I want to talk with you."

We went behind a secluded alley by the college.

"You stitched me up. I was inside when Dad died," I said.

"You traitor you're a honky lover," Matty shouted.

We both lunged at each other and I head-butted him on the forehead, and while he was reeling, locked his arm in mine as if I was a sensei, using his own weight to throw him to the ground judo-style. I couldn't be sure the technique would be a success – I'd only seen it executed in Kung Fu movies – but Matty gasped in anguish as his back slammed against the paving slabs and his knife dropped on the floor. I grabbed hold of his hair, attempted to twist it in my hands, (which was difficult because of the amount of grease he had applied) and I slammed his head against the floor. "You want more do you?"

"No, no, I am sorry man," he bellowed.

I grabbed the knife and marked the side of his face. "Your card's marked don't you ever grass or F- with me again. And stay outta my face man."

I still had strands of greasy afro hair twisted around my fingers and was desperate, in my father's name, to continue the beating. But the beating was taking its toll. A minute of high-stakes brutality, and I was frankly knackered. Matty was blubbering like a baby, so I figured I was safe from retaliation. I loosened my grip and stood up. "Never again. I mean it."

But the rage was still smouldering; I couldn't shake the nagging suspicion. I'd spent ten weeks on remand facing baseless charges, and missed my father's funeral. I had the chance to set matters straight four days later, when our paths crossed again.

It was Saturday night, notorious for trouble, so I was carrying my Japanese lock knife. By habit, I kept mine in my underpants – to avoid detection of stop and search as I was a known criminal.

I was at the main bar of the Caribbean club in the city centre, as usual in a suite that was scammed from a Gratton shopping catalogue and enjoying a second glass of Bacardi on the rocks, when a friend of mine took me aside.

"I just seen Matty Rourke in the first floor bar," he said.

The red mist descended. I suddenly recalled that Matty had looked at me with a bizarre, mocking stare when our eyes had met earlier that day on opposite sides of the street. The staircase was packed with revellers but I barged through the crowds; I couldn't take the risk Matty might take flight.

The upstairs bar doubled as a dancefloor, and its DJ was a reggae enthusiast. Even from the stairwell, the lyrics to Bob Marley's One Love were unmistakable:

"One love! One heart!

Let's get together and feel all right."

It was obvious to anyone in my path that I was far from "feeling all right" that night.

The lighting had been dimmed in the upstairs bar, but Matty's silhouette was clearly visible, slow dancing in the far corner with a skinny girl whose T-shirt and denim skirt could best be described as figure-hugging. There was no way he'd be getting lucky tonight.

"Sayin' give thanks and praise to the Lord and I will feel all right,

Sayin' let's get together and feel all right."

He still hadn't registered my presence when I strode across the dancefloor and grabbed him by the collar, twisting to the right until he spluttered from shortness of breath.

"There is one question I'd really love to ask (One heart!)

Is there a place for the hopeless sinner,

Who has hurt all mankind just to save his own beliefs?"

"I f-ing warned you to stay outta my way," I said, shoving him forcefully to his knees, and flicking my wrist hard so the lock knife opened from its sheath. "Don't ever call me names again."

At the sight of the blade, the figure-hugging girl gasped, backed away, and sprinted for the door.

"I've had enough of you messing me around."

I held the knife vertically above Matty's head, the tip of the blade pointing down, inches from his scalp.

He was begging for his life. "Don't kill me, brudda, please."

Like a tsunami, awareness of the unfolding assault had spread throughout the bar. Nobody was dancing anymore, but everyone was reacting differently. Some had panicked and fled; others were screaming.

"One love! What about the one heart? One heart!

What about, people? Let's get together and feel all right."

I stared into Matty's eyes, like a big game hunter taking a final look at the life he's about to extinguish. I felt no mercy, no emotion except a burning, red-hot hatred. About to plunge the knife deep into Matty's brain.

And then I heard words tumbling from Matty's lips, coughing to project his voice despite his collar being tight around his neck.

"Our Father, who art in Heaven, hallowed be thy name."

His prayers gathered pace. I heard a random assortment of lines from scripture.

"Help me God," he said. I heard him plead with God to help him as he prayed.

For the first time, I shuddered. Matty's prayers were disturbing and distracting. How could I knife somebody who was summoning the Big G? It would be a betrayal of... of who? Angela? Overstones? My parents? Myself?

I couldn't do it, I couldn't complete the deed. As the words "Help me God" settled on my mind, all my rage melted away, like ice left on a beach. I released the collar, and Matty coughed sharply, choking at the abrupt inrush of air. "Cross the street whenever you see me," I said. Then my anger evaporated.

There was no need to push past anyone on the way back down; the crowds parted before me like the Red Sea. At the downstairs bar, a bald but with a rich untrimmed beard man – had taken my stool, but he scampered away as he saw me return. I relaxed my elbows atop the bar, and ordered a cockspur rum. Then I took one of the pre-rolled spliffs from my cigarette box, and held it between my fingers without raising it to my lips.

*

The Caribbean Club was becoming a regular haunt. It was popular with all generations; serious partying started as soon as the sun set, but during the daytime, many elders in our community would gather to socialise, often hunching around small tables playing dominoes or cards and drinking Red Stripe lager. I often gravitated towards its top-of-the-range pool table. Having honed my skills at HMP Shepton Mallet, overcoming the twin obstacles of slanted tables and torn cloth, it was a breeze to pot balls on a high grade surface.

As a confident young man with a bit of swagger, I also found it easy to approach random strangers and engage them in conversation, so my network of friends and associates grew quickly. Many people I met were honest traders striving to earn a crust. But that wasn't always the case, and my presence at the Club drew me to the attention of shadier characters who realised my propensity for violence, and history of brushes with the law, could be harnessed for unscrupulous purposes.

Eventually I was taken to a small pub near the Oxford sorting office – one which doubled as a labour exchange for criminals, where I could meet a wider network of potential associates, as well as trade in stolen goods. (Deals of all types were struck, some involving thousands of pounds, others worth perhaps twenty quid: typical conversations could start "I just got some meat", or "I have a dozen credit cards if you wanna buy.")

At first, it wasn't entirely clear that I was being drawn down a one-way path into the world of organised crime.

In any event, having been identified by talent scouts as 'a person with potential', the steps to advancement within this new world were highly structured and uncannily similar to those facing anyone embarking on a career in big business or the Civil Service. I was interviewed by a businessman called Big Hamish, who had a list of small-to-medium-sized jobs for which he needed talent. He gave me the opportunity to prove my capability.

Later, I appreciated the early weeks were an extended trial period during which I was being closely monitored and assessed, as I completed an initial suite of assignments. The level of diligence was extraordinary – sometimes, two gang members would observe my performance from a safe distance, never interfering regardless of how events unfolded. Feedback on areas for improvement was immediate, blunt and unrestrained. If shortcomings were not quickly addressed, the probationary period would be abruptly terminated (needless to say, I had no recourse to employment rights!)

My trial period comprised a series of street robberies, each one yielding perhaps five to ten thousand pounds. Most jobs relied upon an insider providing critical information on the movement of cash around the city, in return for a cut of the proceeds. The network of informants was impressive – cleaners, disgruntled employees, bank clerks and other professionals. Generally the details would be provided through one or two levels of intermediaries, ensuring I had no knowledge of the original source. Once I'd accepted a task, I was required to conduct surveillance, satisfying myself about certain key facts, before embarking on the crime itself. Sometimes, Big Hamish helped me to case the job, and we'd use walkie-talkies to compare notes after criminal friends in a Post Office had cautioned us that police were monitoring the mobile phone air waves.

Many of the jobs involved cash being transported from business premises – a nightclub, a supermarket, a pub – to the bank, often on a Monday when the sums included the entire weekend takings.

During my preparations, I'd analyse every variable – the route, the couriers, the environment, the bags – before determining the optimal moment at which to strike. Regardless of the size or complexity of the job, there was one cardinal rule, which must never, under any circumstances, be disregarded: I must never set out while off my head on cannabis. Very few robberies unfold exactly as anticipated; there are always unexpected reactions, interventions, developments. A fast response is required, and if one's judgement is clouded by the after-effects of potent weed, things can spiral hastily out of control, with disastrous results.

I developed a close rapport with "Bruiser", an Irishman who'd been raised as a traveller but had become the trusted medic for Oxford's criminal fraternity. He provided a highly valued service for anyone needing wounds stitched or bullets removed, but who needed to stay under the radar and avoid awkward questions. Bruiser was unshockable, and had no qualms about dishing out pain (not just fixing it), but he'd developed an inexplicable soft spot for me; uniquely, this meant there was one voice within the underworld urging me to show restraint:

"I don't think you should be carrying a knife, Marigold," he said.

Marigold was his pet name for me, sometimes coupled with the prefix "Gorgers". Initially, I'd misheard this as "gorgeous", which was flattering if not entirely accurate, but I soon realised he labelled anyone from a non-traveling background as a "Gorger" – meaning somebody with plenty of food on which too gorge.

"I use it to threaten people when I'm robbing," I explained.

"I'm not an idiot. I know exactly why you use it. I just don't think it's good for you."

"What's the alternative?"

"How about fists instead of a knife?" Bruiser had grown up in the era of bareknuckle fighting, and was notorious for the strength of his upper cut.

Bruiser shook his head despondently. He'd been around long enough to recognise when somebody wasn't taking his counsel on-board. I was listening to the words, but ignoring the wisdom.

"I've seen it so many times, Marigold. You'll get a reputation as a knifeman. That means if anyone's got a beef with you, they'll be sure to bring a knife. Probably a bigger one. Eventually, you'll slip up, and either kill someone or be killed. Either way, it won't end well."

Subconsciously, I was equating "old school" with "yesterday's man". I adored Bruiser, and relished it when he introduced me to other travellers as "My son, Marigold", sometimes sparking confused looks amongst those who took him literally. But I paid no heed to his warnings. Our conversations often took place over tea at his house. By the time I rose to leave, my precious lock-knife hadn't been surrendered, and was still tucked securely in my underpants – the exact same place it had been lodged whilst he'd been sharing his warnings.

It didn't take long to settle on the choreography of a street robbery. Firstly, check off three pieces of visual confirmation, verifying the target was the person assigned to carry cash to the bank – who wants to waste energy thieving a shoulder bag packed with groceries and toiletries? Then, there were a couple of priorities: maximise the element of surprise, and dial up the threat level whilst the victim's reeling and disorientated.

The combination of verbal and physical intimidation usually guaranteed compliance, and during my trial period I executed almost a dozen street robberies flawlessly, with a combined yield of around fifty thousand pounds. It was an extremely lucrative occupation – high risk with no guarantees. My bosses weren't concerned about maximising their share – the point of the exercise was to assess my proficiency. I was allowed to keep around two thirds of the proceeds, thirty-five grand during the period, compared with just ten per cent reserved for the informants.

My share was channelled in three main directions – funding my drug habit, partying and smartening up my wardrobe. It was remarkable how attitudes in the Club shifted and evolved, based on attire. All it took was a nicely tailored suit and a dapper silk tie to turn heads, and command respect.

I encountered resistance on just a single occasion during my probation. One target refused to release the shoulder bag and during the unseemly struggle an onlooker had the presence of mind to call the police. Two helicopters were scrambled, the area was cordoned off, and armed officers undertook a building-by-building search. The memory of my tussle with a women initially worried my observers because she wouldn't let go of money, but my reputation was ironically enhanced by my ability to evade detection, which had required quick thinking and improvisation.

"You were lucky she wasn't a trained ninja," mocked one of my assessors. "That would've been quite a sight."

*

As my reputation spread within the criminal fraternity, it spilt over into the wider community. Random strangers would approach me in the street, urging me to interfere in family disputes and to settle perceived injustices. I was accosted by a single mother in a rundown west Oxford estate who was getting no support from her estranged boyfriend.

"My drug dealer's ripped me off, and I'm down to my last twenty quid. I'd love it if you could get my cash back – plus some weed on the side." Sometimes, I'd smell danger, but mostly I was happy to oblige, as if I was providing a public service – the underworld equivalent of the Equaliser.

My gangland career was flourishing. Having earned my spurs through armed robbery, and boosted by positive reports from my assessors. It was now deemed safe to trust me with bigger jobs. My world was gravitating towards London, the city that's lured ambitious young people for hundreds of years. It doesn't matter whether you're keen to make your mark in business, finance, technology, the media, or crime – London was the place to be seen.

I was sent to score drugs from Baron, an associate at a London train station, who informed me the station was a "Drugs HQ".

All I saw was a regular station. There was a lot of buzz and commotion, for sure – commuters queuing at the ticket office, checking departure screens, racing for late appointments – but I couldn't see any of the symbols of a conventional head office.

My frowns betrayed my confusion, and so Baron indulged me with further details.

"That guy," he said, pointing to an elderly porter pushing a luggage cart, "He's my Operations Director; he controls the routes into and out of London for drugs. And him – the security guard – he's on my payroll too. If there are sniffer dogs around, it's his responsibility to get word out. There were dozens more inconspicuous people who all had a part to play in this intricate operation.

I was still reeling from Baron's revelations when Big Hamish decided it was time I met Kenny, who – according to Big Hamish – would provide a healthy stream of high-paying jobs, once I'd gained his confidence.

"He knows banknotes like you wouldn't believe," Big Hamish said. "They could put him in charge of the Bank of England's printing presses, except he wouldn't wear the pay cut. He's got a team of counterfeiters churning out notes – usually for overseas customers – and the likeness is remarkable. Even down to the metallic thread. His specialty is fifties, where it's more worthwhile going the extra mile than with other denominations. Apparently their lab has incredible technology.

"But unless you have a skill they need – holograms, for instance – you'll never see it first-hand. I've known Kenny for four years, and I don't know where his lab's located; not even which part of the country. 'Strictly need to know'."

This was another world for me. What had I fallen into? I'd been hearing rumours about "Kenny" (I doubted it was his real name) for weeks. Outwardly, he was a respected businessman, who moved in high society circles and whose clientele almost exclusively comprised members of the elite – government ministers, judges, media moguls, chief executives, fashion gurus.

The first time I met Kenny, in a bar frequented by City bankers, he oozed charm. He shook my hand, offered me a drink, introduced me to his associates and then whipped out a wad of cash. A very large wad.

"I seem to have fifty thousand pounds too much," he said.

"A nice problem to have!" I commented.

"What I mean is, I'm sitting on an unforeseen windfall because we overproduced for a client in South America. The money's no use to me sitting in a vault, so I might as well turn it to productive uses."

"What would you like me to do?"

"Clean it for me."

"All of it?"

"Every last note. And I got 'em all ready for you!" Before I'd had a chance to ask any further questions, let alone consent to the deal, he thrust a large envelope into my hands. I didn't need an overactive imagination to figure out the nature of the contents.

I was trying to figure out how to diplomatically phrase the question, "What's in it for me?" when, sensing I was slightly standoffish, he put me out of my misery.

"Three grand clear for your troubles!" he announced. "No quibbles, no arguments. Get the job done, and you'll be looked after. You have my word. You've proven you can scare and steal. Let's see how you get on with something that demands a little more patience and brainpower."

I didn't want to disappoint, and – as we left – Big Hamish sensed my excitement. "You could do this easy, Len. You da man!" he said, encouragingly.

He was barely at the door before I pulled out a sample note for visual inspection. To the untrained eye, the likeness was uncanny. The olive green colouring, the windowed thread, the images of the

Queen and Sir Christopher Wren – if not for Big Hamish's briefing, I could've sworn I was handling the genuine article. It was a fascinating project. Offload a thousand of these notes, and I'd have demonstrated that – I had the ability and intelligence – that I could think tactically as well as terrorise thuggishly.

Intriguingly, switching dirty money into legitimate coin of the realm is far more complex than one might assume. My initial gambit – that I'd waltz into a newsagent, pick up a packet of Wrigley's spearmint gum costing fifty pence, and wait for the cashier to count out my change, was time-consuming and prone to incite suspicion.

There was, I found, no single silver bullet to complete the entire job to perfection; I needed to release the cash through a wide network of bent foot soldiers – bank clerks, shop assistants, fairground workers, restaurant staff. The project took a little longer than expected, but I managed to offload the entire cargo within two months with minimal loss (remarkably, persuading the foot soldiers to swap the notes as a gesture of goodwill, rather than for a cut of the takings). In fact, there was even a piece in the Oxford Mail about the "flood" of fake fifties in the city. During the period, I kept the money in my sound system speakers – the left one was used for the counterfeit notes, with the right one reserved for the influx of sound money. One of the under-appreciated advantages of working in crime, was that you knew criminals who knew criminals that committed the crimes. One rarely needs to fret about being the victim of a domestic burglary. (In fact, there have been occasions when family or friends have been subjected to a break-in; it's been relatively straightforward to "let it be known" the goods must be returned; and it's not long before everything's returned its rightful owner.)

Feeling proud and a real sense of achievement, eager to impress, I walked in when I presented Kenny, triumphantly, with the results of my labours. Certainly, a glowing praise, handshake or words of thanks.

In fact, he pushed the envelope to the side of the table, as if it was almost beneath contempt. I guess that, in the organised crime world, fifty grand is just loose change. But I did notice a faint nodding of the heads between Baron and Luther which bought a warm glow inside of me. The cash might have been incidental, but my performance had impressed. I'd displayed an ability of competence they deemed essential – And, with flying colours, I'd passed their test.

10.
Reputation

I was on the periphery of a complex network of criminal activity, whose tentacles stretched internationally, and which profited from illicit activity without getting its hands too dirty at the sharp end.

One of the major preoccupations of the network was the seamless flow of contraband around the country, from the moment it reached our shores, to local distributors. With over ten armed robberies under my belt, news inevitably spread that an adept, streetwise young thug was now on the scene. When word reached Garrett, who ran one of Oxford's drug gangs, he met me at the club and we talked over rum in a quiet corner.

Garrett knew instinctively how to grab my attention. "I could use someone..." triggered a warm glow inside me, as I recalled my rejection by many legitimate employers, from the army to Scholls. I needed to be needed. The combination of special pleading, rum and high-grade weed overcame my apprehension, and before the end of the conversation, I was on-board.

He explained the set-up of his gang. As leader, Garrett took primary responsibility for dealing with the lines of supply into Oxford, as well as major customers such as high rollers or those controlling channels into the prison system. His five or six existing henchmen looked after mid-scale trades, alongside a string of 'soldiers' (the term used for his low-level criminals, those who were being handled). Garrett's challenge was that none were reliable enforcers.

"Many of my customers are supplied on credit," he said. "If they don't pay up, I need someone I can rely on to collect."

Garrett explained his confidence in his existing crew had taken a dive when a recent robbery had ended in a farce. Drake and

Aaron had been charged with relieving a drug dealer from his six kilos of cannabis. They'd threatened him with imitation firearms, but when he'd stretched his arm behind the sofa and produced a genuine twelve-bore, Aaron had panicked and jumped through the window, notwithstanding that it was locked shut, and that they were on the third floor of a townhouse. Aaron's left arm had been shredded by the broken glass, and his right leg had snapped when he hit the ground – leaving Garrett to despair at how hard it'd become to recruit competent staff these days.

But Garrett's ambitions weren't limited to improving his collection rate. He was aiming for the stars. "My plan is to control all drug distribution throughout Oxford."

If he'd diagnosed the necessary steps to achieve this goal, they weren't shared with me. A moment's analysis would have revealed it was no easy task. I was distantly acquainted with a gang of Indian brothers who controlled the bulk of heroin into the city. They had a reputation for exploiting their own people, and were unlikely to surrender their near-monopoly without a fight. Nevertheless, Garrett had charisma and a vision; that was enough to convince me he was the man to watch. I felt privileged to be admitted to his inner circle, and in a short space of time became his chief enforcer, the man he'd wheel out for the most problematic cases.

One of my first jobs for Garrett was to collect almost a thousand pounds from Grumble, a Jamaican drug dealer who'd been trying to keep the extent of his debts a secret from his wife. I was provided with precious little background information, so turned up after midnight ready to play it by ear and improvise. I even left my taxi to wait outside with the meter running. Grumble needed more persuasion than anticipated – he remained obstinate even when I threatened to relieve him of the TV, stereo and keys to his wife's Saab.

"Listen, mate, I'm on the clock. Every minute you f- around costs me money."

"Keep yer voice down, can't yer? Cindy's asleep upstairs."

That was the spark I needed. I bellowed and yelled until Cindy appeared, ashen-faced, at the top of the stairs. "Your man has taken drugs off my crew and won't pay for it," I shouted.

Sixty seconds later, I was manspreading in the back of the taxi, patting the crisp notes in my inside jacket pocket, grinning broadly. Cindy was calling Grumble a "stupid bastard". Her insults, surely the first of many that night, were audible from the end of the street.

In light of my frequent trips to London, Garrett needed me to score drugs from a Ugandan gang in Brixton; it was essential the operation was handled with sensitivity. The undertaking was a sign of his increasing confidence in my reliability.

"I couldn't trust this to Aaron," he said.

His observations about Aaron were spot on. Years of drug misuse were taking their toll on his faculties. Suffering from short-term memory loss, Aaron struggled to remember names and faces – sometimes even where he was meant to be.

My street cred soared as I negotiated good terms with a Brixton gang.

*

I was renting a room from Ingrid, a Glaswegian woman, who lived on an estate near the town centre which had been nicknamed 'Little Scotland' for obvious reasons. She survived on a diet of Southern Comfort, cans of special brew, and cheap cider, many of which were provided by me in lieu of rent. Her other main source of income was from benefit fraud – she had various aliases which kept the dole cheques flowing in.

Seizing an opportunity provided by the soldiers of my new associates, I set up a sideline in credit card fraud. Before the introduction of chip-and-pin, retailers merrily accepted a matching signature on a payment slip as evidence a customer was legit. All that my enterprise needed to thrive was a steady supply of cards and people with the brass neck to walk into Selfridges or a Bond Street jewellers, spot merchandise with street value, and maintain the pretence they were the person named on the card.

Selecting great candidates was the key – ideally, any girl or woman who could forge a signature and was available at short notice. Before letting them loose, I'd ask them to complete a role play ("Imagine you're treating yourself to some retail therapy"), and then demonstrate their finesse forging a range of signatures. After they'd completed a couple of high-yielding missions, I let them buy stuff for their own use on the card, before disposing of the batch and starting all over again. In nine months of operations, I maintained an almost perfect record – no suspicions, no police questioning, no arrests, and only one close shave.

Finally, the chance to earn serious money reared its head. I'd been playing pool at the Club with Frank, a clerk at a Greyhound Stadium and after a drinking session, I learnt what happens to the takings at the end of the night. Before the evening was complete, Frank and I had shaken on the details of our plan.

I gathered together the regular crew – Drake, Aaron and Mitch – and, together, we planned every detail of the operation. I was in no mood to leave anything to chance.

"We need to prepare properly," I emphasised. "Don't treat the dummy run as a bit of a lark. Careful planning is how we avoid jail time. We can't afford to carry anyone who's not committed."

I couldn't have been clearer; which is why my fuse blew when, Mitch was a no-show. I pulled the job, distraught.

My plans required a minimum crew of four people – two big guys carrying out the cash in two large suitcases means safety in numbers. Even with four, the risks were finely balanced; there was no way I could proceed with just Aaron and Drake at my side. If we were a man down, the odds would be stacked against us. We could be interrupted by night security, a passing policeman, or local residents and would have no system of early warning to mitigate against being caught off-guard.

After the long hours spent harvesting Frank for insight and knowledge, and then scouting every approach to the stadium, it was a bitter pill to sacrifice the opportunity. I wasn't prepared to let matters rest. Assuming an equal division of the spoils, Mitch had cost me at least twenty or thirty grand for a night's work, and that was tough to stomach.

I decided to let him know and that I wanted paying!

Mitch lived on a first-floor flat, about two miles from the stadium. I calmly knocked on the door and watched as one of the curtains was drawn back, and the window unclipped from the latch. Mitch poked his head through the gap and let me in.

"Keep your voice down, please," he said. "My girlfriend's in the other room with Social Services."

"You owe me money man" I said quietly.

At which point, the girlfriend appeared at the window in her nightdress, no sign of anybody from Social Services in the vicinity. Mitch had been stringing me along – again! Enough was enough.

If Mitch's mind hadn't been fogged by weed, he might have handled the situation differently. Perhaps an apology, a pledge to reform, or a plea to my good nature, could've calmed me down. Instead, he seemed determined to wind me up.

"Your taking the f- piss and I want my money, you have wasted enough of my time."

Mitch got mouthy even though he had heard my reputation, he was now getting cocky.

"I ain't got that kind of money to pay you, f- of man," he said.

I got up to leave the flat and said, "Me and you are done, but I still want my money."

He was non stop with his endless abuse.

When I got outside the flat, I turned and showed him half my blade. "Look man," I said, "I don't want no trouble."

Mitch repeated his insults as he stepped outside. Would my rage fall away? Could I walk from the scene without having the last word?

"Back off!" I shouted.

I swung my knife before he had the chance to say any more. I'd intended to cut his face – but lost control of my swing. I felt the blade sliding through Mitch's jaw and tongue until the gleaming metal was visible inside his mouth. He was too stunned with pain and shock to utter a word, and backed away towards his house, holding his chin to stem the blood. From inside the house, I could hear his girlfriend calling, "Mitch, you okay? What's happening?"

I climbed into the back of the taxi, the driver had full sight of the confrontation, but to his credit uttered not a single word, except for:

"Where next, mate?"

The knife attack made the front page of the next day's newspaper:

MAN STABS RESIDENT
AND CALMLY WALKS AWAY INTO A WAITING TAXI.

– but there was no mention the police had any suspicions about the identity or motivation of the assailant. For all his faults, it seemed Mitch could at least be trusted not to grass.

There was now no chance we could return to the Greyhound job. The police had enticed Mitch with the prospect of compensation if he'd only sing like a canary. Having no idea about the extent of his confession, the risk was too great that he'd offloaded all the details of the job.

*

Thieving and scoring can be tiring work, and I'd often join up with the crew on Fridays for downtime. After a lucky escape with the credit cards, I met with the crew to celebrate Aaron's birthday at the Oranges and Lemons pub in St. Clements. Arriving late, I was told I needed to play "catch-up" – which involved an excessive amount of rum, with accompanying spliffs. After a pub-crawl, we found ourselves dancing at Downtown Manhattan night club in George Street. Unbeknown to me, I was being observed by a short plump man named Mick. As I staggered towards home, he intercepted me and introduced himself; he seemed harmless enough, and badgered me to join him for a drink.

My willpower was at a low ebb after my consumption, and I eventually agreed to join him for a drink at his place.

By this time, the alcohol and cannabis had penetrated every cell of my body, and I collapsed (rather than sat) onto his sofa. Unfussed by my state of inebriation, Mick continued recounting tales of his life as if I was hanging on every word. Then events began turning weird.

"I'll get some music playing," he offered.

Of all the artists in the world, Mick chose Shirley Bassey for the turntable. Diamonds Are Forever was soon bellowing throughout the room.

"Now something to drink."

A brandy liqueur. It tasted disgusting, so I tipped it into a flower pot. Mick went to refill it, and reappeared wearing nothing but bright green underpants, tight enough to show the outlines of his genitals.

Was I trapped back in Thomas Brown's living room? I squinted at Mick's face – he didn't look like my relative, but how could I be sure?

"I'm not like that, I need to go now," I said, turning away, and edging towards the door.

As I reached towards the door handle, I felt Mick grabbing my shirt, pulling me back.

The image of Brown touching me through my clothes flashed before my eyes. I felt myself being forced deeper into the house – inebriated and exhausted, I was unable to muster my usual strength, and was suddenly consumed with fear and panic that I was about to be raped again. The next half an hour or so was surreal – I wanted to buy time so my head could clear, so I staggered from room to room, Mick following me like an obedient pet – I spouted any nonsense that popped into my head; anything that would keep him away from me. (In my head, I was begging God to come to my rescue.)

We were in the kitchen, and he was blocking my exit with his plump frame. He whipped off his pants, fell to his hands and knees, and he rolled his tongue around his lips, making obscene faces. My head was now a bit clearer, and, as I turned away in disgust, I noticed the vegetable knife on the draining board, a thin six-inch blade with a black handle. I hid it in my pocket whilst he was busy making faces; the blade's tip pierced my right pocket and scratched my thigh as I made the clumsy attempt to hide the knife.

Suddenly I was lost in the memories of abuse by Brown, and the rage rose within me. With all the energy and force I could muster, I stabbed him hard in his bottom. He didn't scream in surprise or pain, but simply turned to look at me, as if he was taking weird pleasure. I clenched my fist and struck him full-square in the face, raining down blow after blow. I kept pounding – the left of his face, the right of his face, until his body was, as far as I could tell, lifeless. I found myself walking through the lounge like a sleep walker;

Everything was jumbled.

I'd only come out for a drink with the lads; had I now murdered someone?

Coming to my senses, I realised I needed to make the scene look like a robbery, but forgetting I left my finger prints, I found two holdall bags and stuffed them with valuables – an Olympus camera, DVDs, jewellery.

By the time I left, the naked body – he hadn't stirred, not the slightest movement, since my assault – I still had no idea whether he'd died at my hands.

I caught an early morning bus back into town.

With the memories still fresh, I couldn't bottle them away, and unburdened every last detail to a captivated Ingrid who was fascinated – and disgusted – by the saga ("Dutty wee bastard," she muttered in her broad Glaswegian accent).

For the next few days, afraid to venture out in case of arrest, I asked Garrett to scour the press for any news about the assault. For my own conscience, I wanted to establish I hadn't actually caused a death.

It seemed I'd gotten away with my crime, and the memories were starting to fade, when a final twist occurred. As often happens, the easy cashflow from her benefit frauds made Ingrid complacent – which also meant careless. Bang to rights, she was exposed by DHSS investigators, and referred to the police for interrogation. It required less than five minutes of gentle questioning, before she uttered the words that were to cause me much grief:

"I don't know why you're wasting time on what I've done, when a murderer's been living in ma hoose."

I imagine the detective dropped his pen at the word "murderer". By the end of the day, Ingrid had traded her cooperation in return for immunity from any benefit charges, precipitating a sequence of events that led, inevitably, to my conviction and return behind bars.

At court I learned Mick was a known paedophile who also had a history of sexual assaults. He survived the beating, although soon afterwards collapsed in the street from septicaemia arising from the knife wound and spent three months on life support.

All together, over the next couple of decades, I'd be spending around a dozen years in some of Britain's toughest jails – Oxford, Exeter, Lewes, Dartmoor, Grendon, Wandsworth, Strangeways. But, despite some horrific experiences, prison (with one exception) served to harden my criminality, rather than assist rehabilitation.

During this period, I was often my own worst enemy; and so it proved whilst on remand for the assault on Mick. I publicly embarrassed the Governor, but he fashioned his revenge with precision cunningly upgrading me from a Category C to a Category B prisoner, and using this as the reason to push through my transfer to one of Britain's roughest, most isolated jails.

Ironically, I figured I'd been performing a public service. One day, I'd offered a mild remark about the calibre of catering in the jail – I knew I couldn't expect refined cuisine, but I expected a basic level of wholesomeness and cleanliness. The next day, I found a piece of a thick piece of rat skin with fur in my dinner. That crossed the line – but, unfortunately I couldn't do anything about it until the doors were unlocked after dinner. I complained to the officers who only offered a replacement meal which I declined. They removed the rat from my food and threw it away; I was angry my evidence was gone. Instead, I recalled the eloquent proverb about the pen being mightier than the sword, and composed a heartfelt letter which I arranged to be smuggled from the jail and mailed to the national press.

The next morning, the lead story in The Sun – was "Prisoner finds rat in food". The newspaper had barely hit the stands before the Bullingdon switchboard was besieged with calls from journalists, relatives of inmates, charities and do-gooders. No doubt the hotline between the Governor and the Home Office was blazing red for the rest of the morning, especially when the story was picked up by media outlets in America and Germany.

Of course, despite being the instigator of this fury, I was largely insulated from the bedlam; while politicians and civil servants were reeling from the frenzy I'd unleashed, I was going about my regular routine – hours spent locked in my cell, some light exercise in the prison yard, a few menial duties, and (of course) overseeing the fair distribution of some cannabis that had recently been smuggled inside. But, despite our detachment from the outside world, it wasn't long before, rumours about the 'rat' story were circulating – one of the screws, who wasn't a big fan of the Governor, struggled to control his chuckles as he slapped me on the back, congratulating me for brightening his day. I was regularly teased by officers "What you having for dinner today Ratattouille or Rat au vin?"

"We got a celebrity in our midst," he said.

I wore a contented smirk for the rest of the day. But, as I've foreshadowed, the Governor had the last laugh. My transfer was swift. In prison terminology I was ghosted, (removed quickly before anyone had time to realise I was gone) and I was on way to Dartmoor, via HM Prison Reading for a short spell, which also housed young offender prisoners.

My abiding memory of Reading Prison was the sleepless nights brought about by the presence of the Younger prisoners, which (contrary to its branding) was not a standalone operation, but simply a landing within the main jail set aside for prisoners aged 18 to 21. In common with kids of that age all over the country, they kept unusual hours, and were not disposed to showing respect to their elders, whether figures of authority or not.

By three or four in the morning, their brains would spill into overload, prompting them to give full vent to their lungs, and bellow abuse from the safety of their cells at the world in general.

"F- life! F- everyone! F- you all!"

"Shuddup, kids, we're trying to sleep!" would come the retort from the landings above and below.

"F- you as well! You ain't the boss of us. F- off!"

At least, they might've assumed they were bellowing abuse from the safety of their cells, but that would be to reckon without the ingenuity of the prison officers, who were as exasperated as the rest of us at the young offenders' hyperactivity and uncontrollable behaviour. One Wednesday morning, the screws picked three of us – myself included – from the landing above, to the cell from where the most raucous screams were originating. Without batting an eyelid, one of the officers turned the key.

"Oops," he said. "Looks like I might've accidentally left the cell door open. How careless! Anyway, I better get on with my rounds. Back in five minutes, and it ain't my responsibility whatever happens between now and then."

Fair enough, we figured. Five minutes to make sure we get some proper shuteye from now on.

Whilst one kept watch, two of us grabbed them by the scruff of the neck, held them and slapped them across the face a couple of times, "Tell us to F- off will you? You ever cheek us again and keep making noise all night while I m trying sleep, you will get more than a slap, now let this be a warning to you." We scolded as if they were naughty kids in the headmaster's office. Convinced they got the message, we quickly got back to our landing before the officers came back.

Swelling with youthful aggression and frustration, the same heads we slapped were once again jammed full-square against the bars to their cells, giving voice to their screams:

"F- life!"

"F- everyone!"

"F- you all!"

*

Dartmoor, the most dangerous of places, so dark, demonic and full of lifers, murderers and hollow empty shell falloff.

Reading Prison was a holiday camp in comparison with what was to follow. A handful of weeks had passed since The Sun's "rat" exclusive, and I found myself staring at the wall of the smallest cell – eight by six feet – to which I'd ever been confined, on the second floor of Dartmoor's southern wing. The next few months would be a severe psychological test and where I'd need all my reserves and restraint to proper "Man Up" and avoid the fate (severe injury; self-harm; depression; the Dartmoor stare and even death) suffered by so many of my fellow Dartmoor inmates.

Dartmoor National Park covers nearly 400 square miles of wilderness in the county of Devon. Its famous high-security prison is located on elevated ground, dominating the surrounding moor, and its massive walls are built with granite, mostly sourced from the area. It was built by the Admiralty in the early 1800s, on land leased from the Duchy of Cornwall, initially to house American and French Prisoners of War, and at one point its population exceeded six thousand inmates. After the POWs had been repatriated, Dartmoor served various functions – during the First World War, it was converted into a Home Office Work Centre for conscientious objectors.

By the time of my incarceration, Dartmoor had cemented a reputation for dealing with many of Britain's most serious offenders, and had been the scene of numerous disturbances, including one occasion when mutineering prisoners had effectively taken control of the jail for a number of hours.

If the prison's architects had been seeking a design that would strike dread into all who approached it, they certainly fulfilled their mandate. Its imposing gateway is built astride two huge granite blocks, with the head of the arch taking the form of a semi-hexagon with a recessed panel on which is carved "Parcere Subjectis" ("Spare the vanquished") – a reference to the site's one-time role accommodating POWs. The flanking walls are built from granite rubble; stand close to them, and they create the illusion of stretching to the skies with no end in view. On a bleak day (of which there were many), the prison's oval perimeter has the aura of a vampiric Transylvanian castle, albeit with the added menace of industrial quantities of barbed wire.

Small wonder that attempts to escape Dartmoor were rare, and most ended in abject failure. The one escapee during my period of confinement – a convict who smuggled himself out neck-deep in pigswill (Dartmoor had an arrangement with a local farm) – was swiftly recaptured and consigned to solitary for a month.

However the most overwhelming assault Dartmoor wields upon the senses is not its grim outward aspect, but the nauseating, unrelenting, oppressive smell.

Slopping out was the norm – the cells had been designed without plumbing, and, in any event, were too small for a regular toilet, and we had to empty our waste every morning, from old plastic buckets into easily-clogged troughs. Inevitably, much of the content never made it to its destination. Some prisoners engineered the opportunity to empty their buckets over the head of another inmate – sex offenders being the prized target. (Most sex offenders requested to be housed on the protection wing under Rule 43, but sometimes they'd try to avoid detection and live amongst other prisoners, but almost inevitably they got rumbled.) Even if one made a genuine attempt to maintain high hygiene standards, one would often be thwarted by the decrepit state of the plastic buckets, which meant urine leaked through cracks in the plastic long before the "out" stage of "slopping out".

If the smells didn't destroy any last vestiges of dignity, there was always the temperature. Evidently, modern air-conditioning or central heating hadn't been a priority during the prison's many overhauls. Through the deep winter months, the cells were near arctic; some nights, I'd toss and turn for hours under my wafer-thin, itchy blankets, too cold to sleep, as ice collected in the cell. At the height of summer, I faced the opposite problem – stifling heat trapped within cells as if we inhabited a greenhouse, bedding soaked in sweat until rank.

I soon became acquainted with a Dartmoor maxim, handed down through the generations, that "Your worst enemy is the man with the blue shirt" – meaning your fellow inmates. Knives were as prevalent in Dartmoor as drugs had been in Oxford, so any new arrival quickly learnt to adopt the "Dartmoor stare". This is a way of maintaining one hundred per cent awareness of potential threats whilst navigating corridors and walkways, typically by edging along with your back to the walk, peering all around in case an assault was imminent. This was a sensible precaution even for prisoners with no known adversaries.

Many Dartmoor inmates had psychopathic tendencies – calculating and evil. Equally, a number had undiagnosed mental health issues. Others were driven to the edge of sanity and despair by the desperate, humiliating conditions. Through boredom or paranoia, there were any number of prisoners who, on a whim, could grab hold of a knife and plunge it between your ribs. The need to be constantly vigilant against assault was exhausting. (Perhaps the fact that witchcraft was regularly practised on the moors infected the culture inside the prison.)

During my first week in Dartmoor, I chatted to two prisoners who suffered different forms of mental ill-health. With Jack, the problems were blatant and self-evident; he looked like a refugee from a horror movie with his straggly, wild, unkempt dreadlocks, and he was often found wandering the walkways naked from the waist down, his oversized trousers having fallen to his ankles. Winston, on the other hand, seemed a pleasant, ordinary chap on first encounter – I recall chatting about his enthusiasm for cricket. The façade didn't slip until we were joined by other inmates, who took the conversation in a very different direction.

"Winston," they enquired, matter-of-fact, "Do you drink your own piss?"

"Oh yes," he said.

That's nasty, I thought,

"One more question, Winston. Do you eat your own shit?"

"Yes, that too," he said, chuckling like a guilty child. "It cleans my insides."

In unison the group of black guys I was with said "Ewww!!" "Narstiness bwoy!" and we quickly turned and walked away.

In general the rule for thriving on the inside for me was to find a group of black prisoners that I could get along with and learn the ropes from, because everybody stuck to their own group or kind. A second general rule was to maintain a low profile and keep your head down.

The faintest hint of camaraderie with the screws could be fatal. Other inmates would leap to the illogical conclusion you were a "f-ing grass", which would be perilous to continued good health. From the other side, the officers wanted to remind everyone who was in charge.

The word amongst inmates was that officers did not tend to work at Dartmoor by accident or by default. Their route to the jail typically followed one of two courses. Either, they possessed a sadistic streak, and had actively sought out a jail where their indulgences could pass somewhat under the radar. Or they'd been employed at another prison, where they'd exhibited a level of barbarity that the governor could not tolerate; since the all-powerful Prison Officers Association made it nigh impossible to fire an officer for misconduct, the easiest retreat for a harried governor was to arrange a transfer to a prison such as Dartmoor, doubtless accompanied by a generous resettlement package.

In fact, throughout my extensive tour of sixteen of Britain's prison estate (In case any editors are reading I could easily be commissioned to write a definitive of country's jails!), Dartmoor was the only site at which I witnessed explicit, rampant racism from officers.

Racist terms were bandied around liberally – but that wasn't the worst of it. On occasions, I'd see screws open the doors of a cell and beat inmates – disproportionately black guys – senseless, whilst another stood guard. Once, I witnessed Sam, a black prisoner and boxer pull a prison officer into his cell, who had been racially abusive to him, and beat up the officer. I never saw the outcome because we were ushered away; but I'd seen enough to know Sam was suffering, I've no idea whether he was transferred, hospitalised or worse – I do know that Sam wasn't returned to his cell, neither on that day, nor in the weeks that followed.

The plans we devised to smuggle contraband were invariably shrewd and creative. Given its remote location, visitor hours at Dartmoor were generous; wives and girlfriends were allowed to spend a couple of hours in the morning and a couple in the afternoon with their partners, with children welcomed – all with permission to return on consecutive days, staying overnight in a local guesthouse. This allowed ample time for drugs to exchange hands.

A favourite trick we devised was to use the plastic centrepiece in the screw-top lid of an average thermos flask. Under scalding water, the centrepiece can be popped out, and forming a convenient pocket for the storage of heroin or cannabis, wrapped in Rizlas (the surrounding cap also makes the content hard for sniffer dogs to detect). The only cautionary note, learnt from bitter experience, is that cold water must be used in the main body of the flask – never, ever anything above the ambient room temperature.

Throughout most of the year, the tension between different people within Dartmoor was off the charts. But, on New Year's Eve, the hostility fell away amidst seasonal good cheer.

As Big Ben struck midnight, a thunderous clamour erupted throughout the jail, and echoed across the moors. United, our lungs gave vent to an almighty roar, and we banged and kicked our cell doors. And the officers, who usually found any excuse to discipline us, were too busy with their own celebrations to bother chastising us for our enthusiasm; they preferred to taunt us about the fact they were heading to the pub as soon as they were off-duty.

"F-ing shut it!"

(Somebody along the landing shouted "Who's shagging yer missus?" to which they shouted back "Not you!")

The nightly call, by the way, occurred promptly at ten. Unusually, cells lacked individual light switches at Dartmoor, so we had no control over when the proverbial plug was pulled. It didn't matter whether we were penning a letter to a loved one, or reading the climactic page of a Jeffrey Archer thriller, the disembodied voice was merciless. Without negotiation, without compromise, without mercy, he would announce:

"Lights Out!"

And then, at a flick of a switch, he'd make it so.

I'd had no warning of this intractable rule, and when I first experienced it, I felt like throwing open my window and yelling across the wastelands "I am not a number, I am a free man!", as if I was Kunta Kinte from Alex Hayley's novel Roots.

I was restrained partly by the knowledge that my audience would've consisted of nothing other than a few bats, moths, and whatever else lives on the Moors at night. But mainly by the fact it wouldn't have been true.

"Lights Out!" – the sentiment sums up the soul-crushing mood inside this secluded and loveless institution.

11.
Demons

During my time in Grendon Prison, I married Mary Nunn who I'd met when she'd been visiting a fellow inmate at a previous jail, and who was attracted to my "bad boy" persona, but who dumped me and marched out of my life shortly after our nuptials. It's a strange life when a wedding becomes a mere footnote to far more significant events.

Grendon was unlike any other prison in which I'd served time. Built within the past half-century, the cells were larger than those to which I'd grown accustomed, with more natural light, and furniture that was a step up in both quality and quantity. It felt a rare and remarkable concession to be afforded a bed so sturdy that, within days, it hadn't induced infuriating back pain. And, like school kids on non-uniform day, we were all allowed to wear civvies – a freedom which, for a while, I was reluctant to embrace, not least because I was squeamish lest my favourite shirts and slacks acquire a musty prison aroma.

However, it wasn't the physical characteristics which made Grendon so distinctive, but its role within the prison service. It offered intense therapeutic programmes for male prisoners – mainly category B and C offenders – through group sessions which, it claimed, promotes "positive relationships, personal responsibility and social participation". Prisoners are required to meet strict criteria before a referral to Grendon is considered appropriate – including being drug-free and with no evidence of self-harm for at least two months, having no current diagnosis of a major mental illness, accepting responsibility for past offences, and signing a "contract" with the therapeutic programme principles.

I hadn't been expecting, or even seeking, a referral to Grendon, and it only arose through a random series of half-chances. In a meeting with a probation officer in Dartmoor, I'd made fleeting and vague reference to a historic instance of sexual abuse. He happened to make a brief note on my file, and a judge who spotted the comment, extraordinarily, used it to trigger a referral. Why my story leapt out and caught his attention is a mystery to this day (perhaps the Big G had finally come through for me?), and I was given almost no notice of the decision.

One week I was struggling to keep my spirits up amidst Dartmoor's austere regime; the next, I was deep into Grendon's induction programme, during which some of the country's foremost counsellors and psychiatric nurses were readying me for the "Democratic Therapeutic Communities". This was the term they used for facilitated, daily, two-hour group discussions involving eight or nine offenders, seated in a circle like participants in a sharing session at Alcoholics Anonymous.

It was all an alien world to me, and, at first, I wanted nothing to do with it. The more I listened to therapists droning on about "psychological wellbeing" and "emotional regulation", the more I felt nostalgic for the simple certainties of traditional adult male prisons, where the screws would shout and swear and bark orders – and never muddy the waters by becoming your confidante, showing sympathy for your predicament, or allowing first name terms to be used.

With my induction complete, I was invited to participate in the first therapy session, where I sat rigid and disengaged for the entire period, like a sulking dumb-mute. The meeting was moderated by two professionals, a therapist and a psychologist, and both gently encouraged me to share whenever I felt ready. Instead, I crossed my arms and glared. I daren't mention a thing about my abuse trauma – partly because I didn't have the words to describe the experience, but mainly out of fear for the response. I was certain I'd be disbelieved, mocked or scorned. That had been the reaction of twelve-year-old Chris Grant, when I'd opened up to him a few hours after being raped. Why would these people, who weren't even my friends, react more positively?

"It's entirely up to you, Lennox. If there's anything you'd like to say, you're free to speak," said the therapist.

I grunted.

"Please don't feel under any pressure. Whenever you're ready."

So I grunted a bit more.

It may be the judge hadn't fully appreciated the types of people I'd find myself surrounded with at Grendon, and had casually bracketed together all offenders with "sex abuse issues", regardless of whether they'd been perpetrators or victims. In the therapy group were three rapists, three child abusers and two murderers.

As a result, I faced the grotesque plight of trying to confront my demons in the company of people who had committed the type of act that had traumatised me for decades. If it hadn't been so uncomfortable, the sheer, cack-handed incompetence of lumping us all into a single group might've been laughable. For days on end, I was forced to sit and listen to vile crimes described in nauseating detail, unable to flinch or flee (I don't propose to repeat the particulars in these pages; most were too gross to transcribe, especially when the sexual element became a stepping stone to a gruesome murder). In any other setting, every fibre of my being would've yearned to spring from my chair, and punch the lights out of men who could violate vulnerable people in such unspeakable fashions – yet being at Grendon had an unsettling calming effect, as if something in the air we breathed was dampening our virility, and neutralising our machismo. I was in the audience as horrors beyond imaginings were recounted, yet my pulse barely registered a change.

Typically, the therapy sessions were before lunch, and in the afternoon I hit Grendon's well-equipped gym. I hoped this might provide a release for the anger and frustration I kept bottled-up during the meetings. I pounded the punching bag, and thrust the weights high into the air, until my body glistening with sweat and my muscles bulged. But even after one hour of hard physical exertion, the inner emptiness was never banished, and I'd return to my cell to toss and turn in frustration. Perhaps my resentment and irritation shouldn't have been a surprise; the Grendon approach is that "building you back up" can only happen once you've been "broken down".

It was a brisk June morning. Eight of us were sitting together for yet another session of therapy, indistinguishable from the rest, and I was feeling as disengaged as ever. The sun had just broken through a parting in the clouds, and I was using my hand to shield my eyes from the glare. I found myself listening as one of the other group members, a man in his fifties named Derek, explained how he'd spent two years grooming a young girl, Sally, who lived on the same estate.

He'd acted the role of the harmless, affable, generous neighbour, invariably courteous and polite, always asking after the girl's health and that of her parents, offering words of wisdom "to keep you safe", and occasionally giving presents.

"Gifts are powerful ways to win trust," he said, "But you must be careful. Too many, or too valuable, and you attract attention. Just enough to stay under the radar but earn gratitude. Ideally, it should be something of a personal nature – either personal to you, or to them. That builds bonds. And if it's a gift that connects to the body, even better. Because then the children associate their feeling towards you with good feelings about their bodies. Something fashionable to wear, or perfume, or make-up."

I don't know whether it was the sunlight, or Derek's words, but I was finding it hard to focus my eyes.

Here was a self-confessed paedophile setting out, without apology or sincerity, his calculated strategy to groom a child towards the moment at which he was ready to pounce.

One trick, he explained, was to pretend his kitten was missing and ask children playing in the park to help him find it, in return for a reward.

I was struck by the patience, the manipulation, the planning, and the total absence of empathy or concern for the consequences on the girl. It seemed that on the one hand, he'd felt an irresistible attraction towards the child he was grooming; on the other hand, he was able to box away her emotional well-being, oblivious to her suffering. At that moment, it dawned on me. When Thomas Brown had raped me in front of his living room mirror, it wasn't due to a spontaneous loss of control; he'd spent the best part of a decade laying the seeds for that moment.

The therapist must have noticed something in my body language or facial expression.

"Lennox," she said, "Is there anything you'd like to share?"

The words no longer stuck in my throat.

I answered her, my voice barely rising above a whisper. "Yes. I will share something. I was abused at the age of eight and raped at twelve years old."

Everyone looked at me, but nobody commented. Hardened criminals, who had committed unspeakable acts, stared in silence. Even the therapist was momentarily lost for words.

I continued.

"And I haven't spoken with anybody about it for twenty years."

Silence again. Finally, the therapist prompted me, gently testing my willingness to open up further.

"Who abused you, Lennox? Was it somebody in your family?"

I felt my mind blocking out my surrounding. I was no longer sitting on a chair in a room at Grendon Prison surrounded by inmates and therapists. I was a disembodied spirit, hovering in my own zone of existence, in a darkened tunnel illuminated only by a faint light source in the middle distance, an intolerable burden weighing down upon my back.

And then…

Words started to tumble freely. Words about escaping from Thornburry with my friend Alan. Words about being confused and hungry and penniless. Words about turning up on the doorsteps of my relative Thomas Brown. And then words about what came next.

I didn't know, didn't care, who I was speaking to. Because, as I talked, the burden on my back was easing. Like shards being chipped from a block of granite by hammer blows. Perhaps, if I spoke for long enough, the entire stone would shatter into dust and dissipate in the breeze.

In the tunnel, I could see the twelve-year-old boy in front of me, Brown's chin nestling against his neck. I found myself describing the scene in my role as an observer – to inform myself of the facts, rather than for the benefit of anybody else within earshot. Details were remarkably vivid – the shape of the mirror, the texture of the chimney breast.

I needed no further encouragement from the therapist, or from anyone else present, as I continued my revelations. I was retelling the story without exaggeration, without vindictiveness. When I reached the moment that Brown said, "I love yo like dat an mi love yo anuda way as well", a massive chunk of granite exploded into nothingness.

Only when I reached the point when Brown undressed me – "Tek dung yo brief, or else you no wat wah appen" – did my composure crack. A tear ran down my cheek, and I wiped it away, self-consciously, fearful I'd be ridiculed. But nobody said a word, not even when a second tear welled up. Or a third. Or fourth.

My voice quivered as I mentioned the touch of Brown's penis against my skin, and the defilement that followed. I described far more than I'd ever shared with Chris or my sisters, but, when I reached the moment Brown had penetrated me, I could continue no further. My cheeks were damp with the freely-flowing tears, and my whole upper body was shaking with terror.

Slowly, my environment came back into my field of view. I nervously looked around for the therapist. What would her eyes betray? Would she, like the others, chuckle at my ordeal? Or worse, dismiss it as a false memory, or a matter of no consequence. I knew many prisoners spun yarns in these sessions to get sympathy and bring forward their release date. As soon as our eyes met, I knew my fears were groundless. She was looking at me with empathy, sympathy, concern, almost affection. She knew every word I'd spoken was the unvarnished truth.

As did everyone else within the circle.

Ian, a two-times murderer, laid his hand upon my shoulder in support. "Lennox," he said, "It wasn't your fault. Not a single thing."

Neil, a multiple rapist, added, "You mustn't blame yourself."

John, whose crimes I cannot repeat, said, "He should die. But you, my friend, should feel no shame. You deserve a good life."

The image of my younger self was fading now. But before it vanished completely, did I notice the faint trace of a smile playing across young Lennox's face? Somehow, across the generations, had we made a connection that had comforted him on that cruel and fateful day?

Unburdening myself of the abomination I'd suffered affected me physically for days ahead. In the gym, my strength abandoned me. I was unable to lift a single dumb-bell – not even the metal bar, deprived of its plates. My appetite deserted me. Walking upstairs required a triathlete's willpower. It was almost a week before I mustered the courage and energy to face another therapy session.

One of the criminals in the group hadn't muttered a single word throughout my story, but by coincidence I found myself alongside him the next day, on dishwashing duty. He had a thin face, almost bald and with watery eyes, and as I scrubbed the plates, he confided in me:

"Lennox, I was like your relative."

I felt my fist tighten. Was there anything within easy reach I could use as a weapon? A fork perhaps? Or a plate?

"I mean, I was that type of man."

He didn't pause from his duties – washing, drying, stacking – but, as he worked, he shared with me the deceptions he'd used to win the confidence of his godson, before raping him in a startlingly similar fashion. "I needed to be focused and single-minded," he said, "Because young boys have a sixth sense when something's not right. One mis-step, one word out of place, and I'd have lost his trust – if that happens, it's impossible to reclaim it. That's why I waited, waited, waited, until he was at the lowest ebb. Until my chance to strike."

"Why are you telling me this?"

"Because the guilt is mine. All mine. I must live with it, because I can never turn back the clock. But, Lennox, you don't need to live with it. Because you did nothing wrong."

"I feel I could've done something to stop it. Perhaps if I'd only…"

"You were twelve years old. There was nothing you could've done. It's too late for me to mend my life, but I need you to promise me. You must move on from the trauma. Don't let it define you. Not for a moment longer."

I would've hit him, but his words seemed to connect with the 12-year-old Lennox. I was overcome with a weird feeling of exoneration. It's funny, I thought. I didn't feel the rage burning within me when all the other sex offenders were describing their crimes, no matter how heinous. But this was different; it was closer to home.

But then the kill switch flicked off. Because it almost felt as if Brown was saying sorry. The words I'd been denied since the day it happened.

*

Released from Grendon, and having begun the "coming to terms with everything" process, I wanted to reach out to people I'd once held dear, and rekindle broken relationships. I saw Chris Grant – he'd secured employment as a lorry driver, but we'd had no contact for years except for momentary eye contact one Friday afternoon. He'd been in the cab of a 20-tonne HGV, and tried to attract my attention. I'd worn my screw face and avoided him. Even when he'd blared in his horn. Even when he parked the lorry and chased after me.

"We were once like brothers!" he pleaded, standing in front of me blocking my path. "What did I do wrong?"

"Don't talk to me. Back off!" I replied. "You've been no brother to me."

"The police warned me to steer clear," he said.

"That was just for the trial. That bullshit stopped years ago."

"You got it all wrong, Len."

"You turned your back."

"You're misinterpreting everything."

"And you laughed at me when I told you what that bastard Brown did."

"We were kids Len, we laughed at everybody."

Chris and I did eventually bury the hatchet, Mummy G, urged us to shake hands "Before I bang your heads together like naughty boys".

Not long after my release from Grendon I was, once again, on the wrong path. And, again, God bore the brunt of the blame. I was impatient for income and stability, and He didn't seem prepared to operate on a timetable that suited me. My immediate challenge was to rustle up funds to pay for my driving lessons – I'd owned and driven numerous cars over the years, and recently concluded that using a forged licence was an unnecessary inconvenience. But unfortunately driving instructors don't work pro bono, so I needed to generate the cashflow to cover their costs.

Carl Simons – with a swept back hairstyle, who I'd met during one of my spells inside – tempted me to practise my driving in his Ford Capri. His specialty was breaking open fruit machines to relieve them of the coins they held for jackpots, but he needed a getaway driver.

My role was to ferry him around Oxfordshire's back roads during the unsocial hours, drop him off at assorted pubs, and social clubs, and then lurk in the shadows of nearby alleys until my services were required. We agreed a fair division of spoils – typically, I'd receive 200 quid from a 700 pound haul – and we could possibly complete three or four jobs in a night. Not a bad yield for knowing how to fire the ignition and operate a clutch.

"I got my very own Morgan Freeman," Carl used to say. It was only a few years since Freeman had won widespread acclaim playing the private chauffeur Hoke in the Oscar winning movie, Driving Miss Daisy.

Unfortunately, our team-up proved rather less sustainable than that of Hoke and Miss Daisy, who, in the film's final scene, are still making waves at the age of 85 and 97 respectively. Our downfall arose due to that classic thief's vice – excess confidence and deceit. One night, after the first burglary of the evening, the Capri's engine wheezed and spluttered but wouldn't fire up. Unwilling to postpone our endeavours until it'd been checked out, we needed a Plan B. I said to Carl:

"Any good at nicking cars?"

"Yes, excellent," he replied. "Wait here with the stuff and keep a look-out. I'll get it sorted."

Moments later Carl returned with a smile on his face, beckoning me to follow him – to a canary yellow Robin Reliant (affectionately known as the "plastic pig" on account of its distinctive shape and fibre glass construction), like the one used by Del Boy whose bonnet was covered with Batman stickers.

"Off all the motors in this bloody car park! Are you bloody mad, Simons?" I vented.

Carl thought everything was a joke and chuckled to himself.

"Anyway, I thought you said you were good at nicking cars?"

"I am," he said. "I just got a brick and smashed the window. Now, stop wasting time and drive!"

With no idea how to hot-wire a car properly, I was lucky it started with a few twists of my screwdriver. Off we drove like the scene from Only Fools and Horses where Rodney and Del Boy are in fancy dress as Batman and Robin.

Within twenty minutes, the vehicle shuddered, its three wheels jerked from side to side, and it came to an abrupt halt – in the middle of the road directly outside St Aldates Police Station! Driving Miss Daisy might have been a romantic comedy, but they could never have included this scene for fear of stretching credibility. Sometimes truth really can be more hysterically outrageous than fiction!

Matters got worse.

A police car approached us, returning from its patrol, so Carl and I legged it in opposite directions. When Carl didn't show at the agreed rendezvous point, I doubled back… right into the path of the police who were giving chase. My attempts to evade the police dogs were to prove unsuccessful. I hid amidst the juniper of a shrubbery in front of a neat end-of-terrace house half a mile from the station, figuring that might confound my pursuers. I hadn't reckoned with the public-spirited homeowner leaning out of the window, jabbing her index finger in my direction as the police scoured the parkland opposite. They got the message, and moments later I was being dragged roughly, my dignity in shreds, from my hiding place. Despite the best efforts of my solicitor Wilson – who increasingly saw me as a long-term client – I was soon back behind bars. Fortunately, they don't "throw the book at you" when the only victims have been a few fruit machines and a clapped-out Robin Reliant. This time, the sentence was nominal, and it wasn't long before I was getting back up to mischief.

*

One day, Big Hamish introduced me to the manager of a travel agency in town, who shared the location of the safe and the book in which the combination number was kept written. "It'll be a cinch, and there's probably around thirty or forty grand inside," he said. He'd "forget" to set the alarm, and leave the small toilet window unlocked so we didn't need to crowbar open the front door.

The plan was simplicity itself. We'd break in after-hours, so nobody would get hurt – no stabbings necessary this time! Even the business' owners wouldn't really be out-of-pocket. Everything would be reclaimable on their insurance. It was the perfect victimless crime, and I treated it as another "Organised Crime Gang Test".

It's often said perfection is achieved through trial and error, and certainly this job involved both trial and error (I'm not sure about the perfection). The plan was for Sticks and I to get the job done in no time – I'd be on lookout (I couldn't fit through the window), whilst he handled the safe. In the event, he struggled with the safe for three hours before emerging from the window, admitting defeat ("I reckon he got messed up about the combination numbers", was his excuse). Apparently the truth was even more bizarre; the manager had forgotten to lock the safe, and Sticks had spent three hours turning the dial back and forth.

I resolved to make a return visit the very next week, this time in broad daylight, and accompanied by Drake – who knew how to wave around a pistol for maximum impact.

"Shut the f- up and get down on the floor," I yelled, as we barged through the front door.

Three staff and four customers cowered in dread. I suspect the closest any of them had previously come to gunfire was watching Clint Eastwood on the big screen.

"Who's in charge?"

"Me," said a slight man, his tone quivering. He was sandwiched between two female assistants.

"Open the f-ing safe now," I ordered.

He was clearly petrified. I grabbed him and, as he yelped, I bashed him on the nape of his neck with the butt of my gun; he collapsed, out cold. I ordered one of the assistants to accompany me downstairs to the safe while Drake ensured there was no funny business in the main room. He bolted the door, and kept his gun trained on the three customers – all were terrified and compliant, although one old lady was too frail to lie prostrate on the floor.

Once I'd emptied the contents of the safe into my rucksack, I ordered everyone to:

"Stay on the floor until ten minutes after we've left. We have guys outside who'll shoot anyone who moves."

Then we legged it to the safe house. It was only half a mile away, but years of smoking meant running was tough. When we reached our destination, I was wheezing like a chronic asthmatic, and collapsed to the floor.

The safe house was being looked after by an 18-year-old soldier called Neil, who was known to Drake. One of Neil's tasks was to take our guns, money and clothes to another safe house, where he'd wait while we rested. More importantly, he was our appointed "stooge" – which meant that, if we were caught, he'd confess and take the rap. For an armed robbery offence, he was probably looking at a minimum of eleven years inside, but the unwritten rule in our circles was we'd ensure neither he nor his family wanted for anything while he was locked up.

We didn't know it at the time, but the police were on the scene minutes after we'd fled. Before we'd even totted up our takings, a lavishly resourced investigation was in full swing.

The police were looking for any "black man with a bag". As Neil casually strolled along the streets to the second safe house, all our loot in his bag, he was hard to miss. He'd barely made it half way when he was ordered to his knees by armed officers, and bundled into a police van.

*

It would be a while before we were aware our stooge had been caught red-handed and arrested on the spot. In the meantime, the labour exchange pub continued as a steady source of scams and hustles, but was seen as coarse and cheap by London high-rollers. For this reason, you could never rely on it for the most "prestigious" jobs, which were generally shared around at upmarket bars in the capital. I'd attended quite a few exclusive gatherings in a Kensington bar, but always as a bit-player, with an observation role. As my name became known to the crime kingpins, I was invited to take a more prominent role. One day, Big Hamish called, and urged me to drop everything.

"It doesn't matter where you are, or what you're doing. I promise you, this could be The Big One."

"How big?"

"If it was a movie, Michael Caine would play the starring role. That's how big."

"You talking more than ten or fifteen grand?" That was the scale of my biggest haul so far.

"Quit yapping, and get yer ass to Kensington. After what you did with those counterfeits, Kenny's dying to get you involved in the next job!"

You wait for Kenny; Kenny doesn't wait for you – so we arrived early ("Better to be an hour early than a minute late"), and made a bee-line for a discrete booth in an alcove towards the rear, out of general earshot.

"He only feels conformable in this one booth," said Big Hamish. "If the owner knows Kenny's on the way, he'll make sure it's vacant."

Big Hamish had warned me that carrying a weapon to a meeting with Kenny was unwise, but I figured my trusty lock knife tucked (as usual) inside my underpants would evade detection.

To the uninitiated, there was nothing special about how Kenny presented himself. He had the bearing of a middle-aged Hatton Garden jeweller, with a stocky frame, and greying hairline, and a quiet cockney manner. The only clue there might be more than meets the eye was the Eastern European muscle who accompanied him into the bar, and then took up a spot six feet from the booth, where he stood unmoving as a Roman statute, arms folded and scowling, his thin eyes scouring the bar for the slightest hint of trouble.

"Great work with the fifty," Kenny said. "They tell me you're a man who doesn't scare easily."

"By the time I was ten, I'd already spent five years standing up for myself against racist bullies in the school playground and gangs. After that, it takes a lot to frighten me."

"And jail didn't break you either? I understand you spent a lot of time in and out of solitary without squealing."

"Never tempted, not for a moment. I couldn't stand to give the screws the pleasure."

"So I hear you can take care of yourself and you got a lot of balls. That's very important for what I'm about to tell you. There's a good chance it'll hit the nationals, so I need someone who can lie low, and not tell a soul about it. And you know the rules. I've seen a few notes about carpentry, shop work, construction work, and some other bits and pieces, but I'm unclear about your current situation. Do you have anything like a regular job?"

"I've been approached by a night club manager to be a bouncer," I replied. "I met the manager yesterday; he promised to let me know in the next few days."

"Don't touch it with a bargepole," said Kenny.

"I might need the cash."

"Take it from me, the cash is nothing compared with what I'm about to offer you. More importantly, you never learn anything useful as a bouncer. If they want to hire you as a bodyguard, that's a whole different ballgame – bite their hands off. You'll overhear enough juicy conversation to keep you in clover for years. But just a bouncer? Not worth it. It's an insult for a man of your calibre."

I glanced at Kenny's minder to see whether a knowing smile was flickering across his face, but he remained inscrutable, surveying the joint with a granite-like expression, no emotions betrayed.

"Right," I said. "A big fat 'no thanks' to the bouncer job. I'll let them know."

"Of course, having a bouncer in your pocket – that can be useful," mused Kenny.

"I agree," I said, wondering whether this was a casual remark, or whether he was hinting at the depth of his knowledge about my escapades. After all, the drug-dealing gang had been feeding the head bouncer in a local club with a steady supply of cocaine, and had recently called in its dues – which had involved security doors being left unlocked and unattended at a preordained time. That particular job had netted around seven grand, which ironically had prompted the gang to withhold the bouncer's fix for a few days. He'd enticed us with the promise we'd make at least double our actual haul.

"Anyway, this is all very pleasant, but you're probably impatient to know about the cash I mentioned," said Kenny. "That's why I wanted to meet again. Let me share some background…"

The back story was complicated and multi-layered. It involved a feud between two racehorse owners that had escalated from some initial petty rivalries into outright hostility. Three weeks ago, matters had reached a tipping point when one of the feuding owners had arranged for the poisoning of a horse owned by the other; the poor animal had suffered a painful and lingering death. For the aggrieved party, this had crossed a red line, and he was now willing to write a substantial cheque to ensure his nemesis met with an early grave. He didn't care how it was done – but it must be timely, terminal and, needless to say, untraceable.

"I assume I'm not being asked to do it for favours?" I said.

Big Hamish chuckled. A lot of deals in Oxford were undertaken on the basis of favours, which was a currency valued more highly than cash itself. If somebody owes you "favours", then establishing how, when and where they should be called in was one of life's great under-appreciated pleasures.

"I wouldn't expect you to do it for less than a hundred," said Kenny. "In fact, I wouldn't advise you to accept the job for a penny less. That's the baseline."

I noticed he wasn't sharing with me the gross value of the job; I speculated it was, in all likelihood, upwards of half a million.

"I'm up for it," I said.

With the deal agreed, smiles broke out across the faces of both Kenny and Big Hamish. Big Hamish was, by nature, a sullen and morose person, so his happiness was a rarity. It suddenly struck me he hadn't been in attendance for selfless reasons; no doubt, his pockets would be lined for having championed me as a willing hitman. How many mouths were being fed from this one job?

I spent the next week focused on the groundwork. I scouted the location – the victim lived in a secluded farmhouse surrounded by open countryside, which offered plenty of options for me. I opted for a sniper's rifle, since it involved the fewest variables.

I discussed the logistics with Big Hamish, who took special interest in the details of the case. He introduced me to an arms' dealer near Salisbury who was able to supply a wide range of rifles – bolt action, semi automatic, even full automatic – without any paper trail. I chose a Remington 700, America's most popular sniper rifle, widely used by big game hunters as well as elite military snipers.

The dealer was enthusiastic about my selection – "You can't go wrong with a Remmy," he said – and offered to spend a few hours in his shooting range training me in its use.

Once I'd dealt with the racehorse owner, leaving not the faintest trail back to myself, or Big Hamish, or Kenny or the client, I'd have proven my worth to my paymasters. As the fateful day approached, Kenny mentioned it might be helpful if I understood more about the money trail.

It could, he pointed out, be a little suspicious if a hundred grand was wired one weekend into your bank account, and it wouldn't take long for the banking supervisors – let alone the police – to trace the transaction back to its source. So I was extended the privilege, rare even amongst London's career criminals, of being invited to accompany Kenny to crime's equivalent to Threadneedle Street –

our very own "Bank of England". It was a vast underground vault, originally built by a water authority to link with London's reservoir system, but it had been forgotten when plans for the sewage system had changed. Now it was the site for row upon row of safe deposit boxes, all used by gangsters and mobsters to park their wealth beyond the reach of law enforcement. I was told that, not infrequently, hundreds of thousands of pounds would be stored in the vault, free from grasping hands, whilst prison sentences were served.

The security and process integrity was flawless and impressive; on par with anything one might see in the legitimate banking sector.

"You'll get fifty the week before the hit," said Kenny. "The rest will be kept in this vault. As soon as death is confirmed, you'll receive a code number, entitling you to collect your outstanding balance."

The buzz of my imminent windfall was exhilarating; it was still three or four weeks before I'd be pulling the trigger.

The night arrived. I dressed in a dark blue boiler suit, imitating a workman, with smarter clothes underneath in preparation for a quick change and getaway. Then I nestled in the thick overgrowth, between two sycamore trees, half a mile from the victim's farmhouse, next to a vast array of daffodils. The contrast between nature's beauty, and the savagery I was about the unleash, couldn't have been more stark. I'd chosen a spot with a wide view of the surrounding area, and which was roughly horizontal to the property (this was important since it meant, as a novice sniper, I didn't need to adjust for the effect of gravity on a bullet as it travelled through the air).

My scouting had revealed the victim to be a man of habit. Bang on cue, just before six in the evening, his Land Rover turned into the track connecting his property to the outside world. The vehicle moved slowly as it approached the farmhouse; the track was bumpy and waterlogged, and, as the fatal moment drew near, I felt perspiration on my upper back and forehead. A few beads of sweat dripped into my right eye, blurring my vision, and I wiped my eyelid vigorously with the back of my glove. It would just be a couple of minutes until he reached the yard; I needed my eyesight sharp as I pulled the trigger.

Moments later, the victim swung his legs out of the Land Rover, and his face came into view of the cross hairs on the telescopic sight. The magnification was uncanny – the stubble on his chin, a scab on his upper lip, grey flecks within the hair, all were visible with crystal clarity, as if he was sitting right across a table. My heart was pounding, loudly and wildly.

The victim was alone – nobody who might be hit by a stray bullet, or who could raise the alarm before I'd had the chance to flee.

"Here we go, Lennox," I said to myself, and pulled on the trigger, sharply and firmly.

I'd been advised that a headshot was unnecessary. The chest provides a larger target, and impact is equally terminal, so the rules of effective marksmanship would logically require me to lower my sights by around twelve inches. it looks so much easier in a war movie but in reality it was totally different.

As the bullet hurtled from the barrel, I'd expected a couple of seconds would pass before impact, as if I was shooting clays on a range; so I was astonished that the result was, quite literally, instantaneous.

There wouldn't be any need for a closer inspection to know whether death had occurred; it was gorily self-evident.

At least, this is how I'd imagined events might unfold, during a frantic and intense dream, two days beforehand.

Everything had, I assumed, been progressing smoothly, Big Hamish called with unfortunate news.

The job had been called off. The reasons were vague, apparently the client was "having second thoughts" about the money involved. I pleaded to speak directly with Kenny – "I'm sure we can work out a deal that'll get the price to an acceptable level" – but Big Hamish wouldn't be moved. Moreover, Kenny hadn't provided me with his own address or phone number, so there was no opportunity to go over Big Hamish's head (this hadn't seemed an issue at the time, but I was cursing myself for being so foolish – why would I not ask for his direct line?).

Was money the real issue? Or had somebody – perhaps superior to Kenny – got cold feet? Had they grown nervous at my status as a person "known to the police"? That a few of my brushes with the law had made the press?

Or the fiasco around the travel agency job?

I realised I'd only seen Sticks once since that night, having gotten used to bumping into him on a daily basis. Had the job been a cover for something else? Perhaps the safe had contained something other than simply cash, and Sticks had been the only one with knowledge of the real purpose?

Or perhaps that was my cannabis-induced paranoia speaking?

I never uncovered the full story; and, to be honest, at the time, I couldn't care less. The immediate concern was my precarious financial predicament, which required my full attention. I'd been snookered; the job had vanished like a puff of smoke, before I'd even received the stage of one payment. I had no alternative but to face the debts I'd incurred in expectation of a sudden windfall.

12.
Pulled Deeper

I was going through a phase when everyone wanted me to bust open safes.

The labour exchange pub had a vendetta against the drinking establishment next door – something petty, probably related to "pinching punters". One weekend, while the neighbour's son was in temporary charge (his parents were in the Costa del Sol), the bosses at my place paired me up with a known football hooligan called Hookie Tom, and "suggested" we might like to raid the place a few hours after last orders. Hookie was the type of repeat offender who could never be mistaken for an angel, looking every inch the thug he was. Eyes sunken and hair receding from a crack cocaine addiction, he'd provoke a fight in an empty room. In fact, that wasn't far from the truth – he was once arrested for crossing the road in an aggressive manner (Or "causing affray" as it said on the warrant sheet).

Since the break-in would take place "on our patch", I figured it would be prudent to be masked. Initially, we pulled stockings over our heads, but realised that wasn't the wisest strategy when I asked Hookie "How do I look?" and he said, "You look like Lennox wearing a stocking!" Instead, we bought a couple of woolly jumpers from a charity shop and cut them into the shape of balaclavas, complete with eye slits. Unfortunately for us, I don't think Blue Peter ever taught the nation's youth the science of balaclava creation, and the fit was terrible. Even worse, the eye slits kept rotating around my face – leaving me blinded, but with my left ear on proud display!

As soon as we'd forced our way in through the side door of the neighbouring pub, Hookie and I went our separate ways. He searched around for any loose cash, while I woke the son from his slumber, to force out of him the safe's combination number. He decided to play the tough guy – "I ain't telling you nuthin!" – leaving me with no choice but to beat the details out of him with a rounders' bat.

In the darkness, and with my ill-fitting balaclava, striking the target was complicated, and so I needed to roll my mask back above my eyebrows whenever I was preparing to land a blow. This immediately compromised my identity – "Lennox, I know you," he spluttered. Strangely, when he later tried to explain the scenario to the court, it sounded so improbable they gave it no credibility. "No burglars are that stupid!" was my solicitor's caustic response. I was saved from prison because my level of incompetence defied credibility.

Eventually, my bat won the day, and the son complied with our orders.

The safe contained five grand, which Hookie and I shared out equally. We spent the next fortnight lying low in Blackpool, only returning to Oxford when the kerfuffle died down – although Hookie couldn't resist drawing attention to himself on the promenade, and even on the pier, flouncing around off his head with drink or drugs. His behaviour caused me such angst and embarrassment that I felt no guilt about keeping secret from him the fact I'd found an additional three grand hidden in a chest of drawers on the landing.

My windfall was carefully deployed across a portfolio of investments – including fancy clothes and some high-grade cannabis, and I never mentioned it to a soul. Not my then-girlfriend, not my drug-dealing gang associates, not the pub owner who'd put me up to it. In fact, the only way Hookie would ever have found out would be if he's reading this book. (Message to Hookie: We're surely past the stature of limitation by now, so please don't pop up with an "in arrears" claim for your half!)

*

I was learning that the money I earned, either in Garrett's drug gang or from my own endeavours, rose in proportion to the risks I ran and the extremes of violence I was prepared to threaten. So my debts forced me to push the boundaries a little bit further, growing more reckless and impetuous as each day passed.

For some adventures, my trusty lock knife wouldn't always be sufficient, so I decided to stock up on my collection of firearms – not a sniper rifle this time, but guns that had more practical, everyday uses. A firearms dealer in Rugby was recommended to me, and I spent a pleasant Saturday afternoon inspecting his catalogue and testing out some of the products.

On this occasion, there were no day trips to the woods. I preferred to trial the weapons on live subjects so I could gain a real-life understanding of how people reacted. I found a little-used alleyway in Castle Street, Oxford, and attacked a man in his mid-thirties with a stun gun, as he was enjoying an evening stroll. As he writhed on the ground, I was oblivious to his screams of pain; I'd gathered useful information which would be of great value when the time came to use a stun gun to extract information from a victim while a proper job was underway.

I'd taken possession of my stun gun, but I still hadn't figured out how to get my personal finances onto an even keel after the racehorse fiasco. Around thirty-five thousand had been blown on indulgences from cannabis to alcohol to criminal paraphernalia such as walkie talkies and guns – which would often be abandoned when making a speedy getaway.

Over the next few weeks, the jobs came thick and fast, but none of them proved as rewarding as hoped, and my desperation grew.

When your luck turns down, disasters seem to follow one another in quick succession. I joined Aaron in the hold-up of a bank branch in a Wiltshire village – we'd selected the site due to the lack of security and skeleton staffing. Everything ran smoothly; the two cashiers were horrified and intimidated by our balaclavas and handed over bags contained twenty thousand pounds without a whimper. But the joke was on us when it came to count the payload – a dye-pack burst over the entire harvest, covering the notes with a luminous pigment.

I'm one of the few people in England who knows how it feels to set fire to a stack of genuine, Bank of England issued banknotes, and watch booty that's worth more than the average household earnings transform into slivers of ash and disappear into the upper atmosphere on an autumnal breeze.

The following week, an attempted heist was foiled since we had a police informant in our midst. IRA bomb warnings had become a daily nuisance in London, and could be guaranteed to divert police resources. We reasoned that, by calling in a threat, a jewellery shop we were targeting would be temporarily unguarded, however, despite a cordon, the cops were wise to our antics. We escaped arrest without even a bangle for our troubles.

*

Re-establishing yourself after a spell inside is an onerous, arduous chore, the career equivalent of ice-skating uphill. Employers have scant interest in hiring anybody with a rap sheet – especially one with "Dartmoor" at the top. Personal contacts go cold with the passage of time, and relationships suffer (Natalie hadn't bought Karen to visit me in Dartmoor, citing the inconvenience of the journey during her hectic life). In fact, there's only one sphere in which your reputation will have held steady, and that's amongst the criminal fraternity. So all paths led me back to the labour exchange pub, where I could hustle for contracts.

One evening, a nervous man wearing bifocals was pointed in my direction.

He'd recently been made redundant, and – approaching his sixtieth birthday – had given up hope of finding alternative employment. But he did have something of considerable value – details, including the combination number, of his ex-employer's Grade 5 rated safe (the grading refers to the maximum insurance value of items that can be left within the safe; a 5-rating allows for cash up to £100,000, and valuables up to a cool million). Gleefully, we shook on how we'd divide the spoils, and I assembled the old crew for their next mission.

The information turned out to be spot-on, but incomplete. "Bifocals-man" had been unaware that a silent alarm would be triggered in the event of unauthorised after-hours access to certain rooms, and we were still fiddling with the safe's locking mechanism when Drake pointed out the reflection of a blue flashing light. Not for the first time, a well-crafted plan was spontaneously abandoned, and we legged it for the rear exit. As I vaulted over the car park wall, I was horrified to spot Big Hamish – who was meant to have been on lookout – casually chatting into his mobile phone, oblivious to our jeopardy.

Drake and I hid in a nearby alleyway but I was fuming at my narrow escape, and Big Hamish's lazy attitude. Arrest would've been the least of my problems; I'd have been caught in flagrant breach of my parole conditions, which would've meant instant recall to the Dartmoor's frigid, foreboding embrace. And that would've meant another year without seeing Karen.

A familiar knotty sensation was flaring up in the pit of my stomach. My rage was, once again, swelling, and this time Big

Hamish – my former connection into London's organised crime syndicates – was the clear and present target.

"We'll teach him a lesson," I said to Drake. "But let's be savvy about it, and not show our hand too early."

"Agreed," said Drake. "I'll follow your lead."

I called Big Hamish on his phone and suggested a get-together "to talk urgently", without mentioning a word about having wised-up to his dereliction of duty.

"Sure," he said, "Pick me up in fifteen at the usual place."

When we arrived, Big Hamish was apprehensive, but sat between Drake and Aaron in the back of the car, and, as we drove off, peppered us with questions about our destination like a tiresome child asking parents, "Are we there yet?" I stopped at a nearby station and topped up the tank with a few gallons as a ploy to fill up two Jerry-cans with petrol. Three miles outside Oxford, we approached the ascent to some woodlands, and Big Hamish realised this couldn't possibly be the location of another job, and demanded:

"What the f-, man?" said Big Hamish. "What's this all about?"

I parked off-road by a small forest in which later found fame as the title of a track of the album Supergrass. But rock melodies were far from my mind that night.

Big Hamish was growing more agitated by the moment. As I frog-marched him into the forest, he started blinking manically, his nose twitching in harmony.

"Now, kneel," I ordered, as we reached a clearing.

"Don't do this," he said. "Lennox, you don't want to do this."

I smashed my fist against the bridge of his nose. He gulped in pain. Then I motioned for Drake to join in the fun, and he kicked Big Hamish in the groin with the tip of his boot. Another yelp, then a snivel.

"Please, Lennox, we've worked well together. We've had good times."

Drake handed me the jerry can, and I disdainfully tipped the petrol over Big Hamish's head. It gushed down his body, drenching his clothes, until he looked like somebody who'd just been caught in a rough storm. Some of the petrol had seeped into his mouth, and he spat it to the ground, still blinking and twitching.

"That's no good to me," I said. "You've let me down. You didn't do the job you were meant to do."

"Lennox – I beg, please, Lennox. You can't do this. You're not a killer."

I struck a match, and held it at an angle so the flame burnt high and wide.

"I'll give you any money you want, Lennox. For both you and Drake. Anything. Name your price."

Drake perked up at this prospect, but said nothing.

"I'll say nothing, Lennox," he was blubbering now. "This whole thing, this has just been you and me, right? Old pals having a lark. It's our secret."

The flame had almost reached my forefinger, so I blew it out, and lit another. The matchbox was brim-full; if I had the time and inclination, this could continue all night. In the meantime, Big Hamish's pleas were increasingly desperate, as he struggled for the form of words that might save his life.

The begging was nauseating. I extinguished the second flame, and dropped the spent match to the dirt.

"C'mon, Drake," I said, "We got better things to do than waste time with this loser."

As we strode back towards the layby, Big Hamish's whimpering was still ringing in our ears.

"Thank ye, thank ye, thank ye."

But we never did see the money he'd promised – rumour had it that he fled to Spain shortly afterwards, and our paths never again crossed.

*

Being active in the drug dealing gang gave me exceptional access to high quality cannabis, and I was increasingly unable to resist its allure.

My use of the drug escalated from a recreational to an industrial scale; I'd light a spliff when I was with friends at the Caribbean club, with criminal associates at the labour exchange pub, or on my own in my flat. I smoked when I was cheerful, and when I was depressed; when I was stressed and when I was chilled; whether I felt romantic or aggressive. Essentially, any mood that struck me was used as justification to light up. More than once, struggling with my addiction, I'd flush my entire supply down the toilet in the morning, only for the craving to return after lunch, prompting me to buy replacement stock. I was decimating not only my mind but my wallet.

The toll taken by cannabis varies sharply from user to user. With me, it was a catalyst to intense feelings of paranoia. I'd mistake harmless Labradors for Rottweilers about to pounce at me and tear out my throat. I became convinced that the residents of the upstairs flat were stalking and taunting me (on the farcical basis that I felt they were arranging their rubbish for collection by the Council in an "aggressive manner"), and created a spear out of a knife and a hoover tube – only to discover, when I confronted my supposed antagonists, that the upstairs flat was occupied by a single mum in her early twenties and her five-year-old daughter.

Worst of all, I was unable to hold down a job – even on the rare occasions I managed to blag an employer into offering me gainful employment. Once, I talked my way into employment in a care home for adults with severe learning difficulties, often caused by brain damage during their early years such as oxygen deprivation at the moment of birth. (The gift-of-the-gab was a vital benefit during the interview process, though it was also assisted by forged qualification and employment documents.) Left in sole charge of the home one night, the cannabis triggered an episode which shames me to this day.

One of the patients was restless, and started spouting nonsense at the top of her voice:

"What's yer name?"

Then she screamed.

I lost it. "F-ing shut up!" I yelled in her face. "Just f-ing shut up."

The scene, if anyone had chosen that moment to wander in, would have been surreal – a carer shouting at a service user who can't help her outbursts.

And then, my body went cold. I was the responsible adult, charged with the responsibility – the awesome privilege – of caring for these brave, tragic, wonderful people. How could I have exploded with such rage, as if I was dealing with some lowlife in the drug-dealing gang?

It was a humiliating, humbling realisation, and I was overwhelmed with self-disgust. I was unworthy of my role; I was unfit to bathe and feed and comfort the people in my care. How could I be trusted to deal with complicated situations; to calm down rather than escalate. There was a simple answer – I couldn't trust myself. The residents were blameless; my temper and rage and mood swings resulted from my pathetic lifestyle, not any fault on their part. The next day, appalled and heartbroken, I fabricated a reason to resign my post.

Once again, the pathway to a better life had stretched tantalisingly before me; once again, I'd fallen at the first hurdle.

*

I wouldn't be able to move on with my life until I closed the book on Thomas Brown. Despite my therapy, the horror of that day lingered. He had been in my head throughout my time with Julie, and when I'd held my own young children Mark and Karen, and during my month of solitary confinement in HMP Oxford's Punishment Wing.

There were so many unanswered questions – Why had he abused me? Was I the only one? Why did he send a glowing testimonial to the court during my first trial? Did he feel remorse or sorrow for what he'd done?

Most importantly, I didn't want my future years to be clouded by the prospect of renewed contact from him – perhaps during another trial, once my latest crimes caught up with me. Boundaries needed to be established. That was the priority – boundaries. Clear boundaries. Then we'd both know where we stood.

Brown continued to prey on my mind, and, one March morning, I resolved: "This is the day. I won't come home today until I've got things sorted."

Brown didn't flinch a muscle when he opened his front door, and found me standing inches before him. He invited me in, although – unlike back in the 1970s – there was no offer of tea and a sandwich.

"Why did you do it?" I demanded. "Why did you write to the court?"

I'm not sure what I was hoping he'd say. Probably something like, "I'd done you wrong, and wanted to make amends." Instead, he mumbled something bland and forgettable.

I could take it no longer. This had all been a mistake, and I turned to leave – only to find that Brown had locked the front door. As I faced him, he cocked his head to one side, staring but saying nothing, his eyes wide with lust.

"Open the door now," I shouted.

Brown said nothing but continued his stares, unfazed by my anger.

"Hopen dis bloodclaaat door now ya ere mi sah," I said, my voice deeper.

("Open the f-ing door now. Do you hear me. Sir?")

This time, my intimidation had the desired effect. But I couldn't shake the conviction that I needed to end matters once and for all.

A week passed, and Brown's stares were still haunting me.

Knowing he was a keen cyclist, it occurred to me there was a foolproof way to end his life – one that, in the unlikely event it was traced back to me, could credibly be excused as an accident. I'd orchestrate a chance encounter between his bike and my car that'd leave him in a crumpled and bloodied heap at the side of the road. I waited across from his house for two hours after sunrise until he emerged, wheeling his bike. I watched intently as he fastened his clips, and started peddling. My course was set, and nothing would dissuade me. I steeled myself to hit the accelerator and speed off in pursuit.

But I'd counted without the infernal mobile phone ringtone! (In those days, phones were yet to become an ever-present accessory; mine had been in the glove compartment, forgotten, all morning.) It was my sister, calling unprompted, to ask how I was, and let me know she'd been praying for my wellbeing. The moment was wrecked as she chuntered on about God and faith. A possible trial was avoided, and Brown survived for an underserved twenty more years.

*

Elsewhere in Oxford, Garrett was still sharpening his strategy to take over other gangs within the city. He'd reluctantly accepted the Indians were too hot to handle, but that didn't undermine the entire scheme; it simply led to different priorities. He was now focused on overcoming, one way or another, a long-tentacled gang led by two Jamaicans on the estate in North Oxford, which specialised in high grade cocaine and weed imported direct from their mother country.

"Jarek and Steve are a problem, Lennox, we need to take 'em out," he said, not for the first time. "Either that or persuade them to work for us."

"You must be kidding!" I replied. "I'm not taking these guys out just because they won't sell for you."

"But there's no one better than you to get them onside."

"Walking up to Jarek's front door for a nice chat? 'Hi Jarek, how about you hand over your business to us – we'll treat you nice, we promise.' – you think that'll work?"

The sarcasm oozed from the tongue.

"I'm not sure you should phrase it quite like that."

Garrett dropped the topic for a few weeks, but he hadn't abandoned hope, and knew exactly how to press my buttons. Our next meeting was back at the club.

"Lennox," he said, "I've come across some very disturbing information."

"I'm not surprised; there's a lot of creeps on the streets."
"But this time it's not your regular punks. It's about Jarek."
"Jarek?"
"You know, the Jamaican gang leader. From Blackbird Leys."
"What you heard?"
"It's not rumours, it's facts. He's been pushing to kids."

I bristled. I'd seen plenty of adults wreck their lives through drug dependency, but even the most corrupt, roughest gangs in London's East End knew that, with children, it usually leads to an early grave. Time for the Robin Hood of crime to come to the rescue, dispensing my unique brand of vigilante justice!

"That's crossing a line."
"I was shocked," said Garret, "But there can be no doubt. He's getting them hooked on weed and then quickly progressing to heavy duty cocaine."
"You sure it's kids?"
"Eight years old, nine years old. It's disgusting."
"What do you need me to do?"

Like a fly in the web of a black widow, I was trapped. Two days later, I'd teamed up with my crew to storm Jarek's home, a semi near the edge of Blackbird Leys, late one evening when his guard would be down.

We were armed to the rafters – Aaron and Drake tucked revolvers under their belts, while I made sure my loyal and long-serving Japanese lock knife was sharpened and ready for the cause safely tucked away in my budgie smugglers underpants. To avoid the risk of early detection, we parked a block away from the target, and strode purposefully towards the property. Fixated on the job at hand, it didn't occur to us that our balaclavas might attract attention.

Little did we know that, at the time, Jarek was under heavy police surveillance, and our every move was being noted by two curious officers in a nearby hideout. No doubt they were thrilled at the sight of looming action – most surveillance ops involve hours of monotony and drudgery. That's why they immediately took the shrewd precaution of summoning heavily armed reinforcements.

There were a few short moments to take advantage of the element of surprise. We stood in formation at Jarek's front door; myself in midfield with Aaron and Drake playing wingers. Drake and Aaron had donned their balaclavas – not just to conceal our identities, but also to increase the sense of horror. I didn't wear anything to conceal my identity; I was there to serve justice.

The plan was straightforward. Knock, wait for the slightest opening, then barge in.

It worked like a dream; Jarek's head was still spinning as the three of us piled into the hallway. Drake and Aaron shoved the barrels of their guns into his face and I swept nick-nacks from his shelves and pictures from his walls in a display of contemptuous power.

We were all doing our own thing. The others had no interest in interrogating Jarek and, having locked Jarek's girlfriend Nicky in the bathroom, we searched the property for valuables. Which left me paired with Jarek. I jabbed my knife to his throat, shoving him into the dining room, where I made him sit at the table, and tied his arms to the back of the chair with coarse, thick sisal rope.

"Make sure your guys don't lay a finger on Nicky," said Jarek. "Or you'll regret it."

Drug dealers can be notoriously sentimental about their ladies, and fear for how she'd be treated would be a valuable spur to securing compliance.

"You're in no position to make threats," I said.

"No? Look at you. Waving yer stupid lock knife around like yer a professional. I know who you are. Yer one of Garrett's boys. He send you?"

I needed to take control of the conversation – at the moment, Jarek was mouthing off, as if I was the one strung up like a chicken.

"You been supplying kids," I said. I meant it as a statement, but Jarek treated it as a question.

"Don't be so stupid. Why would I do that?"

"I know you been. Everyone knows it."

"One – that ain't my style. Two – there ain't no money in it. How they gonna pay me – with the pocket money they earn from their newspaper round?"

I couldn't believe what I was hearing. I was already convinced Jarek was the poisoner-in-chief of Oxford's kids. Now, he was adding the crime of brazenly lying to my face.

"I'm not listening for your stories," I barked. "You'd say anything to get me outta yer hair. I know exactly what type of person you is. Yer scum, that's what you is."

He spat on the floor. "It's been a pleasant discussion, but I got no more to say. So why don't you and yer boys lot me free, leave Nicky alone, and we'll pretend this never happened."

If there was one certainty in my life at that moment, it was Jarek wouldn't be left alone. I called out for Aaron. Having quarantined

Nicky, he'd been charged with rifling through the regular hiding places – behind the fridge, underneath piles of clothes in the chest of drawers, within reach of the attic trap door – to gather up anything of value. He answered my summons immediately, and handed over two holdalls. I turned the first upside down, and tipped out dozens of small grip seal bags, each packed with white powder.

"What's all this?" I gave Jarek an accusatory stare.

"What you think?" he said.

I dipped my finger into one of the bags, and lifted a few granules of the powder to my tongue. It tasted bitter, like vinegar – unmistakably heroin.

"It's high grade stuff," said Jarek. "From the best poppy plants, and cut with starch. You want some on the house?"

"You bastard," I said, "This is the stuff you been pushing to kids."

"Listen, brother – okay, I got a heroin stash. That ain't news. Everyone on Blackbird Leys knows that's my business. How does that prove anything about kids? I'm just a regular professional!"

He was messing with my head, saying anything to confuse me. It was shameless, audacious; but it wouldn't work.

I grabbed one of the heroin bags, tore it open, and poured the heroin into a pile in front of Jarek. Then, another bag. And another.

"What ya think yer doin?" said Jarek.

I moulded the heroin until it was shaped like a mountain, as if it was a scene from Scarface played by Robert De Niro, then grabbed Jarek by the ponytail and pushed his face into it until his nose was smeared in powder.

"You're going ta eat this up," I hissed.

"What the f-, man?" he said.

"All of it!"

"You gotta be kidding, man, that'll kill me!"

"That's what yer doing, peddling to kids. Now it's payback time."

Jarek had been eerily composed when we'd stormed the house, and threatened him with guns and knives. Now, for the first time, there was a hint of panic in his eyes. My word and tone left no room for ambiguity. This wasn't a sadistic game or perverse roleplay; I was serious in expecting him to binge on the opioid until he had the Guinness World Record of overdoses, while I chilled in the corner, feet up, watching the entertainment. I had a general idea of what to expect. Initially, he'd be agitated by the warm flushing of his skin, and weird sensations in his toes and fingers. This would be followed by severe itching, nausea and vomiting. Then his breathing and heartrate would slow, his brain functions would start shutting down, he might slip into a coma. And, all the time, I'd be watching the entertainment, encouraging Aaron or Drake to force-feed him the remainder of the mound if he was losing consciousness.

Which was when events took a bizarre turn.

Jarek, one of Oxford's most depraved and malicious drug dealers, had his life saved by the boys in blue.

We froze for a few seconds and then, in mad panic, the three of us belted up the wooden stairs, like a pack of galloping horses. Without hesitating, both my companions leapt through the bedroom window, landing painfully in the bushes.

A policeman yelled, "They're round the back," and the chase was underway.

Drake was first out of the traps, clambering over a couple of fences to put distance between himself and Jarek's place. Aaron wasn't so fast but gained the upper hand by kick-boxing three police officers, knocking one to the ground and pistol-whipping him brutally in his face. He was overpowered as a horde of officers piled on top of him. I'd seen enough; my escape route was cut off, so the only option was to hide – and the only practical hiding place was a large wardrobe which, as it turned out, belonged to Nicky, and was filled with all sorts of clothes and smelt of Chanel Number 5.

I made a gap in the rail of dresses, skirts, blouses, jackets and coats and knelt at the back covered with any random clothes I could grab. For the next four and a half hours, I moved not a muscle as the police scoured the property; I even resisted the involuntary urge to sneeze as the perfume scents invaded my nostrils.

Eventually, the noise abated. Jarek was taken away for questioning, the downed officer was raced to A&E, and the world outside was stilled and peaceful. Still, like a zoo animal chained to a rock, I daren't move; riveted in my position, terrified lest even my breathing betray my hiding place.

Which was a grievous error. Because, not schooled in police procedure, I'd overlooked the role played by the Scene Of Crime Officers. Long after the pandemonium and excitement has subsided, the SOCO's duty is to visit a location and conduct a painstaking inspection, checking every square inch for evidence. And the presence of a big wooden wardrobe in the corner of the bedroom did not escape their attentions.

I knew the game was up when I heard the screech of the wardrobe door being opening. The sudden light, piercing through the thin materials covering me, was dazzling. I stood to surrender, but the SOCO officers stumbled backwards in fear – all they saw was levitating clothes, as if a poltergeist was in the room. When they'd regained their composure, they backed off like a Kung Fu master ready for action and pulled away the layers of clothes with outstretched hands to reveal the third attacker.

"How long have you been there?" they demanded.

"I don't bloody know."

Long enough that I was hit by cramp from my sudden movement. I staggered from the wardrobe and fell headfirst onto a shag-pile rug. There was no getting away this time.

13. Deals

The high farce of my poltergeist capture was eclipsed by the injuries Aaron had inflicted when he'd pistol-whipped an officer. The victim tragically lost one of his eyes, and had to retire from frontline police duties.

It was a stark reminder that our gang violence didn't exist in a self-contained bubble; it often spilt over and delivered life-changing damage to people who had simply been doing their job to protect the public. Aaron showed no signs of remorse; in fact, he charmed his girlfriend – who was an administrator at the hospital where surgeons had battled to save the officer's eye – into accessing the medical files for additional details, including information about his close relatives and home address.

The data breach was soon uncovered, the girlfriend was fired, and Aaron's declining influence in the gang – he was facing a jail term of at least ten years – meant his attempts to organise "intimidation" were ignored. He was left with no outlet for his obsessive hatred of the police except for verbal abuse ("Go suck yer mudda" was a choice favourite). The entire saga did, however, provide me with a silver lining; the various branches of law enforcement rallied round to ensure the stiffest possible penalty was meted out to Aaron, and my own participation in the break-in flew somewhat underneath the radar.

Even had the prosecution wished to throw the book at me, it would've been an uphill task when their star witness chose not to incriminate me.

Jarek was one of my earliest visitors while I was serving time on remand at Bullingdon. When the screws told me who'd turned up, I figured it was to gloat or mock, but instead he said:

"I told 'em you'd turned up at my place for a social."

"Oh," I replied, almost speechless. Surely there was a catch.

"It wasn't that hard. They recovered two guns and two balaclavas. So there's no evidence pointing to a third intruders. I said you was guilty of nothing worse than popping round for a spliff."

He seemed to be on the level.

"Please, I'll do anything you want," he continued. "Just tell me what you want me to do and I'll do it."

After various discussions, Jarek agreed to sign a statement vindicating me of any wrongdoing, duly witnessed and countersigned. As a bonus, I also persuaded him to deliver a quarter ounce of heroin to me in jail – his hands got dirtier and my pockets got richer. He complied without a hint of protest.

Jarek's continuing denials about dealing to kids played on my mind. In the cold light of day, his words had the ring of truth. Also, had he been guilty, surely he wouldn't be riding to my rescue; he'd want me off the streets for the longest possible stretch. I needed to get to the bottom of matters. I called Garret from a prison payphone – reckless about whether the authorities were monitoring the conversation – and levelled the charge:

"Be honest with me. That whole story about Jarek and children. Was there any truth in it whatsoever? Or was it a figment of your imagination? Your perverted imagination?"

"Why d'ya need to know?"

"It doesn't hold true, not after what I've been through. Was it fact, or did you make it all up? Tell me now!"

"Thing is," said Garret, "I know how soft you is 'bout kids. It's obvious every time you talk about yer own kids, or yer girlfriend's kids."

"You admit it, then, do ya? It wasn't rumours after all."

"Bro," said Garret, "Think about it from my side. How else was I going to persuade ya to do the job? Ya kept saying no."

Did he think a half-hearted attempt at reason would wear me down?

"F-, man, that ain't the point. I nearly killed someone cos of what you said. Now you telling me somethink different."

"We'll all gain when we put Jarek's operation outta business. Not just me, but everyone in the gang. Yer already doing great for us on the inside. You been supplying two hundred quid a day around Bullingdon; that's more'n most of my solders deliver here on the outside."

"F- that, and f- yer two hundred quid. I can't trust anything you say to me, never again. I can't be on yer team if there's no trust. You didn't do one thing to help with my statement so you could keep me in prison earning money for you – and now I find out that my ha-ha trusted friend has set me up. You're dead when I get out. F-ing dead!"

Garrett was rattled.

"Lennox, don't be hasty." He was speaking softly now, but it would take more than a quieter tone to dim my fury.

"Get the f- out of my life!" I shouted, "I'm done with this shit!"

And with those words, my years with Garret's drug-dealing gang came to an abrupt halt. My roles in enforcement and distribution had been occasionally exhilarating, and sometimes lucrative; but many weeks were devoid of any glamour, and a far cry from the world of the Sopranos. Much of my energy had been exhausted dealing with lowlifes and drudgery; threatening violence – and sometimes following through – but usually I'd squander whatever wealth I accumulated and end up almost as broke as when I started a job. Where was the high life? The private jets? The suitcases packed with crisp, maximum denomination notes? The horny supermodels?

I'd given Garret some of my best years, and all I had left was a terrible sense of unfulfilled potential. Emptiness, solitude and waste.

Two days later, Aaron – also on remand at Bullingdon – approached me in the corridor, and let fly a stream of verbal abuse – starting with the insult "Batty Boy!" (he had a vague awareness that I'd been a sexual abuse victim, although I'd never confided any details). In any event, something about his language convinced me Garret had gotten to him, manipulating my co-conspirators as he'd once manipulated me. I felt my fists clenching, and, out of the corner of my eye, spotted two burly prison officers turn their backs dismissively. Probably hoping I'd knock Aaron's lights out after the injury he'd caused. Then, Aaron lurched his head backward, gargled, and spat a clammy ball of saliva directly at my face. As it dribbled down my nose and cheek, I burnt with the desire to wrap both my hands around his scrawny neck, and yank it from side to side until it snapped. I tried to take one stride towards him but... I found I was unable to move my legs. They were literally inseparable from the concrete floor. The more I struggled to pull free, the more immobile I became, I thought "God, what's going on?" All I could do was sway inoffensively from side to side. Aaron watched my contortions with amusement.

"Yer a f-ing loser," he scoffed. "Always were, always will be."

In my mind, I called out to God, "Make him go away."

At that very moment, he marched away, head still firmly attached to his shoulders. Silence descended across the prison wing. Prisoners and staff looked on in disbelief. No longer stuck to the floor, I turned to walk back to my cell in humiliation. I was consumed by a sense of paranoia; I felt I could hear their thoughts. "Is this the guy everyone was so afraid of? What a joke."

That evening, I was approached by Chris Lambrianou, who had been a solider for the Kray twins in London's East End, and was serving fifteen years for his role in the death of Jack "The Hat" McVitie at a flat in Stoke Newington. McVitie had bungled a shooting and, after Reg Kray hacked him to death with a carving knife, Chris and his bother Tony had been charged with wrapping the body in bedspreads and ensuring its disposal.

When the Kray firm collapsed, the Lambrianous were caught within the net, but whilst many sang like canaries, the brothers remained staunch and true to their patrons throughout the trial. In jail, Chris had turned to Christianity, and he was eager to congratulate me on how I'd handled the confrontation with Aaron, and warded off an escalation that would've benefitted neither of us:

"I could see the devil wus trying to egg you to have a go. You wus a solid boy. Resisting temptation – that was a wonderful thing to do."

"Are you crazy or what? I wanted to knock his block off," I retorted.

"God was holding you back," he said. I reflected back on the sequence of events. Could there be any wisdom in his words?

As the trial date approached, my solicitor Wilson Carter – who had arranged my transfer to HMP Woodhill in Milton Keynes, far from Aaron – was in regular contact with the Crown Prosecution Service, and kept me appraised of any nuggets he gleaned.

With Aaron, their only dilemma was the severity of the charges to level: Section 18 Assault of A Police Officer, and/or aggravated burglary and assault with a firearm, and/or Attempted Murder?

In my case, it was nowhere near so cut-and-dried. Apparently, they'd toyed with "Joint enterprise", then with "Aggravated burglary", but the options either seemed too trivial, or too abstract. "Joint enterprise" is notoriously tricky to put forward for deliberation by juries, especially in the absence of corroborating witnesses or a confession.

Eventually, given the conflicting evidence, Wilson and my barrister Jackson Collins managed to negotiate a settlement which allowed me to walk free on the basis of time served. Jackson had a fine legal mind and rare ability to entrance and empathise with juries. I was always keen to have him on my side. Whenever he was defending me, he'd meet me for a briefing in the court cells and, before I was hauled off to the dock, invariably shake my hand and say, "Good luck." He should've been a silk in my view.

"Plead guilty and you'll be out tomorrow," he advised.

"But to what charge?"

"It's a technical charge and very hard to put into everyday language. Think of it this way – you're guilty of basically 'Being in the wrong place at the wrong time'. That's really what it amounts to. Nothing worse."

"You're sure I'll walk?"

"That's the offer."

"Cool, but it's the most bizarre charge I've ever faced."

"Sign the paper! If you want to moan about it, save it for your autobiography."

So that's what I did.

*

The "wrong place, wrong time" deal must have given me a taste for high stakes negotiations because, while my release was being processed, I opened diplomacy on a second front. I'd been chatting with a fellow inmate in the exercise yard – a guy called Daniel, with whom I'd been acquainted since Sunday School days. Daniel shared alarming information about developments in the case of the "travel agency" job which had led to the arrest of our stooge, the 18-year-old Neil, en route between safe houses with our loot.

Despite this being Neil's first offence, and notwithstanding the lack of evidence placing him at the actual crime scene, the prosecution had assigned some of their best people to ensure a conviction and tough sentence. Apparently the use of firearms, the timing (during office hours), and the brazen threats to members of the public, had turbocharged it up their priority list.

But worse news was to follow. Neil, whose identity I'd barely registered, was the cherished grandson of a close family friend who had shown me great kindness as a child – a wonderful gent who would be left devastated and distraught if his "lovely boy" was locked away at just the time when his life should be flourishing. I directed Wilson to do "whatever it takes" to protect Neil from that fate.

"We don't have a lot of cards to play," cautioned Wilson. "They have all the advantages."

"Wrong," I remarked. "I know a shit-ton about stuff where they don't have a clue."

"Stuff?"

"Things I've done. Unsolved cases. How we've gotten away with it. That sort of stuff."

Wilson furrowed his brow. "Let's make sure I correctly understand you, Lennox. You're prepared to talk about crimes that have never been pinned on you. Maybe that you've never been connected with."

"I'll admit to everything," I said. "But I won't incriminate anyone else. I'll draw the line at that."

"Are you sure about all this?"

"Deadly certain."

Wilson was doodling with his biro. "Professionally, I can't advise you to go down this route. In fact, I formally advise against it. You may be turning up stones that are best left in the ground."

"I hear you. But if it wasn't so important to me, I'd never consider it. Anyway it's my decision."

That very afternoon, Wilson sent word to the police that, "Subject to conditions to be agreed, my client wishes to speak about recently committed crimes of which he has first-hand knowledge."

The communication caught the attention of powerful people, and dawn had barely broken the next day before I was ushered into a windowless room in the prison, a few doors down from the visitors hall, which was set aside for legal visits. There, I met with a Detective Sergeant, a Detective Constable, and (of course) Wilson himself – who shivered slightly whenever I opened my mouth, fearing I might blurt our material that he'd never be able to "un-say". No prison officials were allowed inside the room.

My mind was made up. I expressed my intentions with clarity and precision, having had a few hours to contemplate the terms of a deal that should be acceptable to both sides.

"I'm prepared to make a full confession…"

Wilson fidgeted.

"…with very detailed information about my own role…"

Wilson squirmed.

"…sometimes violence was involved, sometimes theft, sometimes both…"

Wilson was spluttering into his tea.

"…all I need in return is confirmation, in writing, that charges against Neil will be dropped, and that I'm immune from prosecution for any of the crimes we cover…"

Wilson stared up at the ceiling, whistling under his breathe, as if he was wondering "How do I make this all stop?"

"...And, so long as I'm not asked to incriminate any accomplices, I'll answer any and all questions you might care to put."

I was embarrassed for Wilson and ashamed at myself because of the numerous times I had led him to believe I was innocent. Now, here I was proving myself a liar. I couldn't look him in the face especially when I started confessing to things. I wondered in passing whether he'd ever defend me again. He thought I was crazy but, as my lawyer, was willing to persist with the process.

He was also meticulous in ensuring the paperwork was one hundred per cent in order before any of my confessions were formalised. He wasn't prepared to take at face value the word of the people who had conducted the interview; he needed documents, signed by people in authority, without any weaselly get-out clauses, and insisted these were provided for review and counter-signature before any further meetings were scheduled. Eventually, wording was agreed to both parties' satisfaction, and he visited me to break the good news.

"Once again, it isn't the route I'd have recommended. But it's your choice, and your life, and my duty is to guide you legally, to the best of my ability, in the implementation of your choices. I've never seen documents as comprehensive as these ones. They provide you with the protection to confess, assuming no double-dealing on behalf of the police. If you answer these questions honestly and openly, the slate has been effectively wiped clean."

The scope of my confession was broad, covering all my activities since leaving St Edward's after my CSEs. Included in the mix were 22 armed robberies, multiple stabbings, thefts, frauds, assaults, drug dealing and possession, firearms discharge, and attempted murder. Was there a single offence on the statue book to which I hadn't pleaded guilty? (Apparently, it's illegal to operate a mineral detector in a national park without the permission of the Secretary of State; I didn't recall ever learning to operate such a device, so that's probably one law I can consider with a blissfully clear conscience!)

Cataloguing my confession took multiple meetings, and neither side was minded to shortcut the process. The police were captivated by every painstaking detail in my account; it was providing them with a rare, unabridged insight into the dodgy dealings, scheming and paranoid tightrope-walking that's ingrained in gang life and culture. I must've been a natural storyteller; they seldom needed to probe me for specifics – despite my years of cannabis use, I found the grim and gory details of all my crimes would pop back into my mind. It was as if I'd had a miniaturised court reporter lodged in my cerebral cortex, making blow-by-blow descriptions of every "what" and "where" and "how" and "why".

I also found the experience weirdly therapeutic and as if a weight had been lifted off my shoulders. Unlike in meetings of the drug-dealing gang, I was able to unload about my deeds and feelings without the lingering dread that, if I said a word out of place, my audience might leap across the room and whack me. The two detectives were intrigued rather than judgemental, and exuded calm reflection not simmering fury.

In the short-term, the legal system was true to its word. When Neil's day of destiny arrived, the facts of the case were laid out in front of the court – a series of exhibits including cash, guns, and disguises which had been found in the accused's possession when he'd been arrested red-handed within an hour of the robbery. The prosecution hadn't even begun to marshal its arguments, but already the material pointed overwhelming toward a guilty verdict.

At which point, the prosecution barrister rose before the court, tugged at his lapels, and announced pompously:

"May it please the court, we offer no evidence against this man."

I was sitting in court under guard because an application for bail was about to be granted me, and, as pandemonium erupted around me, I resisted the temptation to react (I'd had too many briefings about remaining emotionless at all times lest one provokes a Contempt of Court charge). As the judge struggled to exert some authority, reporters raced for the exits, eager to be the first to file their coverage; victims and their relatives were shocked and were verbally abusive and disruptive. Unable to control the public or press, the judge's recourse was to summon the barristers. "Into my chambers, now!" he barked. They bundled up their papers and did as bidden, but it was too late to change the glorious outcome for Neil. He'd now gotten his elusive second start in life; I'd be keeping my fingers crossed that he'd approach it with greater maturity and care than the first time around.

Absurdly, having agreed my deal, the next few months of my life were consumed with uncertainty and stress as the prosecution services combined with the police force to welsh on its terms. After Neil's acquittal, questions about the proceedings had been raised at the highest level – including Parliamentary Questions submitted to ministers by investigative backbenchers – and, once again, I felt the might of the State breathing down my collar. I was released on bail as various legal avenues and appeals were pursued, but with bail conditions so laughably extreme that, if all else failed, one might infer they'd try banging me up for twenty years due to an obscure bail transgression.

I navigated the line throughout this period to ensure there was no cause for anyone to re-arrest me, but it meant a regular existence was tricky, and the prospect of securing or holding down a decent job was essentially zero. I was required to remain at my home address between prescribed hours, and to make myself known at regular intervals at my local police station. I was well and truly grounded.

Ultimately, my fate lay in the hands of the High Court. I wasn't permitted to attend the hearing, so kept a low profile whilst Jackson Collins and the silks argued out their cases. Rather than work myself into supreme agitation, I spent quality time with my then-girlfriend's kids, remembering what it had been like to be a father to Karen and Mark. In my younger days, I might've been restless and unable to concentrate as I awaited the outcome, knowing a ten to twenty year sentence might hinge upon the court's deliberations. After everything else I'd seen, it took a lot to faze me.

Eventually, Wilson called me to announce that, after six months, "We won, Lennox; I have the judgment in writing. Your record is expunged."

As I lit a celebratory spliff, I felt a deep satisfaction knowing Neil was going to be fine, and that I had repaid the acts of kindness shown me as a child from his grandfather.

Wilson had been my rock – almost my father figure – during an unpredictable, bizarre and uncomfortable period of my life, often giving me personal (almost therapeutic) advice during the darkest times. Even when he regarded my actions as risky, he'd worked tirelessly for the best outcome. I couldn't have achieved the degree of closure to my wilderness years – the time I spent racing around at the orders of drug-dealing gang leaders and organised crime bosses – without his steadfast counsel.

The deal he'd negotiated prior to my confession had withstood scrutiny from the finest legal minds in the country – any oversight in the wording, and the document could've been ripped asunder, leaving me vulnerable to criminal and civil proceedings with my own signed statements used as evidence for the prosecution! I was fortunate our paths had crossed years beforehand when I'd first gotten myself into legal tangles; and luckier still that he'd remained at my side throughout my travails. I'd probably be staring at four walls today without the support of Wilson, Jackson and the third member of this legal team, Kayleigh Matthews – who was a remarkable substitute whenever the others were committed to other cases.

The only times I refrained from using this incredible team was when I was too ashamed to let them know what I was involved in and how low I'd sunk. I now send my thanks and fondest wishes to Wilson, Jackson and Kayleigh for their future. I was so glad that they were my defence and not my prosecution.

*

Wilson and I assumed there would be nothing racy about our next appointment with the police; it would simply be to follow-up on some bureaucratic formalities in the wake of the High Court decision. Therefore, we were both a little surprised to be greeted by a grim looking Deputy Chief Constable, who stroked his sideburns with increasing ferocity as he laid the groundwork for his announcement.

"I trust my officers to act with prudence and discretion at all times," he said.

What was this all about? Where was it heading?

"Every day we deal with multiple potential lines of enquiry, and have to make decisions about which could be spurious and which need to be checked out and verified."

I was shifting around impatiently in my seat. It was mid-Friday afternoon, and I had plans to go out pubbing and clubbing to celebrate my legal victory.

The Detective Chief Constable plunged his hand into his slimline attaché case, and produced a brown envelope which he waved before our faces.

"I'm not sure which of you should be given this for safekeeping," he said. I reached out my hand expectantly, but the document had already been handed to Wilson. "It's an official letter to you from the Thames Valley Police Service. I trust it's self-explanatory."

I turned to Wilson, who was unfolding the letter and turning ashen-faced. "What does it say?" I enquired.

Wilson rested his index finger at the start of the second paragraph and traced it along the line as he read. "It says [quote] We are writing to provide you with formal warning of a matter that has come to our attentions. We have received credible intelligence that…"

Wilson paused as he contemplated the rest of the sentence. "You're worrying me now," I said impatiently. "Tell me the rest."

"It says," continued Wilson, "[quote] We have received credible intelligence that a contract has been taken out on the life of Mr Lennox Rodgers and that money has already exchanged hands."

Bloody hell, I thought. "Is that it?"

"There's just one more sentence. [Quote] Mr Rodgers is hereby advised to leave Oxford for his own safety."

I turned to the Detective Chief Constable.

"Who told you this load of bullshit?"

"You know that I'm not at liberty to reveal my sources," he said, shaking his head. "But I kid you not, this isn't bullshit. I wouldn't be taking valuable time out of my day to warn you if I wasn't personally convinced of the information's veracity."

"And how can you expect me to leave Oxford? This is where I was born; this is where most of my family lives. Where should I go?"

"I'm sorry, Mr Rodgers, I'm not in the business of advising people where they should relocate. But I would strongly recommend it's as far from Oxfordshire as you can manage. And I don't mean a few miles the other side of the Gloucester border. Assassins don't respect county borders – with your background, that shouldn't come as a surprise. I mean proper 'far'."

My mind was buzzing with questions. Could I rely on this information? Who would've paid for the contract and why? How had the police obtained the intelligence? Could I count on their honesty – or, after the shenanigans about my "deal", might they be somehow involved (I knew some officers were notoriously trigger-happy) and were using the letter to protect their back should I be found floating in the Thames one morning? Most immediately, was there any risk that my closest relatives could be caught up in it – what if Julie or Angela, or my new girlfriend Rachel found themselves in the crossfire?

I sped to Didcot, a few miles south of Oxford, where Rachel lived in the shadow of the six hyperbolic cooling towers and the 650 foot chimney of the town's famous power station.

"Pack yer things, Rachel. We gotta get out of here."

But Rachel was a Glaswegian gal, stubborn as a mule, and wasn't about to relocate on her boyfriend's frenzied whim. She'd been forced to be tough and grow up fast as, when still young, she played mum to her brothers as her parents had wrecked their lives through alcoholism. Recently, she'd watched on helpless as her previous partner became addicted to glue and alcohol, spent most weekends high, and ultimately took his life after failing to save a friend who'd fallen into a river while they were both sniffing glue.

She told me to pull myself together, and stop infecting her life with my nonsense. So that was the end of another relationship. I'd developed the habit of losing girlfriends and wives in bizarre circumstances, but refusal to join me on the run from hired killers definitely takes the biscuit!

I was eager to verify for my own satisfaction the credibility of the threat to my life, so made a series of phone calls and enquiries to acquaintances who operated on the gangland periphery and would've surely picked up on rumours, had there been any substance. After tapping nearly a dozen sources (with extreme sensitivity – the last thing I wanted, for obvious reasons, was widespread gossip that, "Lennox has a price on his head!"), I was drawing a blank.

I was somewhat reassured the contract, if it existed, hadn't originated from within any of Oxford's gangs. So that left either the London organised crime network (seeking retribution for my assault on Big Hamish), or some deep throat within Thames Valley police (wanting to balance the score after my lucky escape in court). Or perhaps, as I convinced myself after an evening smoking cannabis, the two were working in cahoots. Whatever the truth, it probably wasn't wise to spend the next few months within easy reach.

Hell, if I was headed out of Oxfordshire, why not leave the UK behind. It was nearly ten years since my parents had returned to St Vincents; Dad had since passed on, but Mum was still fighting fit.

Perhaps it was time to step foot once more in the lands where, aged three, I'd been christened Cherry Boy.

14. Roots

I planned on staying in St Vincent for at least six months, which I judged would be sufficient for the 'contract on my life' to melt away. And there are plenty worse places on the planet to pass half a year. Lush vegetation, open skies, clean air, and barrel-loads of fresh fruit bursting with flavour – little wonder I was soon filled with a sense of wellbeing and rejuvenation.

News of my return to the island spread rapidly, and I was bombarded with invitations to meet family friends and enjoy fine Caribbean food – everyone was keen to see what "Cherry Boy" had made of his life. But the role of a "visiting celebrity" wasn't for me; instead, I threw myself into helping with chores on and around the house and lands.

In particular, I relished the chance to finally bond with my estranged mum. I was still burdened with memories of beatings at her hands, and her shouting "Tek im, tek im" on the night I'd been dragged from the family home by social workers to be placed into care.

But I had an unshakeable belief she was, at heart, a good person – she was my mum! – and, with Dad no longer with us, and benefitting from time's healing hands, surely we could rekindle a loving and respectful relationship. At first, the signs were positive. Mum prepared my room, washed my clothes, cooked nourishing meals – the typical things done by typical mums for typical sons. Daily breakfast was a Caribbean fry-up with hard-dough bread and a fresh coconut as a starter, washed down with a coffee or tea; the coconuts were green and I'd drink the milk then eat the fresh jelly at the bottom. Our dogs usually ate the coconutty interior. Some of Mum's habits were a little odd (she insisted I use the beige child's plastic cutlery that had been kept in a drawer since my infancy), but they were charming and endearing, rather than malicious.

So I chortled merrily, happily tucking into my meat and vegetables using nothing other than a four-inch-long child's fork.

I'd been on the island for nearly a month when the opportunity arose to discuss the childhood beatings with Mum. We'd spoken about many shared experiences without anger or blame, including relationships with my sisters, Oxford schooling, and stories involving my dad. But, unless we had an open and frank discussion about the beatings, they would always lurk in the recesses of my mind and it would be impossible to move on.

I wasn't sure exactly what outcome I expected – Was it an apology? A recognition of the hurt she'd caused? Might she open up about her own childhood on the island? Whatever the result, I wasn't afraid of dialogue. At Grendon, I'd participated in numerous group therapy sessions, often sitting with some of the most unpleasant people on Earth. I'd learnt to be comfortable with open discussion, and was able to talk about personal and awkward matters dispassionately, without emotional outbursts or leaps to judgement.

"Mum," I said one morning, trying to balance my cornmeal porridge on my kid-sized spoon. "I wanted to ask you about something."

"Gwarn bwoy."

("Go on, boy.")

"Do you remember that time, when I was eight years old. We were in the hallway, and you answered the phone. A girl from school was calling for me."

"Weh yo gwarn wid dis bwoy?"

("Where are you going with this, boy?")

"I remember it vividly. Her name was Andrea. She sounded like a nice girl."

"Bwoy yo mus lef dem tings in da parss."

("Boy, you must leave these things in the past.")

Her expression showed she was hurt that I'd brought this matter up.

"And I remember your words when you slammed down the phone. You said 'Bwoy, yo tink yar man?' You yelled it."

"Stop bwoy!"

"I'm not trying to blame you – I just need to understand. I just want to clear the air!"

My mum pressed the palms of her hands against her ears.

"LaLa," she sang.

"And then, Mum, you hit me. Not once, but many times. Two of my sisters were on the staircase watching, but that didn't stop you."

"LaLaLaLa," she intoned, her voice louder than before. "LaLaLaLaLaLaLaLa!"

"Then you called Dad and he came and took off his belt. He took me upstairs and he…"

"LaLaLaLaLaLaLaLaLaLaLaLa!"

"Mum," I shouted, "Listen to me. I want to talk with you about this. I need to talk with you about this."

She was shaking her head from side to side, raising her voice whenever she saw my lips move, drowning out my comments. I stood up.

"Listen to me!"

I grabbed her wrists to pulled her hands from the sides of her face, but she resisted fiercely.

Her face twisted into a scowl.

"Sit down, bwoy," she said. "You wus a narty bwoy. A narty bwoy! Anyting wah appen dat wus da reason."

Then she turned away from me and stormed into another room.

If I couldn't have a meaningful conversation with Mum, perhaps it'd be easier with my dad – especially since he'd passed away. I learnt that he was buried under a mango tree down the road in the grounds of our local Methodist church.

One day, I sat under the tree which sheltered the grave, gazing up at its broad, rounded canopy, nearly thirty feet off the ground. It was a typical mango tree, vibrant with colour – long, deep green leaves with light-hued veins, thousands of tiny bronze flowers, and new purple flushes scattered across the canopy.

At first, I didn't know what to say; then emotions welled within the pit of my being and I started sobbing. Although we'd reconciled, I was suddenly filled with remorse at missing out on a proper father-and-son relationship during my first twenty years.

"Why did you go? You could have waited! I told you I'd come. You could've taught me on the lands we could've explored the different islands of the Grenadines."

I lit a spliff and, and, as I smoked it, a mango fell from the tree, and hit my head. I caught it and bit deep into the fruit. It was delicious, and I whispered a thanks to Dad. "You heard me, you're listening."

The only answer was the whistle of the faint breeze through the tree's leaves.

"I'm sorry you died, Dad, and I'm really sorry I couldn't make it back before now. I've been busy. I'm ashamed to say what I've done but you probably knows anyway."

I sat pouring out my heart about everything I've done – the troubles, the broken relationships, and especially all about Karen and Mark. "I know I wasn't a perfect son. And I know there's lots of things we disagreed about, and lots of things I wish you'd never done. You probably think the same about me. But I'm pleased we were able to speak, as adults, when I came back from St Edward's. I'll never forget those chats we had and the time I tried to give you all that stolen money, before Mum sussed us out."

I smiled at the memory, even as tears welled in my eyes.

"I miss you, Dad. Despite everything, I really miss you. I wish you'd never left Oxford, and I wish you hadn't died, but I hope you're at rest now. And I hope that, despite all the drugs and the violence and the carnage, I've done a few things to make you proud. In the future, I hope to do more to make you proud. I miss you, I love you, rest in peace."

*

The following month, Mum took me to Little Tokyo, a fish market built by the Japanese near the war memorial, where the daily catch includes tuna, barracuda, grouper, mahi mahi and snapper. One of my mum's friends had recently opened a small restaurant, and we were tucking into roti stuffed with lamb and vegetables, when Mum pointed through the window at a lady in her forties, walking towards the bay with a group of young children.

"You should introduce yourself," she said. "She's your relative's daughter."

I watched from the restaurant window for minute or two, to see if I noticed any obvious family resemblance. When they reached the street corner, the woman sat on a step, and gathered the children around her to keep them safe from passing traffic. It was clear from her lovely, toothy smile, and the glint in her eyes, that she adored the kids – a dedicated, salt-of-the-earth Caribbean mum.

We caught up with them after we finished our meal. "Hi, my name's Lennox," I said, holding out my hand.

The lady stood up, and introduced herself and the children.

"I'm visiting from England, and this is my mum with me."

"I've always wanted to travel. Hopefully one day I'll have the opportunity."

She smiled wistfully.

I'd known her for just a couple of minutes, but already I felt relaxed in her company. She exuded positivity, and had an ability to make all those around her feel welcome and at ease.

"By the way," I said, "I am a relative of Thomas Brown. I've been told you're his daughter."

Never in my life have I seen a person's demeanour change so quickly. At the mention of Brown's name, her face twisted beyond recognition. The aura of motherly contentment vanished, replaced with revulsion and loathing.

"Never mention that f-ing, name to me," she shouted, and carried on swearing in Caribbean, jabbing a finger in my direction.

My few words had flicked a kill switch. I was speechless as an onslaught of contemptuous anger was unleashed.

"That man is a f-ing disgrace. He should be f-ing dead. I hate him and I hate anyone who says his name."

I looked around. Anyone within earshot would be aware of the explosion of rage and the torrent of language turning the air blue. I noticed pedestrians crossing the road and quickening their pace. The children were rooted to the spot, dazed. Two of the girls were holding hands, comforting one another as best they could. Yet still she wouldn't calm down.

"That f-ing man is the worst kind of animal. He's a pervert."

I cringed with embarrassment. What was I to do?

As he outburst subsided, she backed away and I never saw her, or her children, again.

"What was that all about?" asked Mum.

"I don't know," I said, "as soon as I mentioned Thomas Brown she flipped out on me."

Mum had been negotiating to buy a snow cone from a street vendor – a scoop of crushed ice, layered with strawberry syrup, then another scoop of crushed ice and topped with condensed milk to look like snow, all created in front of you and served in a plastic cup. It's a great way to cool down in the Caribbean heat.

"Remember once I told you about Thomas Brown's strange behaviour. When you used to ask me to take your baked bread to their house."

"Bwoy yo mus forget dem tings meh tel yo."

("Boy. You must forget those things.")

"Did you know what he was like, Mum? Had you heard the rumours?

"LaLaLa."

"Was I not the only one? It's really important for me to know."

"LaLaLaLaLaLaLaLaLaLaLaLa!"

My relationship with Mum was deteriorating by the day. We were quarrelling about everything, from the generous tips I gave her domestic helpers to the amount of weed I was smoking. (She had a reasonable complaint; shortly after my arrival, I discovered the street price was eighty percent lower than anything I'd previously paid; I figured "Why not buy five dollars' worth" and ended up with a carrier bag full of the product!)

Matters came to a head when Rachel phoned to chat. It was hard to coordinate times to chat due to the time difference, and on this occasion, I was out-aided and abetted by Dad's cutlass – to confront another farmer that I suspected of ruining our crops and poisoning our animals (but that's another story). Mum answered the phone, and launched into a blistering onslaught of abuse and accusations about poor Rachel's virtue. Her ill-concealed agenda was to destroy our relationship, motivated by her yearning that I remain in the Caribbean. When I learnt of her clumsy intervention, I couldn't hold back.

"Stay outta my business!" I stormed, accusing her of every wrong thing that sprang to mind.

"Mi nah seh nuting, mi jus seh yo nah deh ya, dats arl."

("I didn't say anything, I just said that you weren't here, that's all.")

Mum was visibly shaken by my hostility, and fled through the side door. But I was in no mood to allow such an easy escape. I stormed through the lounge to our veranda, and, having caught up with her, resumed my monologue.

"How dare you speak to Rachel like that. What do you think you're doing interfering in my relationship?"

"Bwoy mi tell yo aredy mi nah seh nuting."

("Boy, I told you, I said nothing.")

Neighbours were gathering, horrified at our rapidly-escalating confrontation. It was unheard of for a son to speak with such disrespect to his mother, but my lashing-out was no longer limited to the issue of Rachel. My inhibitions had been lowered by drug use, and I was bringing all manner of other grievances to the fore.

"You used to punish me, for nothing. You disowned me."

"Mi pray an pray fi a bwoy an mi geh wah likle devil like yo."

("I prayed and prayed for a boy and got a little devil like you.")

"You took everyone's side against me."

A dozen people were now watching our conflict, captivated but unsure whether to intervene. Then, Buster – my uncle's son – stepped forward. He said:

"Cherry, tap dis tark man, nah tark to yo mudda like dat, it nah good, come Cherry leh we tark."

("Cherry stop this talk, don't speak to your mother like that, it's not good; come Cherry let's talk.")

"Worst of all, Mum, you sent me to that monster Brown. The man who raped me! Why, why, why? Why would you do that?"

Buster was now standing between us, like a chess piece protecting a queen. He was six inches taller than me, and his hands were rough and strong from years of farm work. He grabbed my forearms, and pressed them to my sides, forcing me to calm down.

"Cherry," he said, pushing me away from the scene, whilst I continued to give voice to my accusations. "You must let it go. You'll never know everything she went through. Just… let it go."

As bidden, I "just let it go." But this incident, and my failure to clear the air with my mum, had made an important decision for me… I was heading back to England! There was just one challenge: I was broke, having used up all the cash I'd brought with me – and having been unable to supplement this (Mum, keen for me to stay in St Vincent, had refused to release any of the inheritance money she'd promised). In the end, an uncle and auntie helped arrange tickets off the island with the help of their daughter, Kathy, who worked for the local airline.

It wasn't long before I boarded my flight back to the UK, a full three months earlier than scheduled, much to the disappointment of my family who wanted me to stay and claim my birth right. Although Mum and I made a half-hearted attempt at reconciliation, all other attempts to dissuade me fell on deaf ears. My mind was made up.

*

I landed at Gatwick with little money and limited plans for how to rebuild my life. I was wary about returning to Oxford – who knew how long the apparent "contract on your life" might remain valid? Instead, through a circuitous and random series of events, I was taken in by the monks at the Benedictine Monastery of the Holy Trinity at Crawley Down.

Life at the Holy Trinity is based on the concept of the undivided church – the "one great tradition of mystical and ascetic theology"

– which the monks consider a profoundly prophetic message. Life at the monastery is simple but tranquil, with extensive, beautifully maintained grounds (including a tennis court, no less!) and plenty of time for contemplation.

The tone was set by the Father Superior, Father Gregory, a dignified and devout man, highly respected by the dozen other monks in residence. It took a while for me to adapt to some of their practices – on the first night, after I'd freshened up, I was invited to join them for supper. Throughout my life, mealtimes have been an occasion for conversation; it comes instinctively. I asked the monk sitting opposite me to kindly pass the sauce. He raised a finger to his lips. D'oh! – a penny-drop moment.

"You've just committed a major breach of etiquette," my inner voice lectured me. "These monks, they like to eat… in silence!" Part of me was glad for the silence because my experience in St Vincent was tormenting me like a recurring nightmare. My inability to stay anywhere for too long just added to my sadness of it all.

Holy Trinity wasn't quite as secluded as HMP Dartmoor, but neither was it the most accessible of places, being equal in distance between Crawley and East Grinstead. In the short term, this didn't faze me in the slightest – I was hardly unaccustomed to spending large parts of each day in a small room without company; in fact, it was a rare mercy to be able to leave and return to my room at times of my choosing. But it clearly wasn't a sustainable solution. The monks appreciated this, and kindly assisted with occasional transportation into Crawley, where I was able to sign on, seek work, and scout alternative accommodation. It also gave me the opportunity to extend my tentacles into some of my prior networks, searching for the latest information about the "contract". As one enquiry after another led to a dead end, I knew that even if someone somewhere retracted the contract, wherever I was, I'd always be looking over my shoulder. Would I ever be able to fully rejoin open society?

Having burnt quite a few bridges with my former associates, in my case "open society" meant little more than crashing out on the spare sofa of anyone I happened to know in or around Crawley.

I was existing day by day, only slightly safer and more secure than if I'd been sleeping underneath sheets of cardboard on a park bench. I gave myself a couple of weeks – a month, tops – then the sofa-surfing must cease, and I'd have to figure a way to earn an honest crust. (Or a dishonest one; I wasn't fussy. It just needed to be a crust!)

It wasn't long after leaving Holy Trinity before I was tempted back into old tricks. I'd been introduced by mutual acquaintances to Kieron and his girlfriend Maria. Kieron was an unlikely criminal; he was shy and introverted, a compulsively-tidy 'househusband' long before the term became fashionable. However, his reputation wasn't entirely squeaky-clean; he dabbled in drugs, and his father had been a notorious local criminal.

As a result, it wasn't entirely coincidental when the opportunity to make a few bob through questionable means fell into our laps. We'd been minding our own business in a local Crawley pub (chatting about a drug dealer Kieron knew who might be able to put some work our way), when the barman sent two twenty-something women, who'd spent the past half hour failing to score a bullseye on the dartboard, in our direction.

"You Kieron?" asked the more mouthy of the pair.

"What's it to you?" he replied, barely registering their presence.

"I'm Jen, don't you remember? You use to score speed with my boyfriend a long time ago."

"Yeah, I remember," said Kieron, "You look different."

"I was working but they laid me off."

I could've written the script that followed. I'd been involved in enough inside jobs to recognise a disgruntled employee, in financial dire straits, when I saw one. It transpired that Jen was an assistant at a Crawley branch of Cost Cutters and knew exactly where, when and how the store manager dealt with his weekend takings ("Ten's the minimum," said Jen, "sometimes it's as much as twenty.").

Kieron glanced at me; I knew the wheels in his head had started turning.

He said, "I'll only do it if Lennox is on-board. Otherwise the risk's too great."

I wasn't convinced by Jen's claims. "Newsagents don't make that kind of money."

"Yeah, that's right normally," she said, "But it's bank holiday weekend, so there's no banking until Tuesday. And it's rollover week on the lottery, sixty-eight million someone can win. So everyone's spending for that. You'd be surprised what people spend."

"Why come to us?" I said.

"It's easy money, I can trust Kieron not to rip me off and knowing him gives me some insurance."

And so, like a boomerang unable to escape no matter how hard and far it's thrown, I was pulled back – remorselessly and inevitably – to my old ways.

I nodded silently.

"We're in," said Kieron. "When do we start?"

"It's up to you but after Tuesday it's too late."

For the next two days, we scouted the target from an abandoned car which we parked behind the store's garage.

The store manager, Jim, was clearly a stickler for punctuality. He arrived each morning a fraction before 5:30am, entering through the backdoor which he often left slightly ajar. For the next thirty minutes he occupied himself with mundane preparations for the day ahead – switching around signage, replenishing shelves, sorting the day's newspapers, and finally welcoming the first customer at six.

On the Tuesday morning, moments after 5:30, Kieron and I busted in through the back door; we wanted to maximise the element of surprise before Jim had a chance to settle in, and were so confident of success that, arrogantly, we hadn't even bothered to sort out proper balaclavas. Plus, we didn't want to be too conspicuous when we made our getaway. Instead, we made ourselves very rough-looking and unkempt, knowing that we'd smarten up later. Jim was as resolute as jelly – you can usually tell when a victim is a robbery virgin – which wasn't as desirable as it might sound. When people are terrified, their minds go blank, and they struggle to focus on complying with instructions. Kieron continued to cajole and frighten Jim.

The amount was miserable compared with Jen's forecast; we netted nearly three grand a piece. I guess running a news agency doesn't provide the gold rush she assumed, but it was welcome when one's down on one's luck, and we compensated for the shortfall by helping ourselves to scratch cards and fags. Kieron stored the loot in a black bin bag which he buried in his back garden, whilst – mindful of my training – I used my share of the proceeds to buy different clothes and a nice second-hand car, visit the barbers, and check into a bed-and-breakfast in Brixton, where I could get lost in its large black population until the heat died down.

Usually these precautions are a sufficient guarantee of safety, but Crawley cops are clearly a cut above, and the net closed in rapidly. Someone grassed on Kieron (probably Jen, if she clung to the belief we'd grossed twenty thousand and felt short-changed at her one grand cut). The police interrogated Kieron's girlfriend and hinted she might lose her kid if cooperation was withheld, and – when she told all – the diggers got to work on the garden.

Nobody was surprised when the soil revealed its treasures, including scratch cards with serial numbers that could be directly traced to the Cost Cutters store. The evidence was indisputable, and Kieron was deprived of any credible defence. The police had their primary suspect, but the newsagent had mentioned an accomplice. Aware of my association with Kieron, my picture was distributed to all neighbouring police forces, with a request that I should be arrested on sight.

When word reached me about the arrest warrant, I wasn't too panicked. The British police resources are stretched thin dealing with a long list of ATM frauds, domestic spats, speeding motorists, drunken teenagers and football hooligans picking fights in town centres, racist incidents and a gamut of other offences. I reckoned my mugshot would get lost somewhere in the middle of the in-tray.

But this confidence proved to be misplaced; less than two weeks after Kieron's arrest, driving a second-hand Ford Escort car, I noticed I was followed by police around Crawley town centre. I thought I'd given them the slip, but when I innocently stopped at red traffic lights, I found myself surrounded by armed police ordering me to leave the vehicle with my hands up. I was all too familiar with how the next few hours would unfold – handcuffed; taken in for questioning; offered the services of a lawyer (Wilson dropped everything to shoot down to Lewes, where I was being held); and, before sundown, my arrest was formalised.

I was remanded to HMP High Down, overlooking Banstead Downs in Surrey, which later acquired a degree of notoriety as the celebrities' jail (it housed both former England cricketer Chris Lewis, found guilty of drug smuggling in 2009, and Gary Glitter, jailed for 16 years in 2015 for multiple historic child sexual offences).

At the time, many of the inmates who were Category A prisoners, were arrested as a result of operations at Heathrow airport. I'd never seen tighter security – the entire jail went into lockdown if a single helicopter was flying overhead, in case it had been commissioned by one of the inmates as part of a daring escape plan, and every 14 days Cat A-prisoners would be rotated to different cells to disrupt emerging alliances and networks.

Nevertheless, the power wielded by some of the prisoners was strong, and, being on cleaning duty, I came into regular contact with all of them.

Top of the food chain was (allegedly) a Colombian drug cartel baron, a well-spoken gentleman whose grooming was impeccable and whose prison-issue uniform was always beautifully pressed. He'd been incriminated in laundering money involving eye-watering sums, alongside a string of contract killings, but, according to prison rumour, his vast wealth – which included a fleet of ships used to transport illicit cargo around the Americas – lay far beyond the authorities' reach.

When I first spoke with him, he seemed supremely indifferent to his imprisonment, as if jail was an inconvenient irritation, rather than a serious threat to his business empire. Through his network of informants, he was able to source real-time information on drug shipments, approve shipments and investments, and order hits where necessary. He was also able to continue many of his operations. A fellow inmate was one of his pilots from Colombia, who one evening, confided with me about plans afoot:

"I need to get outta here as soon as," he said.

"How come?"

"My solicitors are arranging for me to serve my sentence in Bogota, not London."

"Why on earth would you want that? I imagine the conditions are disgusting."

"Ha! Believe me, Lennox, I won't be experiencing those conditions. As soon as I'm back on Colombian soil, I'll be out in no time. We have people working for us in high places."

"And what then?"

"I have a long list of instructions, straight from the boss's mouth. My next two years will be committed to making them happen."

Inevitably, ten days later, the paperwork came through approving the international transfer. I watched, shaking my head in disbelief, as the pilot was escorted by armed guard from the premises. As he passed my cell, his head tilted towards me; and, barely perceptible, he winked knowingly in my direction.

Meanwhile, the wheels of justice in the 'Cost Cutters' case were grinding steadily towards a trial – until Wilson had one of those inspired brainwaves that made him such a powerful ally.

It looked like the police were going to proceed without confirming my identity, which was what Wilson had hoped for since it would allow us grounds for an appeal at a later date. In his statement, the store manager claimed to have gotten a good look at the faces of both robbers, and provided detailed descriptions. The police proposed that an identity parade should be organised to determine whether I was the accomplice described by witnesses. The procedures for ensuring ID parades are supposed to be fairly conducted and Wilson insisted every dot and comma of due process was observed as the line-up was assembled. It was quickly evident that, out of pure practicality, we needed to relocate to Brixton (there weren't enough black candidates in Lewes); even then, Wilson objected to the vast majority of stooges proposed – "too young", "too old", "too fat", "too tall", "too black", "not black enough". An artist's impression of the villain had been made available to the media – it looked nothing like me, after I'd spruced up – and our main goal was to have stooges selected who were spitting images of the person in this sketch.

There were sixteen stooges and I was allowed to pick eight – after looking at the artist's impression from Wilson's newspaper, I chose people who looked like the picture. We objected to a few of the candidates (a useful factor for appeal purposes). The police were so confident I'd be pointed out without a moment's hesitation they got quite cocky and sarcastic.

Comically, the store owner shook his head when asked whether 'number four' (i.e. me) had been the culprit, instead insisting it was a toss-up between numbers three and five – both of whom were constables in good standing with the Brixton police force!

If this wasn't sufficient to undermine the prosecution case, it collapsed into nothingness the following week, when a malicious accusation from one of the Crawley police officers that said I'd been "intimidating witnesses" fell apart on inspection (my only phone conversations since my arrest had been either with Wilson or with my sister Angela; the latter had been recorded and the transcript revealed all we'd discussed was my bail conditions). Wilson went ballistic at the trumped-up charge, and took his complaint to the Crown Court, where the judge had no hesitation in ruling in my favour.

The police case wasn't helped by the fact the officer who had fronted the allegation against me chose the week of the Crown Court hearing to debunk to Canada.

If I was a cat with nine lives, I must've now exhausted the first seven or eight. Despite my criminal history being mostly wiped clean, and having navigated clear of the contract on my life, the lure of easy money continued to be irresistible. In all fairness, I should've been alongside Kieron in the dock, facing justice for aggravated robbery. But Wilson's wiles, and my own shrewdness on the ID parade, meant I was still a free man. How would I use my ill-deserved freedom? I made myself a solemn commitment to settle down somewhere and try to live a normal life.

15.
Marley Chan

Often imitated, never surpassed, Bob Marley had an unparalleled ability to infuse reggae music with deep spirituality. Decades after his death at the tragically young age of 35 from a malignant melanoma, he remains a giant of Caribbean culture.

Switching continents and genres, Jackie Chan has been a hero of mine since Bruce Lee died. I was first dazzled by his energy and charisma as a martial artist and stuntman; he has starred in over 150 films, and I could watch them back-to-back and never get bored, especially Drunken Master.

So, when I resolved to abandon my family heritage, it seemed natural to combine the identities of Bob Marley and Jackie Chan to create my new persona.

The idea had been at the back of my mind for some time, but my recent experience bought everything to a head. I'd been appalled at my mum's attitude during my time on St Vincent, and my relationships with my sisters were also strained.

Quite frankly, it was time to move on from the petty squabbles and hypocrisies of the Rodgers family. I would be Lennox Rodgers no more; henceforth, I wished to be known as… Marley Chan.

This wasn't a superficial rebranding. I made everything official, completing all the paperwork for a full legal change of name. The process was surprisingly straightforward, even whilst residing – as I was at the time – in one of Her Majesty's establishments. (I'd been transferred from High Down to Lewes Prison, where I was being held in connection with the Cost Cutters robbery, although my release was imminent as the identity parade fiasco unravelled.)

I was comfortable with my new identity, and, once I got used to hearing it, answered to it proudly and loudly, especially when ordering Chinese takeaways (I also relished the look of astonishment on the faces of the delivery boys, when they asked at my front door for "Mr Chan" and, looking anything but Asian, I merrily quipped "Yeh mon, that's me!"). A hint to anybody else contemplated a new identity – "Chan" has many virtues as a surname; not least, it guarantees supersized portions of Chicken Chow Mein and special fried rice with every order!

In the final week before my release from Lewes, I'd been involved in one of the most vicious confrontations of recent years, with one of the jail's more pitiful inmates, nicknamed Des.

Des was a sorry creature, a real loser who'd never made anything of his life on the outside. He was hopelessly, miserably addicted to anything that gave him a short-term buzz (his sentence related to numerous offences of possession, scoring and dealing), and people added the 'Desperate' to his name due to his extreme behaviour whenever he needed a fix. It was all the consequence of years of drug abuse and failure at anything approaching a normal life. When the craving hit him, he'd do anything for anyone, no matter how disgusting or degrading. He's the only prisoner I ever met who enjoyed having his backside "inspected" (in prison lingo, we treated prisoners to a forcible 'spooning' or 'enema' when they were used as a drug mule and returned from a visit and had nothing to declare or had difficulty retrieving the drugs – I'll leave the details to your imagination). Des was so desperate that he has swallowed drugs without waiting to unwrap the layers of the rather noxious clingfilm in which it's usually wrapped whilst hidden in bodily orifices. However, Des's desperation became a liability for the rest of us when he was unable to contain himself in full earshot of the screws:

Standing outside my cell door, he yelled, "I really need a fix, Marley, I'm clucking. What you got for me?"

"Shut yer face, Des. You'll be heard!"

Other prisoners tried warning him off too, but he wouldn't listen.

"Just something to keep me goin', Marley. I'm clucking here mate. Whatever you got."

Clucking is a term used to describe a very desperate drug addict who is having withdrawal symptoms.

I was trying to settle into my afternoon snooze.

"You trying to tell the whole f-ing jail, Des? I told yer to wait and you keep hotting me up in front the screws like some f-ing grass." ("Hotting up" is prison lingo for drawing attention to something or someone.)

"Please, Marley mate, I'm f-ing desperate and clucking."

I'd had enough. I grabbed Des's greasy hair in my hand and hauled him inside the cell. Realising what was about to happen, my cellmate – a worldly-wise East Londoner – moved into position to stand watch.

The first task was to stop his whines and yelps. Sitting astride him, I balled up a sock and forced it into his mouth. His eyes were wide with panic, but at least he was now silent. I let loose with my fists, punching his head on all sides to teach him a lesson.

"You disturb my sleep again you little bastard and that'll be the last thing you do. I warned you plenty of times to wait but you'd rather shout off your mouth in front of the f-ing screws. Grass me up and you're dead, d'yer ere me, now get the f-k out."

Des knew the prison rules about grassing; if he said a word, it wouldn't be just me who'd try to kill him – nobody likes a grass in prison. "I slipped guv," was his stock response, no matter who interrogated him about his misfortune. The screws knew he was lying, and he knew the screws knew he was lying.

But, as long as everyone maintained the fiction, there was precious little they could do.

In fact, with some screws watching my back in Lewes, I felt chilled that there would be no comeback on me. I was on good terms with some of the screws – two or three of them regularly dropped in at my cell for an illicit spliff – and they'd tip me a wink if there was any danger that repercussions cell searches might be brewing. Besides, they regarded Des as an annoying cockroach who'd received his comeuppance; they'd often turn a blind eye to prison beatings especially on inmates they didn't like – taking them seriously meant more paperwork and awkward situations to investigate.

*

Freed from jail when the CPS dropped the case due to a lack of evidence and the humiliating ID parade for the police, I started building a life as Marley Chan. My first break came within days of release when, living at a bail hostel for ex-prisoners transitioning back into society as well as those on bail whose court dates were pending, I was approached by a group of travellers who needed assistance with tarmacking driveways. What they lacked academically, they made up for in skill with their hands, and their sales patter had to be heard to be believed.

They invariably clinched a couple of orders simply by banging on doors for an hour and a half in one of Crawley's wealthier districts.

This was just the leg-up I needed. Cash-in-hand work that started immediately – admittedly just thirty quid each day, but that seems a fortune when one is homeless and skint, and was a sad reminder of how far I'd fallen. The work wasn't too demanding for anyone physically fit and strong, and there was a glowing sense of achievement at watching a robust driveway taking shape during the course of the day. I struck up a great rapport with my traveller companions – we had a similar sense of humour, we could tell stories for the Olympics, and we revelled in banter. After a few weeks of hard labour, I was granted the great honour of being invited to leave the hostel to live on the travellers' site in one of their unoccupied caravans (my ability to score drugs for them might've also been a factor). At many other times in my life, I'd have rushed to accept this great honour extended to a gorger (a non-traveller with plenty to eat); at that moment, fresh out of Lewes, I felt destiny calling me in a different direction.

I was insecure and unsettled, and feared a life with the travellers couldn't last, so I reluctantly declined their generous offer. Bizarrely, because of my recent troubles, it was no longer difficult to secure instant accommodation when I arrived in a new county. This was put to the test soon after parting ways with the travellers. I was to spend the next five years moving around the country under my Marley Chan identity, hoping that somewhere along the way I could make a happy life. First, I turned up in Cambridgeshire, only to be warned by the local authority housing department that I'd be at the end of a long waiting list before Council accommodation could even be considered – at which point, as if from a magician's hat, I waved the letter, warning someone had put a contract on my life.

Without telling an actual barefaced lie, I implied through winks and nods that I was in a witness protection programme. Suddenly, all the red tape and bureaucracy around the waiting list evaporated into thin air like Scotch mist, and I was offered a choice between two or three fine alternatives where I might lay my hat.

After securing accommodation on the sixteenth floor of a block of flats right near the Lord Protector pub, I thought I'd make ends meet through blagging my way into one unskilled job or another, and set about meeting people.

Strangely enough, my network seldom comprised upstanding members of the local community; it usually wasn't long before I was drawn to the circles of the local drugs trade or some form of violence with someone, and matters invariably descended from there. Huntingdon, a few miles outside Cambridge, was a typical case in point.

My first job was thoroughly respectable but one I'd never do in my home town. The Council provided me with an open-back truck so I could collect major items of litter – beds, fridges, tumble dryers – and I played my part in keeping the country spotless from litter and debris (it was also a role where I could dispense favours to anyone who needing any bulky items removed without having to pay the Council's official, exorbitant price list. I thought I was doing the council a favour because it reduced fly-tipping; they simply needed to ask nicely or tip me a fiver).

A typical evening was whiled away in the Lord Protector pub, which I figured was an unexceptional establishment until I learned of its reputation for drugs and violence. Having struck up a friendship with some Scots and Irishmen from Cork, one evening I saw their true selves revealed after imbibing one too many Guinnesses and whiskey chasers. Conor and Big Hamish clambered onto their chairs and started chanting IRA songs, interspersed with regular shouts of "F- the English!" As tempers flared, I hoped my quizzical expression and exaggerated shoulder-shrugs would persuade the other pub goers that I'd no clue what was going on ("Never met 'em before in my life, I haven't" was my intended look).

Even my attempts to settle down courted disaster. On an adult education course, I met Alison, a mother to three kids, who had recently split up with her boyfriend. One evening, she invited me back to her house for dinner and study time – which just happened to coincide with the time her ex showed up, off his head on crack cocaine, to cause mayhem. With the children shrieking in fear, and Alison repeating "Just get out" like a vinyl record stuck in the groove, the ex turned his attentions in my direction.

"I don't want no bother," I said, backing away.

"Yeah, well, do I look like I care what you want?" he sneered.

"Marley!" shouted Alison, "Be careful – he's got a knife."

She wasn't certain. But his hand was in his pocket; he could be holding anything.

Her warning was all the trigger I needed. Instinctively, I grabbed a vegetable knife from draining boarding, stabbed him just below the shoulder, judo threw him to the kitchen floor, dragged him to his feet and stabbed him again. Before I could do any more damage, he scrambled from the scene.

205

I headed to a friend's house, but had barely had time to calm down with a spliff when Alison called to say the police had showed up, sirens blaring as if gang warfare had erupted. She'd explained I'd acted in self-defence but they nevertheless wished to question me.

I was paranoid and distrustful, but agreed to be questioned. Apparently the ex had accused me of beating the kids (despite never having laid eyes on them before that day) which led me to open up about my own suffering, decades beforehand, at Brown's hands. Suddenly, I found myself offered counselling, sympathy, tea and biscuits – the works. Within twenty-four hours, contact had been made with the police in Oxford, and Brown had been strong-armed from his house, while his daughters watched, for questioning on suspicion of child sex offences. Regrettably, the CPS decided they wouldn't be able to make any charges stick; I'd provided the phone numbers of my mum and sisters, hoping they'd verify having been told about my experience, but the police investigators were met with a wall of silence – my family were united in their desire not to see these matters exposed in court.

In my showdown with Alison's ex, I'd been on the side of the angels, but crime was never far from the surface throughout the years I roved the land as Marley Chan. It was all a far cry from the days when I'd been earning a few thousand pounds in a single night at the sharp end for organised crime bosses. I was now a bottom feeder, loitering in the depths of the aquarium for scraps leftover after the larger, more colourful fish have gorged on the most nutritious pellets and fully sated their appetite. I was drafted into a caper by friends that had volunteered to steal some shopping trolleys for a local under-the-radar business; in the event, I was the only half-way competent member of the team, but my role was limited to driving the truck and showing a bit of muscle if the need arose.

My associates were comically inept, having obtained little or no inside information, and lacking the street smarts to adapt a plan to evolving circumstances. When we delivered our haul, the truck was mostly empty, and the few trolleys they had requisitioned were barely usable. We'd probably done the previous owner a favour by relieving him of the most broken, twisted, rusted items in his stock. Our client signalled his disapproval, and we were left seriously out of pocket – especially me, who'd made the down-payment for the truck hire.

On another occasion, I ran up a two hundred pound debt losing a poker game to Brian, an overweight young man with bushy sideburns who regularly smoked pot in his flat with some young women – the type who don't care what a bloke looks like as long as he can provide a plentiful supply of money, drugs and booze. I lost the poker game and was given a chance to clear the debt if I indulged in a little drinking game, which involved knocking back Jameson whiskey.

I was down to the last shot but, losing coordination, knocked over my glass, prompting everyone to yell in unison, "You lost, you lost." I protested it had been an accident and someone thrust a can of lager in front of my nose – "Get that down ya, and we'll call it quits!" But my stomach couldn't take anymore, and after a couple of sips, everything came back up, spewing into the fireplace and all over the carpet; it was like something from a horror movie. Luckily we were in the house of one of my Irish friends. In a previous life, I'd have scoffed at two hundred quid, barely worth my attention. But now it seemed an insurmountable sum.

This gave Brian the chance he needed to play me. He knew a bit about my violent past from previous conversations.

"There's a bloke owes me hundred-and-twenty for an ounce of cannabis, and he's refusing to pay up."

"Sure, give me his address. I'll get yer cash, no sweat."

"To be clear, Marley, I ain't interested in the cash. The guy's a lowlife, and I need to send a message. You're the guy to send the message, if you don't mind."

Having offered to work off the debt, the unwritten criminal code forbids backtracking – even though I had no reason to follow any codes or rules and had the balls and strength to take everything from Brian, and switch the loyalties of the Scottish and Iris boys. Again, my judgement was impaired by my drug use. And so, less than twenty-four hours later, in broad daylight, I was hammering at the door of a rundown terraced house near Huntingdon station.

A man in his late thirties answered. He matched Brian's description – ginger hair that spiked at the temples, sad eyes, and a rough and weathered complexion. Of course, being a prudent and honourable hired-hand, it was standard criminal protocol to confirm his identity before dispatching any vigilante justice.

"Your name Chas?" I demanded.

"Yeah, what's it to you?"

I wasn't in the mood to indulge in pleasantries, I launched straight into the beating. For reasons that must've made sense at the time I used a knuckle-duster and punched him in the face, which immediately drew blood and hurt my fingers in the process, I knocked him to the floor, and battered him around. The force of my blows broke his nose, and split his lip. "This is a message from Brian."

Back at my flat, I threw my clothes into a black liner, which I dumped in a residents' bin on another estate, and secured my alibi with my Irish friends – the usual routine after a violent job. In the early evening, I headed for Brian's flat, to make him aware the debt was cleared. But, out of shame, I didn't stay long. How far I'd fallen, now reduced to doorstep assaults for lardy lowlife dealers to clear a couple of hundred in gambling debts. Surely the man who, earlier in his career, had been capable of masterminding a complex credit card fraud operation, or implementing twenty-two armed robberies, was meant to scale greater heights?

*

To Manchester, where I figured I would be far from investigators and bounty hunters, and had a fighting chance of staring a new life.

My first impressions weren't great – somebody started urinating against my hub-caps shortly after I'd parked in a train station car park, not noticing I hadn't even left the driver's seat (when he realised his misjudgement, he not only apologised profusely, but invited me to share some weed at his flat-share). The next day, I had breakfast at a homeless café. A bacon sandwich and a northern brew of tea – in Manchester, this seemed the standard answer to any trouble or problem. I was allowed to use their washroom to freshen up and change, so I fetched fresh clothes, an iron, and a board from my car.

It was just a basic steam iron and the board carried burn stains and water marks, but when the staff and homeless folk saw me setting it up, the place erupted with laughter and jokes. "Stay there, I'll bring my ironing for you," said the woman who had made my tea." Not put off, I did my ironing and felt better in clean fresh clothes. After the café, I was admitted, with no quibbles, by a Guest House – I didn't even need to rollout my "witness protection" story.

Odd-jobs and dole money covered a chunk of my day-to-day hostel and living expenses, but I was usually short by the end of the week. Gradually, it was necessary to offload the personal effects I'd crammed into the Ford Sierra (not the ironing board, of course), and, once they'd been disposed of, to sell the car itself. The decluttering process was aided and abetted by Kenroy, a low-level drug dealer who had some connections on the Moss-side estate.

"Myah tel yo bwoy, a mi will deal wid yo tings-truss mi."

("I tell you, boy, it's me who will deal with your things. Trust me.")

Speaking patwa with Kenroy was easy because he was a British-born Jamaican, a few years older than me, who had aged terribly through substance misuse and alcohol. Kenroy boasted he could sell anything – my jewellery, my mobile phone (I could no longer afford the airtime), even my car. The latter was now illegal since I hadn't kept up to date with tax and insurance, and had no doubt been clocked by one or two of the petrol stations where, traveling north, I'd done a runner rather than pay for fuel.

The doubts set in as soon as I'd handed over the keys, and were reinforced when I shared Kenroy's claims with a couple of other hostel residents, who immediately countered with stories of their own – of the numerous times Kenroy had pulled a fast one.

My Robin Hood impulses were awoken. If Kenroy was preying not just on me, but on any vulnerable victim he came across, no one would be safe from his deceit unless he was incapable of carrying on.

Kenroy returned with a miserly £150 from flogging everything I owned and including my Sierra. The next day knowing Kenroy carries a knife I swiped a small knife from the hostel kitchen, as I didn't want him pulling a knife out on me and headed to his room.

"Hey teef bwoy get up!"

("Hey thief, get up!")

He was swift with his denials.

"Mi nah teef yo man Jah Jah no seh mi nah teef yo."

("I didn't steal from you man. God knows I didn't steal from you.")

"Listen man, mi neva teef yo,"

("Listen man, I never stole from you.")

But his claims were falling on deaf ears. I went to punch him in the face and he dodged it and because I had the knife in my hands, the knife caught the side of his face and I carried on fighting him with my fists.

He fell to the floor.

"If you don't want more of the same you better pay me what you owe me."

I wandered the town, making sure to drop the knife down a drain; on my return to the hostel, it was like there had been a murder or something – two police vans, three squad cars and an ambulance.

My claims to be a model citizen with a blemish-free record (technically true after my crimes had been expunged) were undermined when a fingerprint bureau in the United States produced a match between Marley Chan's and Lennox Rodger's. This revelation aroused the suspicion of the officers, and destroyed any trust that had been fostered during our interviews. Police bail was denied, and – despite the best efforts of Wilson Carter– I was remanded to the local Strangeways Prison.

Strangeways is a vast category A jail to the north of the city centre, which had been rebuilt in the early 1990s following three weeks of rioting that had left 147 staff injured and one dead from heart failure.

The prison comprises two Victorian radial blocks and nine wings, and is notorious for – amongst other things – housing Britain's most prolific serial killer, the GP Harold Shipman, and recording the second highest suicide rate of any prison in the UK, with an average of twenty being investigated at any given time. During my eight months awaiting trial, I kept my head down. My years in custody had taught me some basic rules of survival, and "prison's prison" wherever you do your time. I wasn't from these parts – as the officers reminded me at every opportunity (I was called "You f-ing southern bastard" more often than "Chan!" or "Rodgers!"; in fact, a visiting alien would conclude that "southern bastard" was my given name). This meant I had no intuition for the power structures amongst prisoners but something I'd learn along the way. Rather than getting involved, my time was better spent preparing an elaborate cover story for my trial.

And what a story it was! According to my recounting, Kenroy had been assaulted as a result of a falling-out with a local drug-dealing gang.

He'd then grassed on me instead because (a) he was perilously afraid of retribution by the gang leaders, and (b) I'd knocked his crack cocaine into a puddle earlier that day, when he'd been explaining his dodgy schemes for extorting money from the vulnerable. It was a credibility-stretching fiction – but it was supported by a Met Office weather report, obtained by Jackson Collins, that proved beyond reasonable doubt that… there had indeed been puddles in Manchester that day because it had rained. Jackson brandished this document around the courtroom with dramatic flourish, as if it nailed Kenroy's web of lies, and proved, with the conclusive finality of a cast iron alibi, that his client was "innocent of these scandalous charges."

To my astonishment, the jury agreed, and I left the courthouse a free man, no cares in the world.

*

Except that my cares, emphatically, had not gone away.

I had just entered my fifth decade, and was penniless. I'd spent almost half my last two decades in jail, renounced the Rodgers family, turned my back on friends, was estranged from Natalie, hadn't spoken with Karen for years, and didn't have the faintest idea what my son Mark looked like. Moreover, who knew whether the contract on my life was still valid? The only friends who'd stuck with me through the years were my lawyers, although it's a strange friendship where the bulk of the conversation involves preparing for trials or dealing with their aftermath. It wasn't at all clear what the second half of my life had in store. My employment history was a mess – I'd tried my hand at everything from carpentry to construction work to tarmacking to care assistant to refuse collection to shop work, but never found a calling in which I could forge a long-term career. To make matters worse, the years – and especially the cannabis – were taking their toll. I doubted I'd again be able to hold down a job requiring intense physical stamina.

And my drug use meant that, while I could recall certain events with the vivid clarity of an elephant, other memories were a right "two and eight" (Cockney rhyming slang for a state or mess).

After my release, I went back to the Guest House to collect my belongings, only to be told that – since everyone had assumed I'd be locked away for years – everything had been destroyed. In any event, they didn't want anybody in residence with my reputation, regardless of the jury's verdict. The best they could offer was to consider compensation, but even that would need a detailed letter setting out my view of the facts. It was time to head back south.

Ending up in Northampton, I found temporary accommodation through the All Nations church, where I shared a house with a group of friendly Albanians, who earned good money working for a supermarket that was part of the Booker Group of Distributors, and sent much of it to support families back home.

Everything was going well until they offered to introduce me to their sex-trafficking ring – we parted company shortly after that! Once again, my "contract" letter came to my rescue, enabling me to jump the queue of single men and secure a one-bedroom ground floor flat just past Weston Favell and near Spinney Hill. After everything that had happened, I was suffering mental health issues, I had bouts of depression and suicidal thoughts. Was it time to end it all? I wasn't afraid of death, but didn't want it to be painful, and in my ignorance assumed paracetamol offered the kindest route (for some reason I believed I'd drift into a beautiful sleep; the reality is that a paracetamol overdose is one of the most painful ways to go, since it causes catastrophic liver failure).

A pharmacist had warned me that taking too many paracetamol could kill and "Thirty is enough" – which was all the information I needed. I bought five or six boxes from different chemists, and was ready for the final deed.

Firstly, I wanted to be cut adrift from the outside world. The room would be my coffin; I didn't want anyone – window cleaners, Jehovah's Witnesses, life insurance salesmen – intruding into my grief. So I hung enormous black bin liners in the windows, and sealed the door to its frame with duct tape. Then I plucked the battery from my mobile phone, and even unplugged the TV and radio. It felt eerily as if I was back in solitary confinement – alone, forsaken, no prospect of imminent human contact. Would I become one of those melancholy stories which occasionally hit the headlines? – "The body that lay undiscovered for six months, until the stench of rotting flesh was detected in the corridor."

I'd figured out the sequence of my suicide; I'd be mortified if anybody felt the implementation had been slapdash. With the windows blacked-out, I put pen to paper and prepared my suicide note. It wasn't anything Shakespearean; I didn't use it as the excuse to settle old scores. I simply wrote, "I don't want anyone to blame themselves. This is my decision, and mine alone. It's time to check out." In fact, in hindsight, it was something of a missed opportunity; there was plenty of blame I should've dished out. I guess it reflects my state of mind at the time that, even facing death, I couldn't muster the emotion to take a final pot shot at my tormentors. I hated myself and wanted to do everyone a favour.

I filled a jug with rum and coke, and then crushed the pills into a fine powder, which I sprinkled on top of the concoction and stirred in. It was double the amount in the pharmacist's "death warning", but I'd be swigging my favourite beverage. I looked at the ceiling, across at the bin liners, then down at the jug. The moment to check out was fast approaching. Was this definitely the route I wished to take? Absolutely! Was now the time? One hundred per cent! And the place? Yes, as good a place as any! I smoked my final spliff and took some ecstasy tablets.

Thoughts of the crimes I'd committed plagued my mind. The senseless stabbings, missed opportunities to take control of other drug dealers businesses, people I'd hurt, so many broken relationships and two failed marriages, and how my kids were better off without me. Everything was just tormenting me and I couldn't take any more.

I pictured Captain Kirk trying to escape some alien planet and calling up to the Enterprise. "Beam me up Scottie," I muttered and started drinking.

My first sip of the brew that would bring my life story to its conclusion.

I swallowed the concoction.

And…

Spat it straight out again.

The wretched liquid tasted absolutely…

Disgusting!

Horrible!

Ghastly!

Abominable!

"No way am I drinking that shite, dat's narsty yuk!" I shouted to myself, tipping the whole mixture into the sink, and feeling gutted at the waste of so much quality rum. I wanted to die in a nice and easy way, but I thought that was just as bad as cutting myself. Or worse.

I assumed I was venting to nobody in particular but affected by the drugs, I was still tormented with thoughts to kill myself and thoughts of being a failure. Yet I couldn't even do that properly. I was so depressed, I drifted off to sleep, high from the mixture of drugs and thinking of Lennox/Marley – the bungling amateur who can't even complete a suicide attempt with a smidgen of competence.

Should I try again? No way – there was no way any of that vile stuff was getting close to my mouth.

Frankly, I thought, I'd rather die.

16.
The Hand

I was still alive but I wasn't living, not in any meaningful sense.

After my aborted suicide attempt, I ricocheted around the country as if it was a gigantic pinball machine, unable to settle or put down any roots. Oxford, Northampton, Sheffield, Eastbourne, Hastings and London to name a few. I had a girlfriend in nearly every town I moved to and when things didn't work out, I moved on. Many friends were kind enough to let me stay for a few days when I had nothing, but inevitably my acts of violence and crimes brought police attention to their doors, so it seemed right to move on before being asked.

If it wasn't my crimes that made me move on, there was always something else. Finding employment was an ordeal, let alone holding it down for any length of time. On one occasion, I secured an agency job making local deliveries, and needed to borrow a pushbike to get around. Eventually I was able to afford a second-hand car through a company that gave loans to people with poor credit. My major asset was a half decent Ford Mondeo.

Even when I kept my impulses under control, and acted the model employee, catastrophe tended to be right around the corner. One occupation I'd often fancied was bus driving – I had a steady hand and keen eye, how hard could it be? Unfortunately, I flunked the exam when, despite excelling at both the theoretical and practical tests, traces of cannabis were detected in my system.

As the odd jobs dried up, what little income I made, coupled with government benefits, barely covered basic living expenses.

Travelling around from place to place can make you feel like a fugitive – feelings of suicide and failure tormented me – and can be expensive. I sold the Mondeo and off-loaded other possessions – even my iron and ironing board were too bulky to cart around, and therefore now surplus to requirements. It felt weird because what I was carrying around in my mind felt just as heavy as the stuff I'd been hauling around in bin-liners. Gone was the security of having a car to sleep inside, and cannabis to ward off tormenting thoughts. Even regular smoking was a luxury – I was reliant on cigarettes given me by strangers or butts picked off the pavement.

How the tables have turned, I thought. I'm no better than Des. Perhaps I should change my name to Desperate Len.

Finding food and shelter was tough but I was determined not to do some of the things other homeless people did to survive, such as eating out of bins and sleeping in cardboard boxes. I couldn't do it although I did one ponce (beg) a pound from a stranger to buy some rizla papers so I could re-roll the tobacco from a discarded cigarette.

I slept in train stations and hospitals until I was moved on; I fell asleep during the day, weary from so much walking and so little nourishment. I sneaked into someone's garden shed for my night-time kip. Anyone else would curl up on the shed's floor amidst the scurrying spiders. But I nodded off while still upright, and every time I drifted away, I'd slide towards the rake, or a pile of paint pots, and wake with a start. Little wonder that, as soon as dawn broke, I emerged from the shed, bleary-eyed, stiff and still tired from a disturbed sleep.

The worst thing about being homeless is watching everyone else living their lives to the full. It served as a constant reminder of what I lacked. I was hungry, thirsty, tired, cold, guilt-ridden, ashamed.

One day, my desperation for food took me to a busy Pizza Hut, on the Strand in central London.

The aroma of freshly baked bread and melting cheese was irresistible, but I had barely twenty pence in my pocket. I chose the table nearest the toilets, ordered three beers and a family sized "Spicy Hot One" which was helpfully sliced into twelve segments. I'd barely eaten for three days, and relished the flavours that were exploding inside my mouth. The glow on my face at the luxury of a proper meal could've lit up the restaurant for a week, but, as the final chunk of crust was tumbling down my throat, I faced the more immediate challenge of extracting myself from the premises before the bill arrived. As with so much in life, the secret is precise timing and brazen self-confidence. I waited until the servers in my section were sufficiently distracted – I think by a three-generation family being directed to their table – and then strode for the toilets without a single backward glance or hesitant step to betray my true intent.

When I emerged, I strolled out as if I'd already paid. It was like shoplifting from Boots in Oxford all over again. As soon as my feet hit the pavement outside, I knew I'd survived the moment of greatest peril, and bolted towards Charing Cross station, where it'd be easy to disappear into the crowds. (I'd forgotten that running on a full stomach is knackering and often triggers cramps, and I doubled up in agony a few hundred yards from the Pizza Hut. But I'd gotten away with my scheme – which temporarily gave a nice boost to my morale.)

Hunger gets fixed with a single meal, but my other problems were more intractable. I whiled away hours in London's public spaces, weaving through the bustling crowds of Leicester Square or strolling along riversides in Green Park or Hyde Park. In despair and self-pity, I watched regular families enjoying one another's company. Flying kites, kicking around a ball, queuing for a hot dog, negotiating with a street vendor. The smell of food from vendors' carts brought back hunger pangs and the inability to keep hydrated dried my skin and chapped my lips.

Regular, ordinary family activities – all denied to someone with my track record. Every time I'd connected with somebody who might be "the one", the relationship had crumbled before it had really gotten going. Neither of my two marriages had lasted and I was estranged from the mothers of both my children. I often thought about my children during this period and wished I could have been a stick-around dad.

My transient lifestyle, and frequent jail terms, meant my contact with Karen had been sporadic.

Even after everything I'd done to Natalie, she still allowed me contact, no matter who she was with. Often I messed that up too. When she was five or six years old, Karen regularly screamed because she didn't want to leave her mum and come with me; there'd been a terrible tantrum when Natalie bought her to visit me in Dartmoor. One weekend, despite Karen's protests, Natalie said "Just take her, she'll be fine," but I was broken to see my daughter in such a state – I told her that, if she didn't want to see me, I wouldn't force her.

"No," she said, "I don't, never again."

It's haunted me for years that I gave my baby girl an adult choice to make, and Natalie was shocked and hurt that I acted on it.

In the years that followed, I kept in regular touch with Natalie to ask about Karen's welfare; I also sent her birthdays cards and presents – none of which were wanted. The rejection burned me badly and I ignorantly blamed Natalie for poisoning Karen's mind. I even sent photos of Karen back to Natalie because I couldn't bear to look at them anymore, such was the torment. Estranged from Karen, and Mark abducted!

The lowest ebb happened in London, when I reached out to Angela. Growing up in Oxford, it'd been Angela – amongst all my sisters – who always had my back. She taught me many things from a young age and it'd been Angela who comforted me ("Say your prayers every night and never forget God") when everyone else had been imploring the social workers to "tek im" off to a children's home.

It'd been Angels who shared her religious tracts because she thought that, if I had a relationship with God, I could be a better person. Over the years I had short periods of bonding with many of my sisters and that was the nice side of being in our family; each sister was different but they were educated and I learned different things from them all. But my wild side meant that those relationships would be short.

It was common knowledge in our family that Angela lived in a flat in Caledonian Road in the Kings Cross area. It was the depths of winter, and I was hungry, thirsty and cold. From head to toe, my body showed signs of shutting down and, with each passing day, I felt closer to death; my lips were cracked, inflamed and peeling – and I couldn't even produce enough saliva to moisten them. I needed a glass of water, some food, money and a warm place to stay and perhaps even some lip balm. Surely I could count on Angela at my time of greatest need.

The pavement was perilous with frost, and I shuffled rather than walked up the gentle Caledonian Road incline. Eventually, with a light snow falling around me, I reached her address. The house had been converted into three flats, each with a separate buzzer. I pressed the number to her intercom.

It took an eternity for Angela to answer, but the voice through the intercom was unmistakably hers. A single word, but it meant the world:

"Hello?"

"Angela? Is that you?"

"Yes, this is Angela."

"It's me! Lennox your brother."

Silence.

"It's good to hear your voice, Angela. I need help sis," I started telling her what I needed but I got no response.

"Just let me in, Angela. I can explain everything, but I really need some water right now."

Still silence. I didn't understand what was happening.

Then I heard the finality of a brisk click, as Angela replaced the receiver at far end of the line.

Shocked and rejected, I felt like that twelve-year-old boy again who was told by his mother that she didn't want him anymore. In tears and silent anger, I left.

I made my way to Kings Cross Station, and stayed there until I was kicked out by security staff.

I didn't mind dying but I didn't want to let anyone kill me. And I couldn't drink any more concoctions of rum and paracetamol. And I didn't want to die on the streets of London like another down-and-out homeless person statistic.

Ashamed and desperate, I handed myself into Edgware Police Station, and confessed some of the crimes I'd committed whilst homeless. But they couldn't find any evidence, not even from Pizza Hut. I'd gotten stuff off my chest, but was released, and back to square one.

Then it came to me. I knew I was on a strike with the courts, which meant if I was again caught and convicted for a stabbing, then I'd receive an automatic life sentence. So I reasoned that, if I couldn't kill myself, I should pick a fight with someone, stab them, and then spend the rest of whatever life is left firmly behind bars.

It took me a week to find a man who didn't look too vulnerable and was on his own (I didn't want to pick on a man out with his family or girlfriend). By this time, I was exhausted and the shutting down process of my body was further advanced. I felt so ill and needed to rush the deed before I was physically incapable. I didn't have a knife but a bradawl – a tool used in carpentry for making holes in wood – and one evening, at around eleven o'clock, I saw a man in his mid-thirties, slightly taller than me, approaching a cash machine on Oxford Street – alone.

Here's my chance, I thought.

I asked him if he had any spare change, and he grunted "No".

Before he had a chance to put away his wallet, I stabbed him in his face with my bradawl. He shrieked in pain and dropped the wallet; that was no use to me – I wasn't doing this for money anymore but to go to my second home. Prison.

Then, instinctively, I ran. I had no idea where I was running to, I just kept running. Into a really dark alley.

It was difficult to see because it was so dark. It was a darkness I've never experienced or felt before; I couldn't even see my hands in front of me. The only way I could move forward was by swaying from left to right, touching the brick walls on either side of the alley. Eventually, I bumped into some industrial bins and not wanting to go much further, I pushed them apart and collapsed against the wall between them, hoping nobody was giving chase. In my solitude, my adrenalin was racing and my heart pumping; I tried to calm down, I was alert and breathless, listening for every sound. It felt very strange.

The darkness around me was so thick, and suddenly I was surrounded by silence – I couldn't even hear the late night hustle and bustle of Oxford Street. All my baggage of feelings of rejection, hurt, shame and injustice burst forth like a broken dam in floods of tears and my body shook with sorrow. It seemed an eternity before I was able to calm down, and when I replayed in my mind what had just happened, I couldn't believe it.

"Dear God, please don't let that guy have any serious injury, please help him," I whispered, filled with remorse and weeping.

When I looked up, I saw a bright, white arm against the wall in front of me. A strong man's arm like that of the cartoon character Popeye after devouring spinach, but glowing slightly, as if in a Ready Brek advert. Pop-eye and Ready Brek. I froze in disbelief and fear.

Then I heard a voice saying, "Take my hand."

I listened for movement but heard none; I looked for anything attached to the arm, but in the thick darkness saw nothing.

Again, I heard the command, "Take my hand." But there was no mouth – how could there be a voice?

No way was I taking the hand of somebody I didn't know. Then, I realised there was something familiar about the instruction. Could it be God? "But," I reasoned to myself, "I've tried Him and He doesn't work."

I heard the voice say, "But have you really tried me?"

Now I was freaked out and scared; not only could I hear this voice outside of my head but He was answering my thoughts. And I didn't have any drugs in my system!

My mind still reeling, I noticed a row of video clips moving across the wall in front of me like items on a conveyer belt, each showing a time in my life when I'd called out to God for assistance. One reminded me of the time, in the crown court cells, I'd pledged, "If you get me out of this one I'll serve you forever." The others carried a similar theme – cries of desperation followed a soon-to-be-forgotten promise.

The voice said, "Do you like bacon and eggs?"

I thought, of course I do. And I'm starving and homeless. What's that got to do with anything?

The voice continued, "Every time you tried to follow me, you've just given me an egg. I want you to be like the pig – totally committed."

What am I hearing? How do you do that? I thought. Maybe it's like pointing a gun to someone's head. I know that anyone will commit to anything with a gun to their head.

But then I understood. I knew that my heart and mind had to commit and that my choices and freewill had to be surrendered to God. With the clarity of the little boy Joe 90, when information is downloaded into his brain in his computer chamber. Now I understood.

"I want you to choose to do what is right and trust me for the rest. What have you got to lose; you're about to die anyway. Please, take my hand."

My heart sank. Had God just confirmed my fate; that I'm really about to die?

I could see it, I could hear it. But was this really happening?

To my surprise, I wasn't aching and stiff when I stood up to shake the hand. The thick darkness lingered, but bizarrely I wasn't afraid anymore. I moved to take His hand... but all I encountered was thin air. Nothing physical to seal the deal of my lifetime.

I waved my hand back and forth through it just to be sure. But it didn't matter.

"You're right, God, I don't have anything to lose."

I reached into my pocket to pull out my Marley Chan ID and my bradawl. After one last look, I threw both into the industrial bin.

"That's it; that's not me anymore."

*

I walked confidently through the alley – this time without the need to stagger against the walls and noticed two policemen on their beat along Oxford Street. In a moment of urgency, I called out to them, anxious to hand myself in, but they looked at each other, then back at me and then ran off ignoring my call for help. Once I was on Oxford Street, I headed towards Marble Arch, which was abuzz with taxis, night buses, squad cars, tourists. Eventually I found somebody who was able to direct me to the nearest police station, where I waited my turn and then approached the duty officer.

"I've just committed a section 18 and would like to speak to someone about it," I announced.

The rookie officer was startled at this dramatic and unexpected confession. Moments later I was ushered into an interview room, to be joined by two CID detectives, who towered over me.

As we sat down I began to confess recent crimes I had committed, including the "hand" experience. But they insisted I recount my life's story! I declined a solicitor – my goal was still to live out my years in jail – and began an intricate retelling of everything I'd been involved with since my record had been expunged. It couldn't be rushed, and, as the hours passed, my energies were refuelled with regular tea and cigarette breaks.

When one of the detectives ran out of the interview room mid-flow, the interview was halted and the recording machine stopped. "Where's he gone?" I asked. "For tissues," was the reply, "to dab his eyes."

I'd been so engrossed and lost in my story, re-living every moment, that I failed to realise both detectives were in tears. They promised they'd sort out the best possible legal representation, trying to reassure me. I said I didn't care whether Mickey Mouse represented me; I was ready to accept my punishment.

I was introduced to a solicitor who was highly recommended; he nearly fell off his chair when I asked him to "Get me as much time as possible." He said his job was to defend and he wouldn't be able to follow that instruction. At the Magistrates Court, I made no application for bail and was subsequently remanded in custody at Wandsworth prison. Choosing to do what is right seemed to come easier than I thought.

But that was about to change.

*

For many people, the name of Wandsworth Prison will forever be associated with Ronnie Biggs' audacious escape in July 1965, early into a thirty-year sentence for his part in the hold-up of the Glasgow to London mail train, which had yielded around £2.5 million. The Great Train Robber's strategy had been both uncomplicated and brazen – scaling the prison wall with a rope ladder, and then dropping onto the roof of a waiting removal van. While the Home Office was still dithering, in a frenzy about how on earth such a breach had occurred, Biggs was on the other side of the Channel, undergoing plastic surgery and overseeing new identity papers.

Certainly the largest prison in the country, Wandsworth is also, according to some calculations, the most overcrowded. I was assigned to C-wing, Wandsworth's biggest wing. In Wandsworth's case, wings refer to corridors that radiate, like spokes in a wheel, from a central control point.

My time on remand went quickly, I was a fast track and was pleading guilty. I felt a strange peace because I didn't feel I carried any baggage from my past any longer. I'd also lost my cravings for drugs and I refused them whenever they were offered to me. All I had to do was to choose to do what was right and trust God for the rest. I felt happy and was probably the only inmate who wanted to be there; this was now my home again (I'd convinced myself God wouldn't able to get me out of this one!). To make sure I paid my debt to society, I decided to write to the judge and fess-up about the stabbing. I reminded him that I was on a strike which meant an automatic life sentence for knife crime, and now I deserved to have the book thrown at me.

For the first few days, I was in a cell alone, and I passed the time reading a Gideon's New Testament bible with Psalms, which I devoured from cover to cover. I had been warned that my solitude wouldn't last long because of overcrowding, and my immediate thought was "I won't be bothered with them." Then I heard a voice reply "Yes you will, that's who you are; I made you and you are an encourager. You won't be able to stop yourself."

I don't care, I thought, I'm not helping anyone.

Four days after I moved in I had a Nigerian cell mate, a fraudster and drug dealer. Without even realising it, I started being helpful towards him. I couldn't stop myself!

I was getting regular visits from one of the Chaplains called Brian Greenaway. I said, "I read your book in Dartmoor!"

Brian had been acclaimed for his gripping autobiography, The Monster Within: From Hell's Angel to God's Messenger, as well as his habit of wearing a gold necklace with a model shotgun dangling from it, in remembrance of his roots. He'd had an encounter that made him commit his life to serving God and was now a prison chaplain. His wife Jennie often played the piano in the chapel on Sundays. For those who believe, chapel was an opportunity to get out of your cell for an hour and mix with friends.

Having studied criminal law for years in prison and been given an Archbold law book by Wilson for my pains, I started helping prisoners unofficially with their cases – with remarkable results. Anything I didn't know, I checked with Wilson or Kayleigh just to be safe and I referred some inmates who didn't have representation to their firm. I helped prepare defence cases, social enquiry reports, prison adjudications and more for a wide range of prisoners, murderers, armed robbers, arsonists, burglars and fraudsters. At times, I had them queuing up.

The main beneficiaries of my growing legal knowledge were whoever happened to be sharing a cell with me at the time. I helped craft a solid defence for a cellmate who (allegedly) had been one of a group of three who'd scored many kilos of drugs in a logistically complex deal in Switzerland, and been the only one to escape arrest when the police busted their celebratory party. I prepared the defence of "diminished responsibility" for another cellmate who had lived up to his nickname of "Terminator" when he'd leapfrogged the counter at his local police station and started pummelling the officer on duty (Me: "Was it drugs, or had you been drinking?" Vince: "Nah, I just don't like 'em, the police."). Arguably my greatest triumph was securing a minimal sentence – mainly consisting of community service – for a first-time arsonist who was theoretically facing "life". Nobody had been hurt in the fire, and, whilst the law doesn't accept being pissed or stoned as a legitimate defence, I was able to point to toxicology that showed the combination of two different medications he was using can stimulate irrationality and irresponsibility (When in doubt, blind 'em with science – it rarely fails).

One of my cellmates even mentioned to Wilson, who was building a bulging client base on the back of my referrals, that I was the "best lawyer" he'd ever used. I never established whether he laboured under the genuine apprehension that I was legally qualified, but I definitely suspected the "best lawyer" quip was a sly dig in Wilson's direction.

About half way through my sentence, I was given the job of C Wing cleaner, and provided with a mop and bucket so I could get to work. My life was coming full circle; it was cleaning duties at Oxford jail that'd drawn me into the labyrinthine world of how drugs are distributed to inmates. My routine was to begin with the toilets and showers, and move on to the landings and corridors, and my philosophy was that, whatever tasks I was given, I would undertake them to the absolute highest standards, as if they were being performed for the Big G Himself.

Later, I learnt my commitment didn't endear me to other prisoners. When I'd finished my rota, the showers and toilets were spotless, even after the regular occasions when a prisoner had taken it upon himself to smear a wall with faeces, as if it was an art form worthy of the Tate. After I'd tackled it with my trusty bleach and detergent, neither sight nor smell lingered, which set a high benchmark against which to judge other cleaners. More than a few were given remedial duties once their cleaning had been judged wholly inadequate in comparison with the results on C Wing. This resulted in every prisoner coming to my landing to use the toilets and showers.

Having mopped my landing, some prisoners had absolutely no respect. They treated the landing as if they were on the streets. One day, getting to work on the upper landing, I was approached by a prisoner with whom I'd already had a minor run-in, named Raul. He came across my path and I could hear the unmistakable sound of phlegm being fashioned into a ball inside his mouth. The next thing I knew, a huge globule splattered against the side of my wall, and slithered to the floor, in front of me, just by my mop head.

"That was personal," I shouted to him. "F-ing clear it up."

He denied it was him.

I thought, how dare he think he can do this to my floor! The rage was swelling inside me. Beads of sweat broke out across my back, and my body temperature soared, like boiling water. I clenched my fists, preparing to smash the side of Raul's face. Nobody demeans me like that, especially when I'm doing God's work. He needed to be taught a lesson, and there was no better enforcer throughout the Home Counties than me.

I followed him to his cell, my rage mounting. "As far as I am concerned, you're dead, you're already dead! I'm going to take your head off!"

Just as I was about to strike, I heard the voice say loud and clear "What do you think you're doing and who do you think you are? Go and apologise to the guy and tell him you have had a bad day."

I battled internally with the voice. "He spat on my floor," I protested. But the voice reminded me of our deal.

I turned away and cleaned up the mess and said to Raul, "It's alright mate, I've had a bad day and I was just spouting off."

Raul was blissfully unaware of how close he'd come to prematurely finishing his sentence.

"I saw what you did there," said Brian Greenaway, who had been watching me from afar. "You should be very proud of yourself."

That evening, Brian and I studied scriptures together. We read verses and discussed their interpretation, and how we might better embody Christian values in our everyday lives. Brian became my mentor during my time in Wandsworth, and I couldn't be more respectful of the bravery he displayed when he turned his back on his former life and was prepared to help others turn their lives around. If my own decision to reorient my purpose is as productive, I'll end my days a proud man.

My diligence to clean made way for a promotion, and I was headhunted to be in charge of the canteen, as well as prisoners' shopping – meaning I managed their order forms and delivered their proceeds to the cell door. The prison staff who worked in the canteen were so impressed with my work that they used to give me two black bin liners and invited me to help myself in the prison shop to food, toiletries, tobacco and whatever else I wanted. I became more aware of the neediness of those on my prison wing, of how it can be a tipping ground for the homeless. Having been on the streets not so long ago, my heart was moved; I resolved to give out what everyone needed from the abundance that I'd been given. It transformed the wing, and I was so popular that even the prison officers asked me for stuff. I was everybody's best friend and wanted for nothing.

My reputation as an efficient and effective pro bono legal adviser had reached the ears of some members of the Colombian cartel being held in one of Wandsworth's other wings. The "chemist" in their group, arrested within days of his arrival from Bogota and with no fluency in English, was suffering agonies brought on by poor dental hygiene, and his mouth was a riot of abscesses, cavities and inflammation. None of the screws seemed particularly bothered by his torment, probably regarding it as just desserts for all the hurt his work had inflicted. Putting into practice the poignant lesson that it wasn't my role to judge, I spent time getting to grips with healthcare referral procedures and successfully arranged for the chemist to see a prison dentist on an emergency basis. That evening, the chemist (whose jawline was no longer wrenched into an unnatural shape by pain) bear-hugged me in fulsome gratitude.

"You're welcome," I said, wriggling. "Not so hard, please. Wouldn't want my rib cage to snap."

"I'm thankful for your help," said Diego, who was the oldest of the Colombians.

"It shouldn't have been necessary," I replied. "I was only doing what any other decent friend would've done in the same situation."

Diego was my cleaning buddy who was looking after the other side of the landing. He'd previously asked me to get a job in the canteen as money wasn't very good.

The Colombians kept me close and wanted me to help them; they became quite possessive of me. They trusted me like a brother and taught me to speak and write Spanish; in return, I helped them with letters and legal advice. As our friendship grew, we laughed together and played chess at every opportunity.

"Rodjars!" Diego said in his Colombian accent, "I'd like to offer you an opportunity, one for which you'll be generously rewarded. We trust you Rodjars."

It was a lightbulb moment. I knew precisely where this conversation was headed, and it wouldn't end well. After my conversation with The Hand, there was no way Marley Chan would be resurrected, whatever temptations and tests were lobbed in my direction.

"That's very kind," I smiled, "But I really need to get back to my cleaning duties now."

A modest five pounds per week from honest toil with my mop and bucket had many attractions over the short-term riches from the drug trade. Bitter experience of recent years had taught me how short lived are those riches, and how lasting the sadness and wrecked relationships left in their wake.

Eventually the day came when I entered the court to be sentenced.

From the dock, I looked up at the judge, who was holding my letter in his hands.

He removed his glasses to address me.

"Mr Rodgers," he said, "I have read your correspondence, and I have decided not to give you a life sentence. You didn't mean to do this thing."

"What?" I thought. "I've committed a nasty crime and you're telling me I didn't?"

I wanted to stand up and shout in protest. I wanted to repeat the words a previous judge had used to describe me: "A very violent and dangerous man."

Clearly, keeping Wilson away from the court – in case he got me acquitted – had gloriously backfired!

17.
Bali's Story

I was named Bali, its short for Balbinder, and this is my story. My parents had been raised in the Punjab region in northern India, close to the Pakistani border, at a time when education was non-existent and livelihoods were heavily dependent on hard agricultural toil. For a ten-year period following the second World War, and the collapse of the British Empire, the passage of the British Nationalities Act 1948 meant there were almost no restrictions on Commonwealth migration (a freedom that continued until the Commonwealth Immigrants Act 1962, and the Immigration Act 1971).

My parents took the opportunity to travel to England, in search of the "better life". Many immigrants from the subcontinent during that era attempted to adapt and secure those promised riches, and my parents were no exception.

I was the third of their five children, and their second daughter, born about seven years after their arrival in England. During the late 1960s and early 1970s, I was too young to appreciate exactly what was happening in the household, but in hindsight it was clear my parents struggled to cope with the pressures of integration. Their own upbringings had been highly traditional — for example, in the value placed on family structures, arranged marriages, subservient women and a host of daily customs, discipline and rituals passed down through the centuries. When these practices clashed with Western lifestyles, it placed great stress upon their happiness and relationships.

My father took on a labouring job in the building trade in London, where he spent much of his working life. But he fell under the influence of other English and Irish people, also strongly represented in that sector, especially after pay day. As far as I recall at weekends, he'd be drinking and gambling in the local pub for long periods, and this often ended in street brawls or worse. By the time he found his way home, he'd either be bad tempered from the after-effects of too much booze, or bitter at his gambling losses — or both. Inevitably, my mother took the brunt when he was drunk as his brooding fury sought an outlet.

We were in the firing line most days, even when he was sober at times. I spent most of my childhood paralysed by fear and in sibling rivalry, living in an unpredictable environment, when was the next beating or drinking episode coming? By the time I was six, I'd witnessed — and been subject to — domestic violence and psychological abuse.

Having seen extreme poverty, my parents couldn't understand how any child raised in England could ever be considered poor. Yet that was exactly how I felt during my first year at junior school, when I compared myself with my classmates. My mind filled with unanswered questions: how could they talk to their parents like that? Why were they wearing what they wore? How come they have toys? And so many goodies in their packed lunches?

After school, other parents would take their kids to the corner shop, and spend their pocket money on chocolate bars and comics and toys. I was fed and clothed at home, said my parents, surely that was sufficient? I watched an Indian neighbour bring out treats at lunch and break times, showing off her nice bag and clothes. That was it, I decided. I stole for the first time at the age of six; it was just a cheap packet of chews, no harm to anyone, but I got into something I enjoyed, got away with and couldn't resist more. The next year, I raided the teacher's cupboard where the bag of loose change was kept that had been raised during the "Sunny Smiles" charitable campaign (it involved a booklet packed with detachable photos of cheerful toddlers; anyone who donated a few pence got to keep one of the pictures). The teachers were livid at the loss, but I'd perfected a sweet and innocent gaze, so always avoided suspicion. The only people who rumbled me were my siblings, who agreed to keep shtum on condition my pilfering was split five ways.

I was moody for days at the disappearance of eighty per cent of my money, but it did boost our camaraderie as well as the volume of sugar in our system — my dad refused to buy us sweets or toys on principle (what was the appeal? He'd managed perfectly well without them in the Punjab); we had fruit and dinner on the table and these niceties were seen as an indulgence.

I became a compulsive liar, painted a wonderful picture of my home life and made everyone believe I was rich and went to the most exciting places at weekends and was lavished with lots of beautiful clothes and gifts at home.

My shoplifting and stealing from friends and teachers became more brazen as the years passed, and by the time I was eleven, I'd been arrested three times and banned from the neighbourhood corner shop and the Co-op. I had been driven home at times with my father in a police van, having to cope with the embarrassment and shame of "What will the neighbours think?" (a major concern in the Asian community at the time; it seemed a greater issue for my parents than supporting their children).

But the cultural clash between Indian-born parents and their Dartford-born daughter reached its peak during my teenage years, when I yearned for freedom, the typical experiences of any Kent girl hitting puberty. Mum and Dad were preoccupied with their supposed duty to impose a suitable husband upon both me and my sister. I was overwhelmed with self-doubt and regular anxiety attacks; I became painfully thin through under-eating and paranoid about anyone who I saw as having authority over me.

Everything boiled over at the thought of an arranged marriage when, aged 15, I ran away from home during my GCSEs, only to be tracked down by Social Services, and placed with a private foster family. This was a massive culture shock, and not only for me. When it became clear that my demons were being exacerbated by the foster parents, I was passed from pillar to post, culminating in a year-long referral to a psychiatric ward for disturbed young people, where the days merged into one another as an endless parade of needles and drips and whatever it took to manage the psychosis and deal with the anxiety. A relentless regime of antidepressants and other drugs that the experts had prescribed.

My fragile mental state meant that relationships, let alone holding down a regular job, were a challenge. My first paid role was as a computer embroiderer in a local clothing factory, where I turned my hand to producing Formula One badge names for Brands Hatch, fake brand badges sold from the backs of lorries, Nigel Benn T-shirts, and banners welcoming Princess Diana to functions and events.

I wasn't well-paid; if I worked endless amounts of overtime, my weekly wage might reach fifty pounds — in fact, looking back, it'd be easy to argue I was exploited by a hard-line boss as cheap labour. Bizarrely, my natural birth mum worked in the same factory for a while, but never approached me to make contact after I fled from home, and averted her eyes whenever we passed in the corridor.

I channelled my energies into the work, gaining notoriety for my obsession with perfectionist standards, and found it increasingly hard to unwind. Alcohol and, at times, self-harm gave me relief and the willpower and strength to continue. Within a matter of months, I found myself working seven days each week, and supervising a team of five embroiderers. I drove myself so hard that, in the end, I suffered several nervous breakdowns and yet struggled to let go of a role that gave me definition and identity. Workaholism was an internal battle I worked through with a psychotherapist for the next five years. Noticing the pressure I was under, some acquaintances reached out to me — a couple named Linda and Trevor Perry, who I class now as godparents, reached out endlessly and never gave up on me even in my attempts to let go of life, and Angela Hughes who ran the girls' home where I was staying, she patiently stuck by me graciously supporting me. It was harder to opt out of life knowing there were people who cared for me; I spent many evenings battling with the demons, in a darkened room, overdosing, drinking and traumatised by the flashbacks that couldn't be shaken from my mind.

At the same time my childhood friends and siblings were emerging into the exciting and vibrant world of young adulthood, I was still trying to find my feet, and the first glimpse of a better life only arose when I was sofa surfing and taken in by Tim and Ceri Griffiths. Tim was the youth worker and pastor at Dartford's Emmanuel Pentecostal Church, and he ran a household that was full of laughter and love.

He and Ceri had two of their own natural children, Damien and Tara. They had also adopted at birth a delightful Sierra Leonian baby named John while on missionary work in the country, and this had given them with first-hand experience of the "dos and don'ts" of integrating a young person into a different society and culture. Tim was the ultimate calming influence in my life. Whenever he sensed I was stressed or depressed or struggling, he encouraged me to speak openly with them, and was never intimidated or flustered by anything I shared. I was grateful and warmly welcomed by the siblings and into the family, and over time regarded Tim and Ceri as my genuine foster parents, whatever the legal paperwork might say.

Having passed through the system on the inside, and now in a better place having discovered internal peace and faith, I was fascinated by services dealing with mental health issues within the population, and developed strong opinions about how patients could be better supported.

I decided the world of machine embroidery and workaholism would have to solider on without my talents, so I could explore a career as a support worker dealing with substance abuse patients.

My first serious role was back in the psychiatric system working in Vintry ward and then I was headhunted alongside others to develop Bridgehouse. This was an NHS referral unit set up to assist people with drug and alcohol addictions through a short but intensive two-week detox programme using range of therapeutic methods. I soon realised I'd found my true calling — their was a great team and we were working tirelessly and passionately to find ways of providing the best approaches in helping addicts, it was humbling and fulfilling, and, having struggled for so long with similar issues, I found I was able to build trust and rapport with troubled souls whatever their background. It was time to get properly trained, and with the help of Tim and Ceri who were both teachers I booked myself onto courses that would give me fresh insights as well as the necessary qualifications to progress.

By the time I turned thirty, and to my surprise, I was armed with a Diploma in Counselling from the University of East London; I also studied at Lewisham College where the courses covered group therapy.

I was now ready for my next challenge, and it emerged faster than expected. I was given the opportunity to run The Naomi Project in my home town of Dartford by Godfrey Featherstone the Chief Executive and Jean Parks, the Director of Kenward Trust, who believed in me, trusted me and supported me. This was an eight-bed supported accommodation service for vulnerable young women, typically aged between 18 and 50. Residents would be referred for a variety of reasons, including addiction, substance misuse, mental ill health, offending, homelessness, leaving care, domestic abuse or homelessness. The common factor was needing a safe space where they could rebuild their lives away from drugs and alcohol and which — when ready — they could use as a base while searching for housing and employment. The rehabilitation was intensive but never rushed. Many young women stayed at the Project for six months or longer, and the success rate was astounding. For the first time I my life, I regularly felt a glow of satisfaction. I had designed much of the content of the Project's rehabilitation programme with Jean, at the time of Kenward Trust, for example cognitive behaviour therapy and transactional analysis, always with the "twelve step elements," which I knew from my own life was essential in addressing deep-rooted issues and delivered results of real value.

After a childhood spent as an outsider, doubting my self-worth, fearful, hopeless, often crushed and belittled by those around me, it's impossible to underestimate the privilege, humility and the grace of God that I experienced. Me, the black sheep of my own family, had been entrusted to invest my own experience and expertise into the real-life impact of change in the lives of many women at the Naomi Project and to still be able to share in the lives of the women now.

In a different life I might've continued with The Naomi Project until I dropped, but after six wonderful years I feared becoming stale and felt it was time to apply my training to different types of social problems. I applied for a development worker post in Bromley with Turning Point; it was an area reeling from the increasing misuse of prohibited substances in ethnic minority communities, especially by Somalians who had fled a war-torn country, and were still traumatised by what they'd witnessed and experienced. In the 90s, drugs and gang culture was spreading between different minority groups; in the Somalian communities it was often associated with the distribution and misuse of khat to fathers who had nothing to do (khat is a flowering plant from the Horn of Africa and Arabian Peninsula that, when chewed, acts as a stimulant and can lead to feelings of temporary euphoria or loss of appetite).

Of course, many of the problems in minority communities are endemic and will take decades to combat, so it would be wrong to overstate the impact of the interventions I made on behalf of Turning Point and Bromley Council. But, working with a wider team, there were definitely positive stirrings from our engagements with these communities — for the first time, they felt they had a voice; that authorities were paying attention to their plight and the issues they faced. If just one young person turned his back on drugs and violence, just one life was saved from being needlessly lost at the tip of a switch blade, then it was all worthwhile.

As my self-confidence grew, the demons from my youth receded, and I was able to look upon my parents in a different light. With my eyes open, I had a greater understanding of what it is like for many new communities moving to England and their struggles, and was able to consider my own community as people, with their hopes and vulnerabilities, rather than as triggers for my misery. I was able to form a healthier mental image of my dad and mum, and forgive them for how I'd been abused and neglected. One day, walking in the snow to work, I noticed my mum approaching in a car; there was no acknowledgement, no hello, no "Can I give you a lift?" I had made my choices and I knew I had to take responsibility for them.

Every now and then, I'd hear rumours about my brothers and sisters. They were all starting to find their feet, one had entered accountancy, another was a civil servant. Nieces and nephews were entering the world. In the meantime, the years were speeding past; would the time ever come when we could all be reconciled?

I'd been living with my foster parents for almost two decades when I finally felt able to seize my independence. In typical fashion, Tim and Ceri were supportive of whatever choices I made; there was never any pressure to move out, they wanted me to be happy and comfortable with my choices. I felt ready to buy my own place, a nearby flat which I took great pride in furnishing. And of course I still saw them every weekend at church and at family engagements. I would still be part of the lives of Damien, Tara and John – they had all graciously accepted me as family from a young age and I love them all very dearly, they shared their parents with me, for which I will always be grateful.

One Sunday, when the congregation was saying their hellos and settling down, I was chatting with John Pask – a church regular who ran a nearby ex-offender home called the Fathers Arms.

"How's things with Turning Point?" he asked.

"It's going through some changes at the moment, John," I said. "The service is being transferred from the Council to a body called the CRI – Crime Reduction Initiative."

"How does that affect your role?"

"It's uncertain at the moment. The legislation says all our terms and conditions of employment are protected when the transfer occurs; however, that's not necessarily how everything works in practice. It's been suggested my role will disappear and isn't needed after the restructuring. That's typical when you're working with the most vulnerable groups."

"What are you doing about it?"

"I've joined the trade union. If it continues in this direction, there's going to be an almighty Unfair Dismissal case."

John rested a comforting hand on my shoulder. "I'm not an employment lawyer," he said. "But I'm sure everything will work out.

Speaking of which, I'd like to introduce you to somebody who's staying at the Father's Arms at the moment."

"Oh?" John gestured silently across the room, towards a Caribbean guy in his forties, who was chatting amiably with one of the elders. The guy noticed the summons, made his apologies to the elders, and ambled casually towards us.

"May I introduce you?" said John.

The guy stretched out his hand — his forearm bulged with muscle, which wasn't unusual for an ex-con (there's plenty of time for pumping weights when you're on the inside), but the main thing I noticed was his incredible smile. His teeth shone with pure whiteness — lighting up the rest of his face. I felt instantly at ease, and was impressed that his handshake was neither too vigorous nor too overpowering (you've no idea how often I've winced in agony when my fingers have been crushed by over-enthusiastic body builders).

"Hi," said the guy. "I'm Lennox. Lennox Rodgers."

"And I'm Bali."

I haven't seen him around here before, I thought.

I walked away quickly, curious as to why John had seen fit to make the introductions.

During the service I muttered to my friend Sara, "I'm not sure there is a Mr Right out there for me," but when we were called upon to kneel in prayer — meaning all eyes were closed! — she nudged me mischievously, and said:

"What about him, he's gorgeous."

I sneaked open one of my eyes for long enough to realise she was indicating none other than the self-same Lennox! However, my feelings of indifference remained, and I continued in my prayers.

Despite my defiance, I couldn't shake the memory of this character with the combination of charm, his noticeable large muscly arms from years of weightlifting, dark history and a secure presence he carried around him. It was even harder to forget him when he suddenly started popping up at all the same functions and events I was attending. I noticed a couple of voices battling in my head for attention — one of them arguing "Why on earth would you ever start seeing somebody's who's been in jail?" whilst the other was asserting, calmly and a still small voice but insistently inside I heard, "This man is your husband."

Tongues wagged at the amount of time we spent together whenever we found ourselves in the same room — even if we started in opposite corners, gravitational forces seemed to pull us together. One day, John described Tim to Lennox as "Your future father-in-law." It wasn't long afterwards I received an unusually curt text from Lennox saying, "I don't know what you've been telling people, but you're not my girl." As has been the case with a hundred million women through the centuries, a blunt expression of disinterest wasn't enough to deter me; in fact, I regarded it as a challenge. My curiosity was aroused — it was crazy how often we were now circling one another.

One day, I accompanied Lennox as he drove John Pask and his wife Tamsin to the airport; on the way back, he casually suggested grabbing a bite to eat, and before I know what was happening, we were sitting in a booth at the nearby Harvester, tucking into a hearty meal. It was one of the sweetest, most unexpected conversations I'd ever experienced with a guy. On previous dates, I'd become bored senseless before the appetisers had been cleared away, listening to a bombastic, egotistical conversations about their lives. I guess that, being a therapist, I'm particularly in the firing line. Ceri used to say to me during our pre-date pep talks, "Bali if he spends most of his time talking about himself, then forget it!" (On one occasion I had to leave a guy at a bar and call her from the toilets to come and help me make a quick getaway.) With Lennox, for once, my unofficial date was actually showing interest in me. It was a discussion rather than a question-and-answer session.

I opened up about my family, my work with addicts and abuse victims, and my involvement with the many missions and work in the community. He was mildly intrigued that a woman of Indian descent in her late thirties was unattached, but he didn't quiz me about my domestic life.

Then he became more serious and said, "I have been thinking about you." This made me freak inside and want to bolt out of the door.

"I wasn't sure I would want to be with someone so active and with such dominant leadership skills; I've had those types of women in my life and don't need it to be honest."

At this stage I rested calmly back into my seat and pretended not to feel as if I needed to defend myself.

He continued, "But I talked to God and it was as if he pulled me by the scruff of the neck and said, 'Bali isn't dominant, she is bold.'"

He was still talking but by this stage I wasn't listening. Tears welled inside of me. No one had ever been so perceptive or taken the time to think about who I was — not just what I did. It was the perfect thing for him to say to win me over; in fact, it was as if God was speaking to me through Lennox's lips; no human being could possible know me like that. After 38 years on the planet, somebody understood me — and, for goodness sake, it was an ex-con! An out-of-work, penniless, ex-con, but one whose eyes gave a glimpse of charm, kindness and a sense of security.

Our first "proper" date happened a few days later, in Greenwich Park. We walked in random directions, our arms wrapped around one another, talking non-stop — about Lennox's kids, about my foster parents, about some of his lesser crimes, about hopes for the future. We agreed we were in this for the long term.

I lost track of time, but it must've been a few hours before our pace slowed, our talking ceased, and we enjoyed our first chaste kiss. "I think I might love you," he said. My heart fluttered at the thrill and freaked out at the same time. I knew I had been given the heads up so I trusted it would all work out.

The next date involved more food, a game of pool, and — with unintended irony — a visit to the movies to catch a screening of the action comedy starring Brad Pitt and Angelina Jolie, Mr & Mrs Smith (a married couple, each with a secret life as a trained assassin, who are one day assigned to turn their weapons on the other). Things moved quickly from that point, and it wasn't long before Lennox had invited me for a romantic day trip to Paris. At the top of the Eiffel Tower, beneath a cloudless June sky, he bent down on one knee, plucked a ring from his pocket, and asked:

"Bali, will you marry me?"

As far as I was concerned, God had already instructed me that Lennox was "the one". His question merely confirmed that he'd now caught up. So I giggled, knelt down alongside him, laughing at his fear of heights as he held on for dear life to the rail with one hand and said "Yes, Lennox, of course!"

I puckered up and was about to land a full-bodied kiss full-square on his lips, when I noticed he was already upstanding again.

"You had enough already?" I said.

"It's not that," he said, "I just need to get down."

"We've only just got here!"

"But I don't like heights…"

"I sense there's an 'and.'"

"And we gotta catch the Eurostar back to London in less than an hour, so I'm back home by seven."

"Because…?"

"Because that's when my ankle tag bleeps to tell the police I'm safely where I should be!"

I thought, God, I sure hope you know what you're doing up there. One thing's for sure — whatever else you've got in store, life with Lennox sure won't be dull!

*

We were married in the Crayford Baptist Church in front of three hundred people, most of whom crammed into the nearby Slade Green community hall for the reception. Given the estranged nature of many relationships in both our families, compiling the guest list was a task of huge complexity. Most of my immediate family — natural and fostered — turned up, the only significant absentee being my dad. Four of Lennox's sisters were also able to join us for the special day. So many dear friends and family who mucked in a supported our every step, perhaps with some relief and celebration that Bali was finally off the shelf.

The best man ended up being Ricky Walker, a friend Lennox got to know through the church. Chris Grant would've been the obvious choice, but he'd never spoken in front of crowds, and the pressure of saying a few words would have wrecked his day. I'd chosen a bright red dress, while Lennox wore a classic white Indian robe that caused many of his friends to rib him ("You should've warned me; I'd have bought my sunglasses!"). The church service was the longest I can remember, but I didn't care. I loved it.

Tim gave me away and also then married me, my friends made up a huge choir. Music was plentiful — it runs deep in my community, and we were entertained with many performances. One was from my best friend Lynieve, who sang for M. People. We enjoyed a rendition of O' Happy Day by my well-talented foster sister, Tara. There was also a performance from one of Lennox's nephews, one who writes songs for McFly and another who, at the time, had a starring role in Disney's The Lion King.

I insisted on saying a few words — they were brief but heartfelt. I thanked everybody for being part of the occasion, paid tribute to a few dear friends who couldn't join us, and noted that, whatever expectations I had once harboured about the man I might marry, had been well and truly knocked aside when Lennox Rodgers entered my world. We commenced the day with a classic open-top cream Rolls Royce we'd hired for the occasion and ended with Tim's Mercedes. The first chapter of my life was over; I was now turning the page on the next chapter as Mrs Bali Rodgers.

One of the oddities about joining Lennox's life was being introduced to the extraordinary cast of characters he's assembled through his adventures. Naturally, his sisters were all intrigued to meet me, and we were inundated with offers to "stay for a few days". As readers are aware, many of his former associates are based in Oxford, and we took up Julie's offer of hospitality, so I could be escorted to all those places ("the Caribbean Club," "Oxford Jail") about which he'd told such enrapturing stories. The prison had, in fact, been converted into a luxury Malmaison Hotel, and Lennox walked into the place as if he had come home and to his shock and horror they had turned it into a posh hotel. He persuaded the concierge staff to allow us to spend a few moments in the bedroom that had once been his cell.

It was a surreal experience to realise the same space where he'd once experienced things that make my skin crawl was now been charged out to flash businessmen for hundreds of pounds per night.

Lennox was keen for me to meet some of his criminal associates — or, at least, those with whom he hadn't had an almighty falling-out. We showed up unannounced at Trevor Smart's house, and amidst the fog of smoke Trevor's clan glared at Lennox with a look that said, "For goodness sake, here we go again!" The penny quickly dropped, and Lennox explained the purpose of the visit was to announce he had a genuine, flesh-and-bones wife. It wasn't to beg Trevor's girlfriend to wash a blood-soaked shirt — which, back in the day, would've been his opening request from the doorstep.

The most harrowing moment was when we stumbled — almost literally — across Matty Rourke. By now, Lennox had confessed all the darker moments of his previous life, so I was aware of the incident in the Caribbean Club when only Matty's prayers had stopped Lennox from stabbing Matty through the head with his Japanese lock knife. Matty was now dishevelled and unkempt, sleeping rough in the doorway of a boarded-up shop. Lennox squatted on his haunches so he could speak directly to Matty.

"I did you wrong, all those years back," he said. "I was a bad person in those days, a nasty person, and there's no excusing what I did. I don't have the right to ask, but I'd be so, so grateful if you could bring yourself to forgive me."

Matty rolled his eyes, and saliva dribbled from the corner of his mouth. He would've been about the same age as Lennox, but he looked thirty years older. His forearms were exposed, and revealed the tell-tale signs of decades of drugs abuse. He didn't seem to recognise Lennox, and, when he eventually spoke, it was clear that drugs had destroyed his mind.

"You know who I am?" he said.

"Sure," said Lennox. "You're Matty. Matty Rourke. We were once friends and then we fell out. But we can be friends again, if you like."

"Matty? Who's Matty? I don't know no Matty. My name's Lucifer!"

Lennox stayed by Matty's side for longer than I could imagine, chivvying him along, reassuring him, offering one heartfelt apology after another. But nothing was penetrating through the web of confusion that drugs had spun in his mind. Whenever Lennox felt he might be close to a breakthrough, Matty reverted to his default — head back, eyes rolling, regurgitating the same phrase "I'm Lucifer," as if it was a statement of the blindingly obvious.

Of course, the highlight was getting to spend quality time with Chris Grant, who'd been a brother to Lennox since they were scrappy and mischievous little boys playing in the schoolyard together in defiance of the racist bullies. Chris was still a lorry driver, and had settled down with a younger girl called Roxanne (who, as fate would have it, was the granddaughter of Bruiser – one of Lennox's early criminal mentors). I immediately appreciated why Lennox and Chris had forged such a close bind – Chris was painfully shy, but also generous and warm-hearted. Although, truth be told, there wasn't a huge amount of quality time involving me. Lennox and Chris headed straight to the garden, leaving me with Roxanne – who I'd never met before — and didn't re-emerge for nearly four hours! Roxanne and I were struggling to find much common ground, let alone enough to fill four hours, but were fortunately rescued by the appearance of the irrepressible, irreplaceable Mummy G.

"She's a good 'un!" was her verdict about me to Lennox, "She's got a funny accent, but she's definitely a good 'un. Don't you be letting her go!"

Frankly, I dread to think how Lennox would've proceeded if her assessment had been less favourable!

*

As Lennox prepared to (finally) move in with me, he was asked by his friend Rav for a small favour. Rav was a youth worker in Thamesmead who regularly visited the Father's Arms, her and Bobby became very good friends to Lennox.

"I've been trying to talk to this gang of kids," said Rav. "They're called 'T Block'. But, no matter what we say, we can't seem to get through. It's been the same their whole lives – they ignore their parents, the police, social workers. They are a prolific gang known in the area and need help. Something tells me they might respond better if they had a chance to meet you."

"Sure, why not?" said Lennox. "It's not something I've done before. But if you reckon it could do some good, I'll give it a go!"

Rav arranged for Lennox to meet them at a youth centre in Thamesmead. Somehow, he'd managed to corral at least forty of them into attendance — when he arrived, he assumed there might be a half dozen at most. Lennox hadn't prepared a single word, let alone a detailed PowerPoint presentation or a pack of materials for them to digest. But, for two hours, he had them enraptured in his every word. He spoke about his experience of sexual abuse, of being a soldier in a gang, of being in authority in a gang, and of being locked up.

The kids were captivated, hanging on every word, scarcely able to believe his passion and conviction, and that somebody who'd spent twenty years immersed in that way of life could so quickly turn against it. When he invited questions, they flowed without restraint – personal questions, practical questions, factual questions, judgmental questions. And Lennox answered each one precisely, in a down-to-earth manner, using experiences from his life, and without ever resorting to lecturing or hectoring. He only stopped when the youth club manager explained it was already twenty minutes past locking-up time, and even then kids hung around outside to lob further questions his way while he headed towards the car park.

When Lennox returned to the Father's Arms, I was waiting anxiously to see how he'd gotten on.

"I think I've just found out how I want to spend my life," he said.

"You were brilliant," said Rav. I've never seen anything like it. You spoke with such authority and conviction but never patronising, and respectful of the difficulties of growing up in a gang culture."

Lennox quietly said, "They could have been my own children, Bali." He looked emotional. I could tell that a newfound purpose was lighting up inside of him.

"What next? Do you think you can help more?" I asked.

When he spoke, it was as if he'd found the missing jigsaw piece. "I want to refocus kids' lives, Bali," he said.

18. Refocusing

Many thanks to my wife Bali for helping with the last chapter. Our memories of those early days vary slightly, like when two people are looking at the same landscape through different windows, but I can't argue with the overall gist.

The trip to Oxford and seeing what had happened to Matty was one of the most heart-breaking moments of my life. And it's true that, to this day, whenever Chris and I catch-up, we're almost oblivious to everything around us. We get so lost in stories of our childhood and the tricks we played on each other, it's like we never grew up. Most of all, I was really happy when Mummy G met Bali for the first time (no loaded comments along the lines of "What is your intentions with my daughter," with which I'd been bombarded by the parents of previous girlfriends). I was proud of Mummy G and the family into which she'd welcomed me, and I was hoping Bali would love them too.

Anyway, back to our saga. Bali and I were wracking our brains to come up with a name for our new direction, and we'd been going around in circles until Bali remembered the conversation immediately after the T-Block meeting.

"That's it, that's it," she remarked, as her face lit up, "That's what you should call it, Refocus.

For days, images had played on my mind from my meeting with T-Block gang. I kept seeing these young faces that had suffered hurt, rejection, pain and feelings of hopelessness.

Not only could they be my kids; they actually were a mirror image of me. If I was being called to reach these kids, it was just as much for me as it was for them. To my surprise, these kids were going through the same things that had that led me to gang culture and crime. I could see and hear their cry for help. It was a silent cry and it wasn't noticeable to everyone; but to me it drove a deep passion inside to reach out to them.

I'd spent my "working" life operating below the radar, either in undocumented criminal circles, or holding down short-term, unskilled roles. If "it" meant setting up something more official, I'd be stepping into an unfamiliar territory – I needn't have worried because I had a vision of the type of work that might lie ahead. I saw us starting small like a mustard seed, then growing – and working with many other services as Refocus made its impact.

I saw an opportunity to help young people make different choices so they could avoid the same mistakes I'd made. Finally, I could compensate for the years I'd lost by giving back, helping kids of different ages to whom I could be a father and mentor.

It was all too much to take in. I held my head and said:

"Stop! Stop! This is too big, I can't take anymore."

John Pask (who had joined us) laughed as I explained what was happening to me but he fully supported this purpose, and – with his wife Tams—in — would be relentless with his time and advice over the coming weeks. We spent hours around the kitchen table, thrashing out ideas and options for how we could develop Refocus. John had tremendous clarity of vision; I later learnt that he spent long hours praying for our success, sometimes disappearing from our meeting to seek divine guidance. After an evening spent in stimulating but meandering conversation, he was able to summarise the progress we'd made in eloquent and compelling fashion.

Bali was all smiles; from the moment I'd left the Father's Arms, transitioning back into the regular world, she was eager for me to find a worthwhile purpose — both for my own mental stability, and because, in her view, I had so much to offer.

"The surest way to make this official is to set up a charity," said John.

"It'll be called Refocus," said Bali.

"It says what it does!" I added.

"I agree," said John. I can't think of anything that ticks more boxes. We've spoken about how to constitute a charity — from my own experience of setting up The Father's Arms as a charity, I know it's not as straightforward as setting up a normal company. It took us several months to get the status. Charities have tax benefits, so you must satisfy various criteria and pass a public interest test. I don't foresee a problem, but there's paperwork to complete for registration with the Charity Commission. Luckily, I know just the organisation to assist."

John referred us to Bexley Voluntary Services, where we were introduced to a lovely lady called Carol Britnell who walked me through numerous forms, collated my responses, and helped assemble the necessary supporting information.

Carol's magic worked its wonders, and amazingly three months later, we received official confirmation from the Charity Commissioner's offices. It was a heart-warming moment. Charity registration number 1150441 – the digits became ingrained in my mind like my prisoners number. The excitement of being a charity was surreal and Refocus was now official!

I was grateful during this time to Tim Griffiths, my church pastor Bali's foster father who seemed hopeful and encouraged me with the vision, and Andrew Rogers the Church accountant, who gave freely of their time and expertise. Andrew was also our nominated Treasurer, overseeing the setting up of our general ledger, banking mandate, and annual reporting. The contrast with my previous life couldn't have been greater – I was used to money men who devoted their ingenuity and energy to keeping cash flow as undocumented and untraceable as possible.

Of course, having a registration number was the beginning, not the end, of the journey. Our immediate challenge was cash. There wasn't much we could do to further our charitable aims without a steady source of funds.

This was where Bali excelled. She had the imagination to identify a vast array of people and organisations with both money and motivation; she also had the tenacity to persevere, never abandoning hope at the first brush-off. Incredibly, she was still holding down her regular management job at the Kenward Trust while supporting me in my efforts to launch Refocus upon an unsuspecting world. As soon as she clocked off work, she'd head home, and bury herself for hours in application forms, especially grant and donation applications.

Her success rate to me was staggering. I knew how to rob money from people, but no idea how to ask for it to be given freely; that was unheard-of in the world from which I'd come. The first breakthrough came courtesy of the Tudor Trust, an independent grant-making charitable trust with around £250 million of reservoo, which funds "organisations working to support positive changes in people's lives and in their communities." The Trust shares out between £15 million and £20 million pounds annually, and applying for a donation involves a two-stage process which Bali breezed through. When the call came we were asked to see the Trust at their offices and were interviewed. A few short weeks later we received a letter confirming an award for a grant.

Bali shrieked with delight – shouting "Oh my gosh" several times annoyingly, without explaining what had happened. I couldn't quite get my head around the impact this money was going to have on Refocus, and the people we sought to help. After a year and a half, we had the comfort and credibility of a funding guarantee to cover our costs for at least twenty-four months. That gave us a magnificent window to launch something really special.

In 2006, the idea of using ex-offenders to share their stories when reaching out and communicating with vulnerable young people was not always viewed approvingly. However the majority saw value in what we were seeking to achieve, and argued passionately that "people such as you" should be encouraged to reform and rehabilitate, not be defined or condemned because of an unwholesome past.

Potential benefactors were genuinely intrigued; some had faith in our mission from the outset and couldn't do enough to assist our work. We found numerous other supporters around London, especially in areas like Bexley and Bromley.

A gentleman by the name of Nigel Sedierer was our second significant grant advisor. He introduced us to Colyer-Fergusson Charitable Trust, a Trust established in 1969 by Sir James Colyer-Fergusson to support charitable causes in Kent, which pursues the vision of a "fairer and more equal Kent", with a particular focus on young people and rehabilitation. In the Trust's own words, "Even in the most deprived areas, local people have the personal resources to strengthen their communities, if they can operate with equal opportunities on a level playing field."

Refocus was seen as a strong match with the Trust's goals, and they enthusiastically joined the Tudor Trust as one of our invaluable backers.

We had legal form, and we had a financial cushion. The next challenge was to contact services offering to speak with kids at risk of offending and those who needed educational support. At first, the task seemed daunting – which types of organisation might wish to engage us. We needn't have worried, because those who used our services in the early days, unknown to us, very quickly spread the word.

Penny Stotesbury was a youth worker for Kent County Council who opened doors for us to go into youth services and schools; she became a key partner in many projects. PC John Brooker and other police were great partners to work with in Kent and Bexley. Godfrey Featherstone, CEO of the Kenward Trust, allowed me to join as a sessional worker, alongside his youth workers, until I found my feet. We were quickly inundated with invitations to talk with vulnerable young people, especially those who were at risk of being dragged into criminal activities, who had been caught using illegal drugs, or were attracted to gang life and culture. Our popularity spread so quickly that we were working all over Kent and South East London. We really stretched ourselves and took on everything anybody threw at us. In the small amounts of spare time available to me, I studied and trained in youth work, substance misuse and management training.

Not everyone was willing to acknowledge the crime epidemic crimes, especially amongst Kent's youth. Little did they know at the time that turning a blind eye to problems would bite them in the butt, ruining the chances to prevent crime through early intervention.

Broadly, Refocus' services were aimed towards young people aged between 11 and 17, although we worked with kids as young as eight, as well as others well into adulthood. We collected a pool of resources and soon we had visual aids and tools aplenty, all geared to "Refocusing lives by giving hope and living the message". Due to the diversity of issues within the community, it was essential to tailor our programmes, workshops and one-to-one sessions to accommodate a wide range of needs.

Our bread-and-butter were workshops that tackled topics such as crime exploitation and its consequences, drugs and alcohol abuse, gangs, and anti-social behaviour – which were greatly needed by schools, pupil referral units and youth clubs. Over time, we added workshops on other vital matters including bullying, domestic violence, self-harm, risky behaviours, attachment issues, gang issues, and coping with a parent in prison. We attached to some of these workshops the chance for a young person to be a prisoner for the day to demystify the glamour, and show them first-hand what their lives would be like if they made wrong choices.

We also helped poorer families who struggled to get support from other services for their children. The impact and outcomes of our work was regularly measured; Social Services and parents noted quite a change in many young lives. The prison service recorded a 98 per cent success rate with young people turning away from crime after having their eyes opened to some of the realities of a life of crime.

Typically, we'd take participants through a sequence of discussions and activities, enabling them to appreciate their worth, understand any unmet physical or psychological needs, identify patterns of behaviour that might be misplaced and generational. We incorporated David Kolb's model of the four different learning styles and this helped us accommodate students with short attention spans or other learning needs, and made our workshops and sessions as interactive as possible to maintain positive engagement.

Possibly the most personally fulfilling area of Refocus' work has involved one-to-one mentoring. If schools, Social Services or Youth Offending Services came across young people at high risk of having their lives derailed, but with a (heavily veiled) potential to reform, I was asked to mentor them since "they won't listen to anyone else." The Refocus team was invited to work with individuals on a sustained basis, mentoring them towards a positive outcome. As with all mentoring, it was never in Refocus' remit to preach or to judge – our role was to work with young people as they considered their life choices, providing them with insight, information and experience that – hopefully – would inspire them to change their thinking and choose the right path. But, in all cases, the final decision was theirs.

I'll never forget one of my earliest workshops. Bali worked with parents whose kids had been caught with cannabis or other drugs and I helped the same kids on a programme called (DISP) Drug Intervention Support Programme. The initiative involved the police, the Housing Department, the Youth Service, a drug service called Grey Zebra, and a branch of Kenward Trust who helped adults come off drugs and alcohol.

The programme was an alternative to prosecution delivered on a Saturday in most areas in Kent. When Refocus joined, it was struggling. But young people would listen to someone who had been there and done it and got the proverbial T-shirt. The new approach had an enormous impact; people took notice and made positive changes to turn their lives around.

At the same time, Bali's invaluable work with the parents helped reconcile family relationships, showing parents how to listen to the needs of their kids, and support them with more quality time.

The young people seemed fascinated with stories of prison life. For many teenagers, especially those that have overdosed on

American prison dramas, there's a strange, edgy fascination with the idea of being locked up – as if it's a rite of passage that confers glamour, status and respect. "Don't mess with this dude, he's an ex-con," is their delusion. My approach was slightly different. I didn't dwell on the rights and wrongs of being sentenced, or the embarrassment of letting down loved ones (that was covered separately, in one of our "domino effect" sessions). Instead, I burrowed into the grisly details, exploring the reality of being an inmate with gut-churning frankness without using scare tactics.

"Everything I say to you may never be your experience but if you continue to make wrong choices, then at some point in some prisons, you may experience these things." I'd then explain a typical prisoner kit-bag, holding up each item in turn.

"Phil," I said, "would you wear Ted's boxers, sitting next to you."

"F- off man, that's disgusting. Why would I want to do that?"

"You don't get to be so choosy in jail. They give you boxers that have been worn by, perhaps, hundreds of inmates before you. They do boil wash the boxers and sheets, but they can't always remove every stain. I have seen the odd brown stain and sheets with lots of dried white dots all over it."

"I'll wear my own clothes then."

"In some prisons, you're allowed one or two of your own clothes. But, mostly, everything you own is taken from you on arrival, never to be seen again until the day you're released. You wear the same clothes every day until kit-change day, which is normally at weekends."

"F- that. I'll go commando."

"Going commando is your choice, I suppose, also quite brave. Sex is forbidden in prison but it happens all the time; officers are giving out condoms on request."

"Shit! I'm not having that! If you're so clever, what we should be wearing?"

"You tell me. In my experience, there's only one sure-fire way to continue wearing whatever boxers you like, and that's to stay out. In prison, there is a saying: 'If you can't do the time, then don't do the crime'."

"OK, man, I get it."

Later in the same workshop, I asked what happens if you drop the soap in the prison showers. To dispel any myths I described them a typical shower setting. For a laugh, I threw a bar of prison soap on the floor and asked them to imagine themselves in the showers with no screens. "How would you pick it up?" I asked.

The role play was creative and hilarious and loosened the mood. One person managed to lower himself, keeping his backside against the wall throughout the manoeuvre. Another had one hand clasped against his bottom, the other to groin area. The truth is that, in jail, most guys shower in boxer-shorts for privacy; you're fine picking up soap as long as you don't thrust out your naked backside blatantly or provocatively. There are also security cameras in the showers although that isn't the perfect deterrent to violence or sex since, in desperation, prisoners can smear soapy water over the lenses.

Prison food was another favourite topic for the young people because they all smoked cannabis and often had the munchies (hunger pangs are a notorious side effect). "In some prisons, you get fed twice a day, with your first meal served you at 11:30am and your second at 4:30pm."

I described how your breakfast pack consists of a small helping of cereal (emphasis on small) in a sealed bag. The good cereals such as Weetabix, Coco Pops or Rice Krispies are usually swiped by the kitchen boy, leaving only bland stuff – usually bran flakes. The breakfast pack also contains a quarter pint of milk in a small carton, tea bags, two large sachets of sugar and one dried coffee sachet. Most prisoners eat their breakfast in the evening because they're so hungry, meaning there's nothing else until 11:30am (you can stock up from the prison canteen shop, but that requires skills in money management which are rare amongst inmates).

"How do you like your mashed potatoes?" I asked.

"Creamy," answered one participant.

"Smooth," said another. "And nicely warm. Not too hot, not too cold."

"You can forget all about 'nicely warm' in jail."

"Don't we get the chance to heat it ourselves?"

"This is prison we're talking about, not a cookery class. You eat what you're given."

A main meal of toad in the hole with mashed potato and vegetables seems nice in theory, but in reality the pastry is usually burnt and the sausage is hard. The mash is lumpy and you can still see some black eyes where the potatoes haven't been peeled properly. And sometimes a bit of spit if the cooks felt like adding some moisture.

"The vegetables are hard and bland – all the goodness has been boiled out of them," I added. "It's all been prepared in the early morning and re-heated."

To make matters worse, I described how salt is provided in a wooden box into which prisoners take turns putting their unwashed hands to dole out the contents – you'll be fine if you're not squeamish about where their hands have been!

"No pepper is allowed because it can be thrown into prisoners' or officers' eyes, or chucked on the floor to throw drug dogs off their scent," I added.

"Holy shit, that sounds bad. What happens if we leave everything on the plate?"

"That's an option, of course. But if you leave everything that tastes foul, you'll be very hungry for a very long time.

We recognised it was important not just to frighten young people into rethinking their lives, but to be realistic and to hold out a vision of a positive future. After all, even the most bloodthirsty horror movie usually ends on a lighter note. So, in the final few minutes of a workshop, we'd pivot from gruesome details about skid marks and spit-soaked mash, and underscore the benefits of a solid career and a stable family life. "You happen to live in a country that values entrepreneurs and self-starters," I said. "If you buy your BMW through building a business, rather than dealing drugs, no policeman's going to turn up on your doorstep one night and impound it. Wouldn't it be great to drive a car without worrying whether it'll still be yours in the morning and spending every day and night looking over your shoulder?"

As our reputation flourished, our funding sources grew more diverse. Around two-thirds of our income involved paid-for contracts, with Kent County Council and other statutory and voluntary bodies such as Bexley Council, Bexley probation, the Kent Drug Action Team, Bromley Council, Learn Living Peckham, Kenward Trust, schools in Kent and Medway, primary care trusts, housing associations, Kent police, liaison officers. The remainder of our revenue originated with foundations and trusts, with Esmée Fairbairn Foundation, The Lottery, The Brook Trust and Children In Need being added to the roster of supporters that had begun with The Tudor Trust and Colyer-Fergusson Charitable Trust.

After a couple of years, the order book was sufficiently stable for Bali to join Refocus on a full-time basis, looking after the administrative side of the charity as well as being involved in some of the front line service delivery (projects that didn't depend upon "what happens behind bars"). Even with Bali and I working together, the workload soon demanded more resources, and we offered positions to some of the exceptionally talented people who had prospered as a result of the programme. One of our earliest hires was a former traveller and offender, who, having turned around his life, wished to "give something back."

;Recognising that Refocus would be my life for the foreseeable future, I figured it was time to get myself properly qualified. I already possessed a legion of qualifications in fields such as carpentry from my various career false starts, but this time I was in it for the long haul. I signed up with the Chartered Institute for Personnel Development, the professional body for those specialising in human resources and people development with 150,000 members worldwide, and took a course in training management. Other courses I completed included youth work level 2 with London Youth, neuro linguistic programming with David Perridge at New School in Sevenoaks, Kent. and mentoring. This allowed me to hone my skills and comply with current laws, policies and procedures.

I didn't realise the full impact I was making with my workshop sessions until people started stopping me in the streets, either to thank me for my insights or to ask my advice about tricky situations. Once, a young person sat outside a restaurant patiently waiting for us to finish our meal and came up to us and thanked us for helping him through a difficult time. Another time I was shopping in the centre of Dartford, and, whilst queuing for the cashier, overheard a ten-year-old kid near the entrance whispering about me to his parents. "Look," he said, pointing with zero subtlety directly at me, "That's the man I was telling you about. The one who stabbed this bloke in the backside so he wasn't raped."

I felt embarrassed because I was sure I hadn't spoken about my near-rape experiences to kids of his tender years; I later learned that some older youths who had been in my session had shared this information with their younger siblings.

Notwithstanding the "backside" tale, it was stories of my prison experiences that inevitably captivated my audiences. I'd been pondering how I could ramp up the impact, when, one day, Bali mused:

"If they're so interested in your life inside, why don't you show them first-hand?"

It was an inspired suggestion. Over the next few days, I wrote to prison governors throughout the country asking for the chance to bring a group of Kent kids onto their premises. It took hours to compose a note that struck the right tone. Before I could agree to take young people to any prison, I always went to see things first and discuss any risk assessment issues. I didn't want to scare the kids needlessly, and therefore needed to concentrate on those on the verge of encountering the criminal justice system, who would benefit from a better understanding of the reality of prison. It also allowed me to say, "Don't take my word for it, come and see what prison is like for yourself." The first prison to respond positively was HMP Glen Parva in Leicestershire, which delighted me – they operated a hard-hitting "last chance programme" for young people in nearby towns, and I managed to persuade them to extend it to kids I'd bring along for the day.

Glen Parva's proposed itinerary meant being on-site by nine thirty in the morning. If we'd been based in Loughborough or Derby, that would've been a cinch; from Dartford, the challenge was slightly more complicated. The kids I planned to take had to assemble at the Dartford Crossing at 6am – travelling from different parts of Kent, some of them needed to be out of bed by four. I feared an almighty list of no-shows, but was proven pleasantly wrong. Everyone who'd signed up for the visit was in the minivan bang on time, and, having beaten the commuter rush around the M25 and up the M1, we arrived at HMP Glen Parva ten minutes earlier than expected. For the next five and a half hours, my gallant band of kids were treated as roughly and rudely as any of the regular inmates. When one of them, Craig, was deemed to have been star-jumping half-heartedly during gym warm-up, the entire group – inmates as well – was told they'd be spending more time on "wimpy" cardiovascular exercises, much to the annoyance of the actual prisoners who were missing out on valuable time in the weights room and who threatened, "Wait till shower time."

Some of the group grumbled they wouldn't be showering, and one boy said, "I ain't getting raped." I was chuckling at their naivety, but also took pains to reassure them they were safe – a prison experience is what they wanted and that's what they were getting.

Another lad, called Chuck, refused to follow orders, and started swearing and kicking things around. Someone pressed the incident alarm bell and prison officers rushed from everywhere – there must have been at least forty of them which terrified my group but certainly made the point. They restrained Chuck (now classified as "the violent offender") and consigned him in a punishment cell for a couple of hours. When they let him out, he was one of the best behaved on the group. After that, no one else tried to push at the boundaries, reality had hit them all, and with it came a compliant silence.

After dinner, the group went outside for exercise in the yard, with two warnings: not to retaliate to any verbal abuse, and not to stray too close to the walls in case nasties were dropped from cell windows. Prison officers creased with laughter as the prisoners engaged in non-stop, highly inventive, mickey-taking of the kids in my group, until they eventually calmed matters with a curt call of "Enough now, lads."

The kids who accompanied me to Glen Parva all fancied themselves as hard nuts and wannabes. They were nominated by Pupil Referral Units, the Youth Offending Service and the odd referral by the police who tried to help some youth make a change before he gets in too deep with his criminal behaviour. This meant they had a wealth of deep-rooted baggage such as exhibiting psychotic or antisocial behaviour, excessive aggression and rage, or attention deficit disorder, and a lot of their behaviour was made worse by their heavy use of drugs. Driving back home down the M1, the mood in the minivan was one of great relief that the ordeal had come to an end and they were free once more. They implored the driver for a pit-stop so they could all indulge in a much-needed cigarette and a well deserved McDonalds.

One little guy said, "I swear to you, if that arsehole in the gym had said one more word to me, I'd have punched out his lights. That's all it would've taken. Just one more f- word."

We all rolled with laughter. The prisoner he had in mind was a six-foot African guy with eighteen-inch biceps, who now travels the world competing in body building tournaments.

After that, having spent nearly six hours being insulted and berated and deprived of their independence, tiredness hit home. I started work on writing up the experience, for our own records and to send to the prison. It had exceeded my expectations in all respects, and was an experience I was keen to repeat.

*

They say the essence of great comedy is timing, and I could never have been a stand-up because mine has always sucked. Refocus was just hitting its stride when the global financial crisis knocked the economy off course – and with it, the budgets of local governments and statutory bodies. Refocus was in the firing line, because we were the ultimate discretionary cost. Far easier to cut funding to a small charity than to lay off staff members with employment contracts and trade union membership. For a few nervy months, I feared we wouldn't make it through another financial year, until one of our trustees said me we needed to sharpen our messages about the outcomes of the work we'd delivered. Even though we had been able to show some fantastic outcomes with feedback from young people, parents, teachers and other services, somehow, it just wasn't enough.

Our research revealed that, in our first few years, we'd touched the lives of a remarkable 9,500 young people, 90% of whom found our workshops or programmes of personal value, and 75% of whom subsequently made a conscious decision to reconsider their behaviour around bullying, drugs or knife crime. In one programme, 53% of 200 participants had pledged to stop their use of cannabis; in another, 45 (of 135 I'd spoken with in group sessions) had requested one-to-one mentoring. In the most recent year, we'd helped 156 young people in alternative curriculum schools and centres, with 30% deciding to stay in their education or head to apprenticeships, employment or college; we'd also trained and mentored 15 ex-offenders, six of whom were quickly in paid employment with the balance volunteering.

The results from our intensive nine-week programmes were possibly the most astounding. Over the period, we'd worked with 600 kids on a one-to-one basis and had recently been asked to support ten young people on the verge of exclusion. At the end of the intervention, six of the ten had reversed course. Not surprisingly, our folders bulged with appreciative correspondence. For the first time, I collected together many of the enthusiastic, unsolicited testimonials, provided by our beneficiaries and by the professionals who commissioned our work. There were far too many to include in this chapter, but the following provide a flavour:

"I am convinced Refocus will have a lasting and positive impact on the young people they work with."

"For a group of young men from one of our housing estates, the 'Inmate For A Day' programme was a high impact, no holds barred experience of life inside and has really made them think about the choices they make."

"[He] is now back in education and has been top of his class in most of his subjects, has a healthy relationship with his mother and no longer spends time with local gangs."

And I can't resist adding a couple of comments from young people themselves, shortly after experiencing our prison visit programme:

"I need to stay away from crime."

"Never realised before how you get bullied in prison."

"I better stop getting in trouble."

I'd been told by the trustee that it wouldn't be sufficient simply to tug at the heart strings in our communications. Local and government officials respond with greatest zeal if a cost-benefit analysis demonstrates a solid, hard-nosed financial return from early intervention. When young people are stopped from travelling down the road I'd once taken, the numbers are dramatic. The Ministry of Justice estimated, at the time, that the average annual cost of keeping a prisoner locked away is nearly £35,000. When pupils are excluded from education, the direct costs of the Pupil Referral Unit – about £15,000 annually – is just the tip of the expense to the taxpayer.

Over a lifetime, the cost – including damage to future employment chances and social costs from crime and substance abuse – quickly mounts up to a staggering one-third of a million pounds. And, whilst they have the ring of truth, those were not Refocus' numbers but from a 2007 government commissioned report entitled "The National Behaviour and Attendance Review". When these figures are piled one on top the other, the total estimated cost to the economy from failing to break the cycle of young people entering the criminal justice system exceeds £11 billion, more than half the entire budget of the Transport Department.

If the one-year re-conviction rate for young offenders leaving prison (73%, compared with 47% for adult offenders) can be reduced by a few percentage points, the financial, social and community benefits are immediate, worthwhile and widespread.

As the financial crisis worsened, the funding world changed, and we were told we needed to upscale our applications and become much more business minded. Our bids had to be even more outcome based and identify the cost benefit equation. Neither of us had the time to take a fundraising course, so this hardened attitude started to cause problems.

Bali and I drafted and published a booklet about Refocus' track record which, to this day, is a testament to the impact we were making. It contained a brief synopsis of Refocus' history, contained bios of myself and Bali as co-founders, and described our volunteer network, services, governance and future priorities. In the final pages, it highlighted the "outcomes and achievements" which are at the forefront of every single workshop we run and programme we design. I'm exceptionally proud of every item on the list, and would like to close this chapter by re-capping on them:

Provide young people with hard hitting real-life workshops and intense mentoring, as an alternative to prosecution.

Reduce offending and re-offending behaviour around Knife crime, Drug using, Violence crime and Gang culture.

Equip and empower young people from low to high level crime, with tailor made, hard hitting, innovative and creative programmes to address subjects such as bullying, gangs, grooming, drugs, knife crime, self-confidence, respect and crime.

Empower children and young people with early intervention and prevention workshops, to stop exploitation and grooming into crime/sex/money laundering/gangs/drugs.

Increase the positive role models and peer mentors from different BAME (Black and ethnic minority backgrounds).

Reduce the proportion of vulnerable 15 - to 17-year-olds from being excluded and becoming NEETs (not in education, employment or training), using one-to-one mentoring and teaching conflict resolution as alternative solution in school. Empower families and communities by providing solutions and support.

Work in partnership with the Police, Council, Early help, parents, Faith groups, Youth services, Probation, Youth Offending Teams and schools.

This truly remains the heartbeat of Refocus.

19.
Full Circle

It was difficult to imagine the media would want to contact me and take an interest in the work of Refocus. Other than BBC's Crimewatch programme, was there any desire to cover these deep-rooted issues? How could we possibly compare againts't breaking news from Parliament and Number 10? Or the latest celebrity divorce? Or the midweek Premier League results? I had a platform to voice the cry that many young people felt, but in the UK's population of 66 million, our interventions surely would seem microscopic and inconsequential.

But I believe every child matters and even if only one child is saved, it's worth it. I was shocked when I found that, after all, there was a willingness to give attention and priority to the societal challenges we were highlighting.

It all started with a passing reference in the Evening Standard to "gangs in Kent". The police were flatly denying their existence, while Refocus was being quoted as a charity working to eradicate the effects of Kent and South East London's gang culture on its youths. Clearly both statements couldn't be true, and BBC South East News decided this was a story that merited journalistic investigation. We agreed to discuss our experiences on-screen through journalist Colin Campbell and set up for the reporters to meet, and interview, a young kid we were helping with gang involvement, on the condition that his identity was disguised when the programme aired. As soon as I'd made the commitment, I was excited at the opportunity to justify the need for the work we were doing – but also a bundle of nerves.

"I've never been interviewed on TV," I offloaded to Bali.

Bali reassured me that it would be fine. "Just tell it as it is. You're good at that," she said. "Besides, they're just people, and it's not like you haven't been interviewed before, in job interviews, police cells and under oath in courtrooms, when it was your liberty at stake. What's the worst that can happen?"

Bali offered to provide some media advice in the run-up to the show, based on her experiences dealing with the press while at Turning Point. She recounted her experiences and how she'd learnt to get focused on the points you needed to make, and never to be thrown off balance by an unexpected question from the interviewer or someone else's interjection.

"It might be helpful to write down some bullet points on a piece of paper," she said. "But don't keep looking down when you're answering, and don't worry if you forget things or make mistakes. That's perfectly natural. Relax and be yourself and have fun doing it."

While we rehearsed, Bali lobbed non-stop questions, giving me valuable experience of keeping to my central message of the challenges facing vulnerable young people surrounded by gang temptations. Bali had a sixth sense for when I was veering off track and kept returning me to the point. Her trickiest questions included, "So are you saying the police are lying or they just don't want to scaremonger?"; "That's enough about local gangs, tell us about when you were in a gang?"; "Which political party is most effective at tackling crime?"

As I went off-track to a direct question, Bali steered me back to the notes on my piece of paper. "Try to remember that you're not there to endorse one party or another," she said. "We're a non-affiliated charity and we'll work with politicians of all types to make a difference."

"But that's not what they asked," I countered, naively.

"Doesn't matter. You can't be expected to comment on other people's experiences, because you're not them. Keep coming back to what you've seen and heard in Kent and South-East London; nobody can contradict that. Keep it real." Her training was extraordinarily helpful.

When the crew arrived for the interview, it was like the paparazzi were in town – reporter, lighting guy, sound engineer. However, I held my nerve and concentrated my remarks, as Bali had suggested, upon areas where Refocus had direct knowledge. In fact, Colin Campbell wasn't as demonic as I'd feared; no-one spent the time trying to trip me up, or promote a hidden agenda, the team was constructive and reassuring.

When I re-watched the interview on a DVD – in the era before catch-up TV, programme-makers often sent a physical DVD to anyone who'd participated upon request – I was pleasantly surprised at my coherence and fluency. Although I did promise myself to cut down on the "ers" and "umms." (Typical example: "We, er, set up the charity because, umm, we wanted to make a difference, and umm felt umm, that working with young children who had, er, made some wrong choices would umm yes be a good intervention. Y'know.") Throughout my childhood I had suffered with a stutter and when I was under pressure I found it difficult to communicate and now I was being asked to fire answers back at a speed I never done before.

The most moving part of the show was set in Dartford's Central Park, 256 acres of ornamental gardens and informal open spaces at the south end of Princes Road. I was interviewed on a park bench, the River Darenth in the background, alongside a sixteen-year-old kid with whom I'd worked, and who was bravely willing to share his experiences. He'd been drawn into gang culture shortly before his fourteenth birthday for "something to do", and because "all my friends was doing the same."

He was hooked on cannabis from a young age which spiralled into drinking eight cans of cheap lager every day, and his need to sell drugs and do robberies to fund his habit. "Once I'd started, it became harder to stop," he said, shaking his head, overwhelmed at the memory of a youth spent dealing with psychological issues, an absent father, being bulled in primary school, addictions and gangs – all at an age that should be filled with optimism and excitement for the future. Colin and his news team were true to their word and their professionalism; this wasn't their first rodeo.

The boy was treated with respect and filmed in silhouette, with his words being subsequently dubbed by an exceptional voice artist. Even his own mother would've struggled to recognise him. The impact was extraordinary and gave Refocus more recognition with the general public, who called the station – and us – with questions and often to seek help with their own kids, as they struggled to figure out whether they were hanging out with a "group of friends" or a "gang". The issue was now firmly placed on the public policy agenda with the local council.

I learnt that, like many other professions, the media is a close-knit community, and word spreads quickly. Refocus' name was picked up by many other journalists – initially, incoming enquiries were from local press and radio, but increasingly we were called upon by national broadcasters too. Generally, if the journalists seemed prepared to give us a fair hearing, we embraced the opportunity, even when we knew some of our most searing comments would be edited to fit the available air time. We live in a media age; unless the public is aware of an issue, it's an uphill battle to make a change. Most importantly, I wanted to demystify the widespread impression that young people, who've had a rough start, are somehow evil or beyond hope. The dice rolls differently for each one of us – my dream was for parents to think of every unfortunate young drug soldier with love in their heart, because that child could so easily be their own son or daughter.

I learnt there was a strong correlation between bad news hitting the headlines, and calls from broadcasters and production companies asking me to share my insights. In August 2011, following the shooting by the Metropolitan Police of the 29-year-old Mark Duggan in Tottenham, London endured five days of rioting, arson and looting, which quickly spread to other towns and cities in a wave of copycat violence. More than 3,000 arrests were made across the country, causing a bottleneck in the court system until arrangements were finalised for extended – even all-night – hearings.

Five people died, and property damage ran into the tens of millions of pounds (one source put the estimate as high as £200 million) before the mass deployment of police officers began the slow process of restoring order. I was interviewed for ten minutes on Sky News alongside former gang member Timothy Clark, and was blunt in my assessment. One of the points I emphasised, which seemed to resonate, was about the lack of opportunities for ex-offenders attempting to rebuild their lives after release. "It's hard to get a job. It's hard to get a bank account. You learn to do time inside, but it can be even harder trying to live a normal life outside, so don't do the crime if you can't do the time or cope with the consequences."

I remarked, "Kids struggle to cope with boredom? That's why it becomes a merry-go-round. If there aren't any youth services to provide guidance, support and activities, it's not long before you're back on the gang treadmill and then back inside."

"Very sensible words of advice for our justice system," said the presenter, "I hope everyone's listening."

In the madness of the moment, the scales of justice tipped in response to the public outcry, and there were examples of spontaneous, low-level looters receiving harsher sentences than those involved in knife crimes. Over the year ahead, there would be a domino effect. Vulnerable people caught up in the heat of the moment would fall into the eager hands of organised crime networks, and be schooled in far darker ways.

A few years later, the explosive statistic was released that London was suffering from a higher murder rate than New York City, largely due to the soaring levels of knife crime. Politicians searched for easy, soundbite solutions – "bring back stop-and-search", "harsher penalties for carrying a knife" – although, as the murder rate escalated, there was a rising sense of helplessness and desperation (London Mayor Sadiq Khan was widely criticised for admitting it might take "ten years" to get the levels of violent crime under control).

Once again, Sky News, Radio 5 Live, LBC and others were queuing up to air my observations and opinions. In one interview, I pointed out the high proportion of fatal stabbings which are black-on-black crimes. This was a fact which an over-sensitive white establishment was reluctant to acknowledge, but, in my view, problems cannot be effectively addressed through practical on-the-ground measures, unless the will exists to understand the reality and tackle the grass root issues. I'll be setting out my suggestions in more detail in the next chapter.

Not all my media work was in response to tragedy hitting the front pages. The most fulfilling appearances were those that shone a light on the power of positive interventions to redirect young lives onto a better path. For a number of years, the work of Refocus was in the spotlight as a beneficiary of the BBC's Children In Need campaign – an annual telethon which, since 1980, has raised over one £1 billion for disadvantaged children and young people. One difference between Children In Need and most of our media coverage was that, in this instance, I wasn't required to trudge up to London to be interviewed in a studio setting. Instead, the filming took place at local venues such as Leeds Castle in Maidstone, Woodville Halls, and our offices on the Dickens Estate in Gravesend. This allowed viewers to witness activities at first-hand. It was always a magical moment when the cameras started rolling; even the most cynical young kids spruced themselves up so they made a good impression on TV.

Ten years on, you might expect me to be an accomplished old hand at the media game. The truth is spontaneous interviews still have a tendency to throw me, especially when forced to think on the spot with the dazzle of camera lights all around.

I still feel the proverbial butterflies in my stomach as the interviewer pitches his first question; it's hard to comprehend that every random word that tumbles from my lips is being broadcast, by the miracle of technology, into a countless living rooms. Bali's advice is as priceless today as in the beginning. I still jot down relevant bullet points, commit them to memory, and do my utmost to remain calm and speak from the heart. I remain passionate about Refocus, and speaking on behalf of the communities we support is a great responsibility.

*

It was one thing discussing the work of Refocus on television and radio; it was quite another to open up about my own family. Nothing could prepare me for the deeply personal experience of appearing, with Bali, on the Channel 4 documentary "Jailbirds", which explored the impact of prison upon loved ones on the outside.

We were interviewed at the offices of the Koestler Trust, near Wormwood Scrubs, surrounded by prisoner artwork, all of which had been submitted during the previous twelve months by offenders, secure patients and detainees. One of the Trust's more enduring activities is to organise an annual exhibition, at the South Bank centre, that displays prisoners' paintings, music, writing and sketches.

In one of the most emotional moments of the programme, Bali explained why the creative works of prisoners can have such a profound emotional impact:

"This is an opportunity for offenders to express themselves. I imagine they'd be a lot more bottled up inside if not for this outlet. Looking at their pictures and artwork, you can sometimes tell what that person is going through. It can give you a connection that's sometimes not possible just from going to visit them."

But I'm getting ahead of myself. "Jailbirds" had selected us to share our experiences not because of my own regular stints behind bars – I couldn't paint a picture to save my life – but because of another family member. One who hasn't appeared in these pages since he'd been abducted to Florida in 1985 by my first wife, Susan. Twenty-two years and nine months had passed since I'd last seen him in the flesh, when Susan had escorted him through the security checks at Heathrow Airport for a "short holiday with his grandparents." My beautiful first-born, Mark.

The circumstances of my reunion with Mark were troubling, to say the least. One of the reasons I'd refrained, for two decades, from reaching out was the illusion he was living the American dream. Perhaps he'd been captain of the school basketball team, perhaps he'd been accepted by a top college to study law of medicine, perhaps he now lived in his luxury condo with his swimwear model girlfriend in a gated community. After all, isn't America the place where anybody, no matter their background, can be elected President if they work hard and play by the rules.

In hindsight, these thoughts might have been my coping mechanism for dealing with my failings as a father – all those years ago, when I'd allowed Susan time with Mark, I'd ignored the wishes of not only the civil courts but the hospitals doctors, health visitors and social workers.

Tragically, the American Dream hadn't been Mark's story after all. He'd been neglected by the Preston family and struggled with addictions and abusive relationships. Before his twentieth birthday he'd served time for drugs offences and robbery. Unsurprisingly, during the period he was incarcerated, the American authorities concluded this wasn't somebody they wanted in their country. His right to remain was revoked, and arrangements were made for him to be flown back to his country of origin, accompanied by a handful of other British citizens who had overstepped the mark.

I knew nothing of these developments until I was contacted by the organisation, Missing People, with whom I'd been registered for some time. The charity "offers a lifeline" to the 180,000 people who run away or go missing in the UK each year, so that "every missing person is found safe." When they contacted me to explain that Mark was in the country, the moment of which I'd dreamt for 22 years, my mind filled with sadness and disappointment. Partly, it was the circumstances (whatever happened to the college degree and the swimwear model girlfriend?). Also, I harboured serious doubts about the reality of what I was being told. During my own spells inside, I'd come across multiple fellow inmates who'd stolen someone else's identity, impersonating them in furtherance of their own interests. Perhaps the real Mark had been the victim of such a scam.

The Finsbury Park charity, Prisoners Aboard, had supported the so-called Mark in his resettlement, and had been in contact with Missing People to coordinate our reunion. A time and place were arranged – the early afternoon, outside a centre the charity ran in Edmonton. Bali could hardly contain her excitement – "It's finally happening!" she screamed down the phone. But I headed there with deep reservations. Why would I want anything to do with the man who'd taken Mark's identity? What type of person would put relatives through such a charade?

My scepticism wasn't relieved when we finally set eyes on each other.

"Dad, it's great to see you," the potential-imposter said, flinging his arms around me. I hugged him back, half-heartedly. He looked nothing like I imagined – and nothing like me. For starters, his skin tone was all wrong. Plus, he was shorter than either Susan or me. And he was rough looking, with stubble and unkempt dreadlocks. I still pictured my Mark as a clean-cut college boy, the "big man on campus". The gulf with between my perception and the person hugging me was unbridgeable.

On the other hand, I didn't have it within me to turn my back and abandon him. I offered him a drink at a nearby pub – strangely he chose orange juice (which had been my nickname for him) – and listened patiently and with sadness as he recounted his tale of how "it all went to so wrong." Apparently, everything had been blown out of proportion, it was all a huge misunderstanding, the authorities were under political pressure to "toughen up" and he'd been caught in midst of a witch-hunt. As this young lad was speaking, I thought, "looking at how my life went wrong, who am I to judge Mark on his?" Then, the belief he was an imposter forced its way back into my consciousness. How could I process all these thoughts?

When I introduced Bali to Mark she couldn't understand why I was so doubtful as she recognised the match to the polaroid of his younger self on our book shelf, and tried to reassure my doubts. We took him back to the temporary bedsit with which he'd been provided – a curtain-less room, empty except for an antique firearm, visible to anyone who'd peered in through the window. The threadbare carpet was so sodden from leaky pipes that it squelched underfoot and a smell of damp lingered all around the place. "At least I haven't seen a rat for a couple of days," he said. Both Bali and I were stunned that prisoners abroad could dump someone so vulnerable in a crack house, living amongst rats. No wonder the British government is broke – I later found out the taxpayer was paying out six hundred quid every week for this hellhole.

The firearm wasn't one of the registered fixtures and fittings; Mark had "acquired" it (it hadn't taken long for him to fall in with local gangs), and, despite the drawn-out period of official resettlement, nobody had bothered to explain to him there are certain items which don't raise an eyebrow in the States (being readily available at K-Mart as part of the weekly shop), but happen to be illegal in countries without a second amendment. Fortunately, the Metropolitan Police were running one of its occasional "weapons amnesties" at the time, so, despite his protestations that he was being left "unprotected", I persuaded Mark we should take advantage of the no-questions-asked policy, and turn the gun over to the authorities.

My mind was made up. It didn't matter whether this was Mark or an imposter (eventually, he confirmed his identity by producing a photo of him surrounded by the Prestons, leaving me scratching my head as to why he waited so long, but also angry at myself for being do doubtful). Here was a young man in need, right now, of support and love and family.

After much persuasion, he reluctantly tore himself away from the local gang and accepted our offer to cover the rent for a house-share arrangement in the Kent village of Stone, famous for its medieval castle built from flint (a 40-foot tower remains standing to this day), and its close proximity to the Bluewater Shopping Centre. Surely, being surrounded by our friends and family it would assist his rehabilitation, especially since he was house sharing with an upstanding man in his thirties who held down a regular job as a local bus driver. We even helped Mark find employment in the kitchens of a local Harvester.

After our enforced twenty-two year separation, everything seemed set for an untainted happy ending, especially as Bali and Mark bonded quicker than I had. Bali "got" him more than I did, and they shared a passion for cooking.

I'll never forget the moment when, whilst listening to music on his phone, Mark said, "Come here, Dad, I'll introduce ya to some music ya've probably never heard before."

"Who's that?"

"A bloke called Michael Jackson."

"What kind of dinosaur do you think I am?" I chuckled at the unintended insult.

I'd been a loner most of my life, unable to sustain a relationship – or even, with the exception of Chris Grant, a friendship – for more than a couple of years. Now, I was in a close family unit – myself, Bali, Mark. When he settled down with a nice girl, the jigsaw would be complete. I hoped this contentment could last the remainder of my days, and made plans to introduce him to his sister Karen, who was anxious to meet him.

But the family unit wouldn't even make it two years before it was torn apart. Looking back, I've asked myself a hundred times whether there was anything we could've done differently. Perhaps the scars from Mark's upbringing ran too deep. Or he'd never fully recovered from the time, in Florida, a freight train had clipped the side of his head as he raced across the tracks, leaving him hospitalised and with unfinished surgeries, dependent on prescription drugs to null the pain. Perhaps he simply found more kinship and fellowship with the drugs gangs than with his blood family.

Whatever the reason, I'll never stop reflecting on those magical days, and thinking wistfully about an alternative world in which Mark remained a permanent fixture of Kent life, settling down, marrying, having a family of his own. A world in which he and I stayed tight, speaking every day, confiding in one another; a typical, loving father-son relationship in an ideal world.

The first sign that we weren't living in that idyllic alternative world came when Mark was fired on the spot by the Harvester for unruly behaviour, exacerbated when he nipped outside for a quiet spliff to calm his nerves. Shortly afterwards, he was evicted from the house share for (in the words of the landlord) "turning it into a doss house"; as guarantors, we were asked to certify the damage, and knew immediately we wouldn't be seeing our deposit back.

The carpets and walls reeked with the smell of weed; nasty stains were ingrained in the upholstery, and the toilet, sink and bath clearly hadn't seen a squirt of Jiff throughout the tenancy. As tactfully as possible, I asked Mark why he'd wasted this opportunity. Was there a hint of remorse; anything to demonstrate he'd learnt from the experience, and wasn't stuck in a cycle of despair and self-destruction.

He glared at me as we argued; then he turned away, unwilling to listen to any more. Briefly enraged, I held him tight against the wall.

"You will listen," I said. "You know the work we do and you pull this shit." I wasn't just referring to the Harvester fiasco. I'd also learnt he'd been drawing kids into a gang, and had recently put a knife to the throat of a 15-year-old boy who owed him ten quid for some cannabis.

Mark mocked me. "Go on, do it, hit me," he said. "You know you want to."

I was weighed down with guilt when I realised he was right.

"Dad," he continued, "You can't live my life for me."

Again he was spot on.

"I'm sorry, son. Yes, it's your choice," I said, and released my hold.

I shuddered. His facial expression was all too familiar. It revealed the toxic combination of arrogance and contempt which had once filled my heart, when I'd been enforcing debts on behalf of drug-dealing gangs. No matter how we might try to reason with him, and alert him to the danger he was creating for himself and those around him, our advice was increasingly met with contemptuous silence. He was hell bent on destruction. Later that week, he even blurted out he might need to kill someone to deal with the extreme rage he was feeling.

Having just got my son back, this was like the worst nightmare. I felt broken inside – I'd lost him once, was this now happening again? Now, I must make a choice – would I save my son, or other people's? I was reminded of the deal I'd made with God in that alley a few years ago – to "Choose what's right and trust me for the rest." It would be hypocritical to teach kids to take the right course if I wasn't prepared to do the same.

The words of encouragement I used in my mentoring sessions echoed back, haunting me: "The best thing you can give your kids is a good example on how to be a decent human being,"; "If you don't want to change, you won't change; you have to want to change for this to work."

We decided to report Mark's gang activities, including the knife incident, to the police. It might destroy our relationship, and blow apart the family unit, but I had to think of other people's children. It was an awful choice, but I'd prefer to lose my son rather than see him kill someone else's son and live with the regret.

To my astonishment, the police admitted to knowing about some of these activities in the area but wouldn't be acting upon it at this stage. My heart sank. Both Bali and I were broken because we felt the situation was urgent.

It was little consolation to learn that, when the inevitable happened, amidst the horror and carnage the life that was lost was not Mark's own.

Every gory detail of the appalling events that led to Mark's arrest, and subsequent conviction, were recounted during the week-long trial in late 2008, which Bali and I observed throughout from the public gallery of the Old Bailey. Mark had come under the influence of a crack dealer named David Smith, who had also been deported from America; in fact, they'd been nicknamed "Jock One" and "Jock Two" on the streets of Tottenham on account of their accents. Smith had established himself in the north London drug scene, dealing crack and heroin to prostitutes and other addicts from his home in

Green Lanes, and had recruited Mark to "work the night shift" at a crack den in Edmonton.

One evening, Malcolm Berry, an 18-year-old customer at the den, had been taking drugs with a girl, a heroin-addicted prostitute. When Amy accidentally knocked over Malcolm's crack pipe, he'd taken a replacement rock from Mark, saying "You know it's only a tenner, I will settle up later."

The following morning, Smith learnt of this, and was livid at the "disrespect", inciting Mark to accompany him to "teach him a lesson." Inevitably, after the night's drug binge, the "lesson" got out of hand, and during their violent attack, Mark stabbed Malcolm no fewer than nine times, leaving him with a punctured lung and jugular. Malcolm managed to stagger from the house, but there was no saving his life; he collapsed between two parked cars, and died as the road turned red from the free-flowing blood. The judge summed up the tragedy of the scene: "This was a planned piece of retribution, pure and simple. You decided Malcolm had to be taught a lesson. He was obviously a terrified young man desperate only to escape. This was a wholly joint attack on a defenceless young man. All for ten pounds."

The pair were found guilty by an 11-1 majority, and Mark was sentenced to serve a minimum of twenty-two years, meaning he'll be almost fifty before he's eligible for parole. Watching the trial stirred many emotions in me – his attitude and behaviour were eerily reminiscent of my own at a younger age (it was pure fortune that none of the stabbings I inflicted ever led to death), which meant that, in theory, he had access to the best possible advice – from me! – about how to protect his interests as the legal system closed in around him.

But it was an uphill struggle – we had unfinished baggage, we're still getting to know one another, and who listens their parents anyway? So, with the cocky disdain of a twenty-something, Mark ignored my every suggestion, with devastating results. With the weight of DNA and witness evidence against him, I'd advised him to plead guilty (taking the case to trial added seven years to his minimum sentence), and, remembering my own mauling in the witness box when standing trial, argued that under no circumstances should he expose himself to cross-examination (the inconsistencies in his testimony were mercilessly exploited by the prosecution barrister).

At every turn, he preferred to rely on his own gut instinct, and his legal aid counsel was content to follow Mark's instructions without a murmur of disapproval. I even advised against using his statutory right to lodge an appeal; there were no obvious grounds, and he ran the risk of his sentence being increased. (Fortunately for him, he caught the appeal judge on a good day, and the sentence was unchanged, although, from her ruling, it was evident that an increased sentence had been seriously contemplated.)

Bali and I have stayed in close contact with Mark throughout his imprisonment – hence our appearance on the Jailbirds programme. As Bali explained to the viewers, visiting a jailed son – or step-son – can be exhausting, not simply due to the travel involved, but also from dealing with the emotional trauma of the visitation process.

As with most lifers, Mark's own wellbeing fluctuates from week to week, although his artistic talent has given him a focus. The Koestler Trust has sold a number of his works, and his art has been used in Refocus' promotional materials. He's even turned his hand to sketching scenes from my life, and his illustrations adorn the chapter headings throughout this book. As Mark was being led from the dock after the verdict was passed, I'll never forget the harrowing words of Malcolm's mum, whose scream of "I hope you rot in Hell!", alongside a colourful stream of obscenities, sent an icy chill through many spines in the courtroom. My hope for Malcolm is that this journey in prison will help change him for the better. I once said to him, "Every time you have a bad day in prison, don't complain but remember you're still breathing. Malcolm's family don't have their son anymore. We still have some hope but theirs was lost with their son."

The irony isn't lost on me that, while Refocus clocks up success stories from our work with vulnerable young kids wishing to turn around their lives, neither Bali or I were able to save the person closest to us from self-destruction. To my mind, in no way does this undermine the work of Refocus; in fact, it reinforces one of the principles we advocate at the beginning of every single mentoring session. We can show young people the value of a different path, we can nudge them along the way, we can even use our network of contacts to open up career opportunities. However, achieving success is a joint enterprise between Refocus and our mentees.

As Mark once said, "You can't live my life for me." And, at Refocus, we're forever conscious that trying to live someone else's life will never end well. We can play an influential, sometimes pivotal role; but the ultimate choices rest with the young people themselves, and never with an outside agency.

*

Mark is now ten years into his sentence, a period that's seen twists, curves and endings in the life stories of many people who, for good or ill, have made a mark upon my life.

Chris Grant is still with Roxanne, and a father for the tenth time, but his career as a lorry driver was bought to a premature end as a result of a back injury and an unexplained blackout. To his lasting credit, he reinvented himself as a qualified electrician, passing his exams with such distinction that the college invited him to stay on as an assessor (he declined). He specialises in major home renovations.

Mummy G is firing on all cylinders; having retired from a long and distinguished career in management roles (she had a knack for being obeyed), she worked as a carer, before finally, officially retiring. She's not as mobile as in her youth – her hip replacement has seen to that – but her mind is as active and agile as ever. Her instinct is still to fight in defence of "Little Lenny" if she figures the odds are stacked against me, although hopefully I'm better able to figure out my own solutions these days, and was deeply troubled when I finally summoned the courage to discuss my abuse at the hands of Thomas Brown with her. Her shock at my ordeal was matched only by her disappointment that I hadn't confided in her, so she could've "put things right".

Thomas Brown died a few years ago as dementia and old age took its toll. He doesn't really deserve any more commentary than that, although – bizarrely – it was the second time I'd been informed of his passing. For reasons that still don't make sense, my sister had told me of his death three or four years before the grim reaper finally caught up with him, and I've never established whether this was an honest mistake or part of a conspiracy to "even out past ills." Brown was never made to account for his crimes on earth, and his fate now lies in the hands of higher powers.

Bali's foster father, Tim, sadly passed from leukaemia around the time Refocus was celebrating its tenth anniversary, after nearly a decade spent in and out of remission. He was one of my best friends who had such love and care for others and was immensely popular with his church and countless others of all ages and backgrounds, especially the homeless. He and his lovely wife Ceri had been missionaries in the outback of Sierra Leone, and became legends with the local people as they embraced them with love; it was this love that had prompted a woman in the village to ask Tim and Ceri to adopt her son as their own as she lay dying shortly after childbirth (there are now kids around Sierra Leone named "Tim" in his memory). Ceri continues the ministry they started together, supported by their kids Tara, Damien and John. It has been an absolute honour and privilege to know such a lovely family and to be part of it.

I continue to be part of Linda and Trevor's lives, Bali's godparents who – knowing my sordid past – watched over me like a hawk when she and I started dating. Trevor's words of warning had been motivated by his genuine love and concern for Bali, having helped her throughout her struggles with mental illness. I have the utmost respect for them and enjoy the many wonderful times we spend in the company of their family.

With the passage of time, I've been fortunate enough to forge bonds with all Bali's siblings, as well as her nephews and nieces. The first time I ever experienced a chilled-out, warm-hearted Christmas, filled with togetherness, fun, love and laughter was with Bali's brother, and his lovely wife and their three amazing kids.. The Griffiths, the Grants and other amazing families help my Refocus workshops to be grounded in the real world, one to which kids can relate.

Bizarrely, another character who has helped me confront my demons has been my dentist, Adrianna Moulson, a wonderful lady from Transylvania in Romania who has always been patient, kind and understanding. I had been traumatised by my childhood experiences of a racist school dentist who'd pinned me down and knelt on my chest to administer injections and then hadn't even completed the treatment leaving me in agony. Finally, I undergo dental treatment without the welling up of pain and bad memories (I'd once threatened a prison dentist by saying that, if he hurt me, he wouldn't "leave this room alive"). Adrianna holds the top spot and her brilliance as a dentist and knowing how to build trust with a patient who carries these types of mental scars.

My family are doing well in their lives and spread out in different parts of the country. My daughter is chasing after her hopes and dreams, and is very happy in doing so.

My mother passed away during these ten years. Passionate, troubled, wonderful, scheming – she'd been a bundle of contradictions from cradle to grave. There were times I hoped never to see her again, but also times when it gave me deep satisfaction to be reconciled. Her shortcomings were many and glaring, and I can never forget the beatings I endured for no purpose (as I'm sure she would never forget my naughtiness as a young boy); but she also had a deep sense of duty as a Caribbean mum, and worked tirelessly to exercise her responsibilities. Yes, she had her fault – as do we all. She was, after all, human and my mum. I mourned her passing and spoke at her funeral to pay tribute to her "giving and forgiving" nature, adding that "I forgive all the wrongs that have been done to me by anyone in this room", knowing many in the congregation who fell into that category. I also asked forgiveness from any who felt I'd committed wrongs against them. I was honoured to be one of the pallbearers who carried Mum to her final resting place, and – in accordance with Caribbean tradition – joined the rest of the family by the graveside to sing her favourite hymns with passion, enthusiasm and joy.

20.
Looking Ahead

Kathy suffered sexual and psychological abuse for most of her teenage years, leaving her lacking in confidence and self-worth to the point that she retreated from the world around her – wearing a hoodie whenever she left home, and, as if that wasn't enough, growing her hair until it dangled like a curtain over her face. Kathy was diagnosed with dyspraxia and dyslexia, which affected her physical coordination and made it difficult to thrive in education which later affected her confidence and her abilities to achieve. Her vulnerability and personal circumstances made her an easy target for criminals in Kent and before long, Kathy was groomed by a drug dealer, who later became "her boyfriend" and she consequently became addicted to drugs and involved in crime. Kathy was sentenced to three years and six months in jail for supplying drugs on a prison visit to her than drug dealer boyfriend as well as her involvement in street robbery, car theft and shoplifting. On release, she was more withdrawn than ever, facing an insecure and frightening future.

Refocus attended a school where Kathy's mum was working, and afterwards the mum told Kathy about our work. This prompted Kathy to think, "That's what I want to do", and she contacted us with the help of Christine Williams, her then mentor at The Prince's Trust. From the moment Bali and I met her, it was clear Kathy had deep-rooted issues that she was struggling to deal with. She shifted around uncomfortably in her chair, and barely made eye contact – spending half an hour staring into her lap. On the other hand, we recognised a lovely person hiding inside, waiting to come out; the world had thrown its worst at Kathy, but she hadn't been totally crushed. If the unique, lovely, curious and exceptional individual within was willing to come to the fore, it would be our honour to guide and support her along this path.

Kathy's progress was phenomenal. The breakthroughs with Kathy were gradual, our team made Kathy feel at ease and laugh a lot and pretty soon she was ready to unveil herself and remove her hood and show her face to the world. With some girl time and a little makeover, Kathy put on a dress for her next meeting at the Prince's Trust; her mentor and her boss walked right past her – the transformation had been so dramatic, they didn't recognise her! As the weeks passed, Kathy grew in confidence and achieved her Youth Work Level Two certificate with two merits, with the organisation, London Youth.

To top off everything, Kathy was nominated for a Young Achiever Of The Year Award through The Prince's Trust; she and her family were invited to attend the Awards Ceremony in London, attended by His Majesty, The Prince Of Wales. Kathy was a runner-up – an incredible achievement. It was a bittersweet occasion; she'd remarkably summoned up the courage to share with her parents the stories of her abuse on the same night as the event. At last, they could understand the reasons for her troubled behaviour.

Within two years, Kathy's assurance had grown to such a degree that she became one of Refocus' paid members of staff. In this new role, she shared her experiences with young girls who were themselves at risk of grooming, exploitation and even suicide – even bravely returning to the prison where she'd once been an inmate to offer empathy, encouragement and practical solutions as a staff member. Kathy is now in a stable relationship with her partner and in 2016 gave birth to their wonderful and bright-eyed son, Owen; she remains a valuable member of the Refocus team, and I can't begin to count the number of girls throughout Kent who owe their liberty, health and resilience to the interventions Kathy made in their lives.

*

By the age of 14, Ben – who I mentioned in the last chapter – was already immersed in gang culture, addicted to cannabis and devouring around eight cans of cheap lager every day. The combined effect of drink and drugs had taken its toll on his body – despite his tender years, Ben never had any problem getting served, even at off-licences and pubs that had the strictest policies about checking the ID on anyone appearing to be a minor.

His behaviour was out-of-control; not only had he been kicked out of school, but his parents had been threatened with loss of their Council house. By the time he was referred to Refocus, his family and the authorities were at their wits' end.

Today, Ben is an outstanding and diligent stonemason. The road to rehabilitation was fraught with peril – not least, his lack of a bank account or passport creates numerous obstacles to honest endeavours. Ben's determination has enabled him to overcome such hindrances, and – like Kathy – he is keen to share his experiences so that others might gain. He's been one of Refocus' most in-demand volunteers; stand him in front of a classroom, or a group of offenders, and the impact of his life story is immediate. Ben is particularly effective with kids who've been excluded from mainstream education and those who have experienced bullying. He'll work with them on the domino effect of making wrong choices at a young age as if standing at a crossroad together. Kids are shown two roads – the first carrying negative consequences with more downs than ups; the second demanding hard work, but with a brighter outcome.

I couldn't be more proud of the person he's become.

*

We were asked by a prison if we could mentor and help Jermaine after his release from a second spell in prison for drug offences and violence. The authorities were desperate to trial a new approach after everything else had failed. Through one-to-one mentoring and restorative justice we helped him identify the root causes of his troubles. He recognised much of himself in the other kids we were helping, and was able to share with them the pitfalls and consequences of wrong choices.

The transformation in Jermaine's life, in a short period of time, has given me as much satisfaction as anything else Refocus has achieved. He has settled down with a beautiful partner and child, and competes at the highest level around the world as a professional body builder.

As if that wasn't enough, Jermaine is also eager to give back.

He's unafraid to expose his mistakes when talking with young people about his experiences, tackling difficult and complex issues. Jermaine was one of the model ex-prisoners who was chosen to appear in the "Last Chance" programme about young offenders institutions; there was nobody better to comment, because Jermaine certainly made the most of his own last chance, redefining his priorities before it was too late.

*

Refocus can – and has – made a difference in Kent, and South East London but, however hard we work, we can never do more than scratch the surface.

More effective solutions on a national scale are certainly needed; we're all reminded of that whenever we glance at a typical day's news headlines. "Man jailed for stabbing former friend to death with Rambo knife," "Father stabbed to death trying to break up row outside nightclub," "Former gang member warns 10-year-olds go out with Rambo knives," "We've been destroyed say family of teenager murdered by flat mate," "Four murder arrests after teenager fatally stabbed in south London" and "Teen killed in London's fifth fatal stabbing in six days" are amongst the dozens of similar Evening Standard stories that have sent a chill up the spines of Londoners in the past few weeks alone.

In the pages that remain, I'd like to offer a few thoughts, based on my own experiences. During my years of childhood through to adulthood, I internalised the disease of hate and rage, it was like carrying around an imaginary charge sheet from which I held my family, my community and society to ransom and these were my deep-rooted issues. I saw myself as a black man inhabiting a predominately racist society and my experiences of rejection, anger, pain and hurt, coupled with my excessive drug use, exacerbated the deception which resulted in my displaced irresponsible behaviour.

As I aged, the debts accumulated. It took me forty years to reclaim my own identity, uncoloured by what others said about me, or what I thought I was owed or needed to have. In the end, all that was required was to let go of my baggage, stop my drug dependency, and cancel all debts – freeing myself to discover me.

Over the last fifty years, my knowledge of the consequences of a "wasted youth" has accumulated as I've viewed the problem from multiple perspectives, as petty criminal, enforcer, drug dealer, armed robber, prisoner, victim, volunteer, mentor, personal coach, commentator and speaker. If my observations can save other lives from addiction, incarceration, violence and death, then my efforts will have been worthwhile. Change doesn't have to take place so late in life; we can intercept the journey on which young people are travelling using many approaches.

I believe my story pinpoints issues and highlights solutions to societal problem which have infected so many of our young people in communities across the country. The problem needs to be tackled from the "inside out" – the criminal justice system, rehabilitation and resettlement back into community, society and in our families.

For me, my early experience of the care system and jail led to over twenty years on the wrong side of the law. I learnt about crime and drugs during my years in care, yet before I was sent down, I knew a handful of criminals; by the time I was released, my network of underworld contacts was large and sprawling. Prison was my LinkedIn – a place to network and build relationships with all the most undesirable sorts of people. Moreover, on release, potential employers wanted nothing to do with me, making it even harder to resist the temptations of a few hundred quid for an evening of not-so-legal endeavours. In my view, all prisons should segregate the violent criminals from the vulnerable first-timers, which can be identified through the initial assessment process. Hardened inmates can smell a naïve, low-level offender a mile off, and quickly scheme and bully to ensure that person is in their debt.

Many first-timers are already disorientated by their new surroundings, especially when overcrowding has led to all the furniture and fineries being removed from cells in favour of bunk beds, with three or four men crammed into space designed for one or two. To make matters worse, non-violent or first-time offenders, who may suffer from mental health issues, are putty in the hands of gangs and criminals who for some sick reason want to exercise their power over someone who is easy prey. Instead of prison acting as a deterrent or promoting rehabilitation, this practice leads to precisely the opposite effect. A person whose crime may have been a minor irritant to society is transformed, under our watch, into someone who will clog up the justice system for decades.

It may be argued that prisons aren't configured for inmates to be separated in this way, which in some cases is true – although it's surely more cost effective for the taxpayer to adapt prisons (and build more, where necessary) than bear the cost of ruined and lost lives. In any event, prisons already single out specific groups, such as sex offenders, who often occupy a dedicated wing, now called the Vulnerable Prisoners Unit (VPU) for their own protection. Some celebrities also often receive special treatment when they are deemed to be at risk of victimisation or extortion ("My mates are out to rape you; for a bit of protection money, I'll make sure you're OK."). There are five or six special dispersal prisons for particularly violent and dangerous prisoners serving long sentences, and it's not uncommon for lifers to be afforded separate arrangements.

Some prisons have a separate lifers wing because of the psychological issues associated with coming to terms with their long sentence, which can make them quite volatile during their first few years (and so they can "make a home" of the place where they'll be spending the rest of their lives). Prisoners who qualify for enhanced status with special privileges are often given cells on separate landings so they need not have the fear of bullying from other inmates. Segregation can be made to work as is proved in the above mentioned cases and as it does in the segregation units for prisoners who are being punished.

Visitations are also a valuable tool – currently used on occasion to maintain order and discipline, but also with great potential as part of prisoner rehabilitation. Prisoners detest closed visits with a vengeance (the type where the inmate and visitor are separated by a toughened glass screen – as recognised in numerous American prison dramas). Nothing gets in or out and they're cheap to install. The UK is almost unique in developed countries in the denial of conjugal visits, when prisoners are allowed to have sex with their partners. I've only seen intimacy officially sanctioned on a single occasion, when a governor was moved by a tragic story involving the death of a child whilst the father was inside.

I've never understood this blunt and rigid policy. It surely increases the risk of family breakdowns – how can a prisoner be expected to reintegrate rapidly into the community when the first thing he confronts on release is the fact his partner has moved on? And, when prisoners have no moments of intimacy through which to calm their anxieties and tensions, this inevitably increases incidents of testosterone-fuelled violence and rape within prison. Again, conjugal visits would be a privilege earned, who'd want to mess that up? (Officially, sex in prison is a strict No-No, but – as mentioned earlier – when I was in Wandsworth prison inmates were able to get condoms on request; the screws knew it was happening anyway.)

One of areas that is a massive downfall is the justice system in our country, it really struggles with sentencing. Many times judges don't use their power to dish out justifiably long sentences, or pass inconsistent sentences; other times, they seem out of touch with current affairs and are letting offenders off for serious crimes. Don't get me wrong – I welcomed a bit of leniency when my own neck was on the line, but I often felt the victims are neglected by the system.

I'm aware of one woman who was forced to drink bleach while her husband beat her; because she was educated and had a degree, the judge decided she wasn't vulnerable and could rebuild her life and spared her husband prison. Recently, a young man attacking a car driver with a zombie knife in public was spared prison because he had been the victim of an attack the week before. In such cases, how can we say, "Justice has been served?"

Criminals should serve the full length of the sentence passed, with any reductions left to the discretion of the prison in which time's being served. I'm sure that if drug dealers did seven years for possession of class A drugs and up to life for supplying (as stated in British law), we'd see a reduction in the number of drug dealers on the street – not least because the culprits are behind bars. This rule should apply to all types of crime; you serve every day unless you become eligible for a reduction.

With criminals suffering from psychological trauma, prison officers are not equipped to provide professional help. If not for the support I received from leading psychiatrists at Grendon, I would never have come to terms with the sexual abuse I suffered as a child. No ordinary prison officer could have provided the help I needed, and it took a long time at Grendon before I felt ready to disclose what I'd suffered. Ironically, a shorter sentence would have served me less well. The length of my sentence gave the opportunity for root issues to be tackled and rehabilitation to take shape.

Prison has to be a place of detention to protect the public. It has to operate strict conditions to keep order and discipline; it doesn't need to be inhumane and should provide the help and support prisoners need to rehabilitate. Time is a great healer.

Juvenile offenders who commit serious crime should be sent to detention centres to follow a strict regime of education and training with regular assessment by external professionals who understand the teenage mind. Routine and clear boundaries with proper support available to every young person serving a sentence, to avoid stigma or ostracization. This approach is vital if the young person is to de-criminalise and rehabilitate, let alone rebuild their life and emerge with the skills and education they need.

In our experiences of mentoring young people in schools, we are finding too many young people are being referred when it's late in the day, and they are already falling through the net. We are passionate and very determined to help vulnerable people avoid the criminal justice system, and too many times hear the words,

"Why didn't I get Refocus when I was younger, it's too late for me now!" They feel their choices have been made and their lifestyle set. That's why being in a young offenders unit should be a second chance and an opportunity for services to unpick the bad behaviours before they are fully ingrained.

Which brings us to the next crucial stage in resettlement. To avoid the dangers of reoffending, the resettlement process could incorporate ex-offenders as part of the team, to support and mentor the prisoner for release as they understand the issues that will face them when they go back into the community. A successful resettlement means prisoners will, at some point, need training, apprenticeships, employment and support – not the type of the pretend or tokenistic help that some statutory services provide, due to lack of funding and huge case loads.

Prisoners nearing their release date can be part of some sort of halfway housing scheme and whilst they integrate back into society. Other prisoners taught me to write "No fixed abode" (NFA) on discharge papers because it means you receive a more generous discharge grant – most of which ends up being spent on drink and drugs. The temptation to return to crime after discharge was hard to resist, especially if released near Christmas when you suffer from the guilt trip of needing to buy presents for loved ones. This is why so many prisoners find themselves homeless so soon after discharge. Occasional meetings with a probation officer aren't enough to give focus or vision to an ex-offender's life, let alone enable one to get re-established in the community.

Every one of us has a stake in the rehabilitation and resettlement of ex-offenders. For the individuals, it means a more fulfilled, settled life. For society, it avoids the vast cost of dealing with crime and its repercussions. And for potential victims, it frees them from the trauma and fear of a horrific, scarring experience. Which is why it beggars the senses that, in defiance of all logic, the budgets for rehabilitation, early intervention and support services have been slashed in recent years.

Refocus, despite our track record, has not been immune from this slash-and-burn mentality, and we've found it difficult to sustain and finance the same numbers of interventions that we used to deliver. But this isn't a plea on behalf of Refocus; all organisations that believe in the power of early intervention have had to tighten their belts since 2013. In the beginning, the funding constraints were manageable – we all worked a little bit harder to ensure we delivered the same for less. But over the years, people who want to keep their jobs have spent more time writing impressive bids to secure funding than fulfilling the contracts requirement. That's why so many small charities struggle, with results that have painfully filtered through in the crime statistics.

My prison experience means I can suggest to government various simple, cost-effective and practical measures to assist the mental well-being and rehabilitation of offenders, whilst also clamping down on criminal gang activity within jail. The Home Office has, for some time, been struggling with the issue of smartphone use in jails – they are increasingly smuggled in, and used by prisoners to direct illicit and illegal operations. Prisoners pay up to a thousand pounds for a mini smart phone. Various options have been scoped to address this issue, including the installation of expensive blocking technology that costs the tax payer an absurd £300m to install and £800K annually to maintain; another much-discussed idea has been the introduction of targeted telecommunication restriction orders (the latter has been severely criticised by, amongst others, Lord Ramsbotham, on grounds of the large number of court orders that would be required and the potential for these orders to be undermined through the smuggling of new SIM cards).

My proposal has been for the mobile phone Nokia 6110 to be made accessible to all prisoners, with the handset and airtime paid for by prisoners through the existing system of canteen credits. The central benefit of this solution is to provide prisoners with an opportunity to maintain relationships with the outside world (such as with family members, or their solicitor), albeit in a tightly controlled setting. The handsets allow calls to be made to recognised numbers on a prison pin-list, and have the capability to send text messages, but constraints can be programmed – for example, calls cut off after ten minutes, and texts after thirty characters. In addition, the phones are designed without cameras or social media access, are fitted with tracking technology, are tamper-proof, and both SIM and battery are sealed inside. If desired, a host of additional security precautions are available, such as stamping each phone with the prisoner's N.O.M.S (National Offenders Management Service) number at the time of purchase.

I have written to senior politicians advocating this elegant and cost-effective solution, and have yet to receive any reasoned objection.

At Refocus, our commitment to the cause is undimmed. We continue developing new ways to reach young people, rationally as well as emotionally. Our core conviction remains that self-disclosure enables us to connect in ways that other services cannot. If vulnerable or cynical people arrive at a mentoring session, or to listen to a talk, filled with scepticism ("What can he possibly know about my life?"), this quickly dissipates as I willingly disclose my history of drug abuse, gang culture, offending and imprisonment, coupled with Bali's openness about her mental health history and the past experiences of other team members.

Our content is packaged into thematic programmes, and concepts that have recently struck a chord include "Doing time outside" (aimed at those adjusting to life outside their cell walls) and "U CHOOZ" (for those on the cusp of the criminal justice system). These programmes prepare and equip individuals for a positive life in the community by exploring behaviours to break the cycle of reoffending.

Topics we cover during sessions include goal setting, barriers and pitfalls to leaving prison, generational patterns, counting the cost, getting it out of the system, breaking the cycle and many more, and are often tailored to suit particular groups and individuals. They tend to be hard-hitting and often uncomfortable – doing the right thing doesn't mean doing the easy or straightforward thing. But it's never been more necessary than it is today.

Our VIPP ("Violence intervention prevention programme") is our new intensive mentoring service, dealing with issues arising when different levels of violence have been displayed. We apply a multi agency approach to engage with young people, and to build relationships over the longer term. This is based on the new government violence strategy using a Public health approach to include all public services to address the level of gangs and knife crime in our communities. We work with the family as well as the young person in enabling and equipping them with the tools to identify the signs of grooming, drugs and crime.

I'm often asked to outline the next 'big idea' for Refocus. To be honest, I won't be entirely unhappy if we do nothing other than persevere with our current set-up until the day I need to hang up my boots. It's extremely productive, fulfilling and gratifying work. But I am chewing around ideas to take our service to the next level of impact. In the light of the increase of youth violence we are exploring how we can extend the capacity of the VIPP through converting an abandoned warehouse or factory into a makeshift prison – complete with cells, kitchen area and so on.

The prison design would pull no punches. The sights and experiences would approximate a real prison and role play exercises would involve real inmates and officers. The aim would be to provide young people on the cusp of being drawn into the criminal justice system, as well as their parents or carers, a glimpse of what awaits if they don't refocus. I am a believer in "learning through experience" – it's not enough to tell young people, they need to live it. As Benjamin Franklin said, "Tell me and I forget, teach me and I may remember, involve me and I learn."

My idea means they'll be shown the life that awaits them if they make those kinds of wrong choices. For vulnerable and at risk kids, the goal will be to remove the desire to be a wannabe gangster; for those with loved ones inside, they can start to empathise and therefore offer better support. I should emphasise the prison wouldn't be designed to scare anyone but give real life experiences, increase mutual understanding, provide education and give answers to questions. We can all be affected by violence or youth crime – parents, businesses, education services, sports services, prisons, emergency services, faith groups, social services, YOTS, Probation. That's why we all have a distinct role to play.

The VIPP aims to target some of our most vulnerable young people and I'd like to see us help them more. I think that, in today's society, our young people are given too much choice and often left to their own destructive devices. Rather than being guided and supported to make choices, subsequently they are then drawn into the criminal circles. If it's clear a young person isn't engaging in education, the risk is they'll opt out as they're moved around schools before ending up in a PRU (Pupil Referral Unit) which can be a crushing blow to their self-esteem. An alternative solution would be, at an early stage, to offer a starter job, or an apprenticeship or training based on their capabilities; this will give a rocket booster to their confidence.

Criminals are investing money to make money; they generate huge amounts from targeting and luring vulnerable young people, then grooming and training them. To compete, we need to do the same.

There are so many people with some sort of colourful past but have changed for the better. Many of those we have helped now want to offer their skills and time to mentor others. I'd love to use my skills as a training manager to equip them all, so I could have more Refocus workers acting as role models and mentors on the VIPP programme and running the service in the community. It's important right now to break down barriers between communities; as a young man, my neighbours the Grants didn't shy away – their kindness have me that all-important glimmer of hope which rested within me throughout the dark years. Maybe I wouldn't have changed or had any trust at all if it hadn't been for people giving me some positivity in my early years. In a multi-cultural society it's not acceptable for each community to look out for its own, to the exclusion of all others. Just as harmful is when communities turn on one another due to internal power struggles and jealousies – hence the so-called "black on black" wars. Our society is built up of diverse communities of gifted human beings who can reach out to each other, look out for one another and be an extension of family for others.

Cultural diversity is one of the country's strengths – we have one of the world's most diverse populations. Let's not make that an excuse for a fragmented society. Above all else, every human being deserves a fair shot at success. If this means we look out for one another's kids with as much attention as our own, the result will be magnificent. They say it takes a community to raise a child, and parents can fail their children for many reasons over which they have no control – poverty, single parenting, social housing, disadvantage, the trauma of war, mental health and many other issues.

The racial issues primarily exist because of the poor areas, lack of opportunities and lack of positive role models, which creates hatred towards oneself and others, which as we know is then displaced onto the wider communities.

Sometimes, when these arise in black and ethnic minority groups, they are brushed under the carpet and not directly addressed for fear of being racist, or politically incorrect. If we don't talk about these issues amongst ourselves and in the wider society, the problem may be buried from sight, but it will still exist and it will fester and grow, like a silent cancer.

Family is where it begins. As we know, there's no perfect family, but the love of family unit has been the solution for many. It certainly has played a major part in my life, Bali's and others who have turned their life around. The feeling of belonging and people believing in you, caring enough to nurture and support you. We hope that one day we too can open a four-bedroom family house to take in young people, teaching them family values, supporting them in the transition to positive choices, and giving them a chance in life.

I raise my hat to those families and single parents who have done a fantastic job with their kids; almost every day I see how they are making a difference. A lot can be learnt from these positive people, and I would encourage parents who are struggling, to firstly speak up without the fear of social services involvement and be willing to admit they need help to local neighbours, community, to reach out and learn and be helped by these incredible role models who can help to build a family unit within a community.

*

My own story has been shaped by the experience of growing up in the mid-to-late twentieth century in family circumstances that were unusual, perhaps unique, even in that torrid and bizarre era.

The eighth child but the first son. Deeply religious parents who beat me for the slightest transgressions. A home filled with the sights and sounds of the island they'd left, not the land to which they'd come. A local family who took me in and spoke of adopting me. I was a father, twice over, at a young age, but separated from both mothers and children – either by circumstances or by an ocean.

Would my journey have been different if i wasn't black?, with a more conventional upbringing; if I'd had the chance to refocus at an earlier age? Perhaps, but I also believe that, for all my parents' failings, for all the questions to which I never received an answer, there was – mixed within their harsh words and harsher fists – an unmistakable slither of love. And it was that love which enabled me to reconnect with both of them in my adult years.

The same strain of love which, during my darkest, loneliest days, saved me from ending my journey prematurely or descending to a point of no return.

I have a new family now. When Bali entered my life, and shook up my world, we've forged something that's far stronger than either of us could create alone. That doesn't mean I no longer regard my blood relatives, or even Chris and Mummy G, as family. It simply demonstrates that family isn't static; as our relationships evolve, the family structures around us renew and refresh themselves.

As I reflect on the work of Refocus, I look across our small office, a stone's throw from Dartford city centre. Bali is furiously typing away on her laptop; she looks up at me, smiles, whispers a few words of encouragement, and then gets back to work. We're surrounded by things that remind me of what Refocus has achieved over the past decade – our most funniest moments as a team, testimonials from those who've supported us and those we've helped, stimulating material we use in our training and mentoring, bound copies of proposals over which we've slaved, DVDs of various TV interviews.

And also, more ominously, evidence of my previous life – in the form of Mark's illustrations of Lennox when I was "breaking bad".

I can never forget those days; they're a part of what has made me into who I am, and I refer to them almost every day because self-disclosure is such an inherent theme in our work.

The phone rings, and I turn back to my desk.

Who's calling this time?

A journalist seeking my comments on the latest outbreak of violence in London?

A social worker with another case requiring intervention?

Or one of my mentees needing urgent guidance lest he make an awkward situation worse?

Whoever it is, I'll approach the matter, as I do everything, with determination and humility, hoping that the evil that was out to destroy me has been turned around for good. Praying the work we do makes a real difference.

So that not just I, but all those we support, will continue Breaking Better.

How you can help?

Refocus is proud of its diversity and sees the importance of making sure we are a needs-led service, reflective of our communities, ensuring our youth forum contributes regularly to help shape and improve our services. We have worked with the lives of many young people in and around South East London and Kent, yet the disease of gang culture and knife crime stretches far beyond the locality where we operate. That's why we're proud to celebrate the work of organisations the length and breadth of the country who are developing innovative and results-focussed approaches to tackling this scourge in our society. We embrace the "Public Health Approach" in reaching young people as individuals with addictions, which treats gang culture as a health problem and promotes building a rich comprehensive network of expertise to address all aspects of the well being of young people today.

Over the coming months, we will be calling on these organisations – charities, social enterprises, local government agencies, and many others – to work together in partnership, sharing ideas and experience in the public interest. As a catalyst for greater collaboration, Refocus is delighted to be involved in the creation of the **'Safer Communities Alliance'** – a forum bringing together great initiatives with similar origins that have proven their effectiveness, so that we can be a more powerful voice lobbying for positive change in our communities. Together we are stronger, so please visit www.safercommunitiesalliance.org for more information.

If you're a concerned individual, we encourage you to make contact with the leading organisations in your community that are working to turn around the lives of young people – and to offer whatever support you can. For some people, the best contribution you can make may be to become a "Friend of Refocus" donor (contributing towards core costs, staffing, mentoring, resources, and other vital expenses). For others, it may be giving your time or expertise to support a community intervention project.

If you're an organisation like Refocus, please don't hesitate to pick up the phone to Lennox, Bali or other members of the Refocus team (Tel : 020 3405 1787). We would love to hear from you and share our ideas for future collaboration and the evolution of the Safer Communities Alliance together.

We're a small team with enormous dreams! A vital motivation in writing Breaking Better was to demonstrate how even lives that seem beyond redemption can be rescued and turned around. Please help us to extend our reach – forging a Britain where every citizen can escape the trap of being defined forever by youthful mistakes and excesses. And can instead seize practical support to build a successful career and a fulfilling life as part of our wonderful society.